Boston

A Century of Running

Boston

CELEBRATING THE 100TH ANNIVERSARY OF THE BOSTON ATHLETIC ASSOCIATION MARATHON

By Hal Higdon

Rodale Press, Inc.
Emmaus, Pennsylvania

Copyright © 1995 by Hal Higdon

Printed in the United States of America on acid-free ∞,
recycled paper containing a minimum of 10% post-consumer waste ♺

Cover Photograph: Clarence DeMar wins his seventh Boston Marathon in 1930.
Page ii: The start of the 96th running of the Boston Marathon, April 20, 1992.
Page vi: Looking down Commonwealth Avenue in Boston, the John Hancock Building looms
ahead to inspire marathoners during the race's last three-quarters of a mile.

Senior Vice-President and Editor-in-Chief, Rodale Books: Bill Gottlieb
Vice President and Editorial Director: Debora T. Yost
Managing Editor: Sharon Faelten
Editor: Lee Jackson
Art Director: Debra Sfetsios
Cover and Book Designer: Maureen Erbe and Rita A. Sowins, Maureen Erbe Design/South Pasadena, California
Photo Editor: Susan Pollack
Photo Researcher: Andrea Schulting
Copy Editor: John Reeser
Production Manager: Helen Clogston
Manufacturing Coordinator: Patrick Smith

Library of Congress Cataloging-in-Publication Data

Higdon, Hal.
    Boston: a century of running / by Hal Higdon.
        p.   cm.
    Includes index.
    ISBN 0–87596–283–1 hardcover
    1. Boston Marathon—History.   I. Title.
GV1065.22.B67H54 1995
796.42′5′0974461 dc20   95–4112

Distributed in the book trade by St. Martin's Press

2 4 6 8 10 9 7 5 3 1 hardcover

OUR MISSION

We publish books that empower people's lives.

RODALE BOOKS

DEDICATED TO ALL WHO

FOLLOWED IN THE FOOTSTEPS OF

JOHN J. MCDERMOTT

Contents

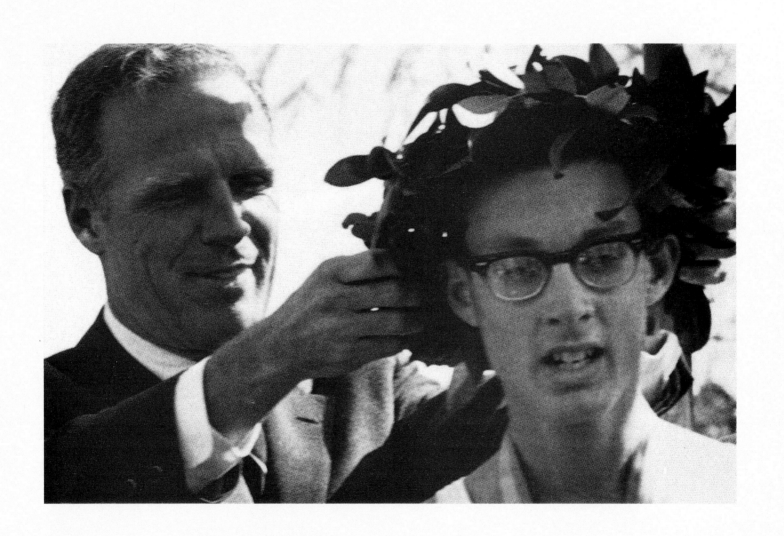

THE BEST BOOKS GENERALLY fall into one of two camps: They take you to places you've never been or return you to familiar places you want to visit again and again. This unique volume, Hal Higdon's *Boston*, reaches both camps. Whether you have dreams of one day completing the Boston Marathon or memories of many Boston runs, you will find these pages filled with wonder and inspiration.

And perhaps an unexpected chuckle or two. In reading *Boston* I knew I would encounter tales of the marathon's gloried history, of the unforgettable course, of the great champions who have found themselves drawn back year after year and sometimes decade after decade. What I didn't expect were the vivid passages that would trigger long-forgotten Boston memories—memories that, once unleashed, elicited a warm laugh.

Two of my favorite memories both come from the first Boston I ever ran in 1965. Even though a runner might one day win Boston, he or she will always remember moments from the first Boston with razor clarity. I was 18, a college freshman, entered in my first marathon, driving 100 miles north from our Connecticut home with my father.

The trip was uneventful until we reached Hopkinton Green, where, for the first time, I noticed a light covering of snow on the rooftops. Snow in mid-April seemed totally absurd to me! Much like the notion of running 26 miles, 385 yards. What was I getting myself into?

The same thought struck again as I ran through Framingham, just past the marathon's 6-mile mark. I had felt good as the several hundred of us poured out of Ashland and snaked through Framingham. The miles passed easily. Then I encountered something for which I was totally unprepared: A small triangular sign, bright orange, in the middle of the road, reading "B.A.A. Marathon—19⅞ Miles to Go." What a ridiculous number, I thought—and what a stark reminder that I had never once in my life run that far. Once more, I felt trapped by the absurd. Still, I kept going and I felt terrific every step of the way. This, I might add, has never happened again in the dozen or so Bostons I've run since then.

I mention these two anecdotes because I'm sure Hal's book will trigger many personal recollections for all readers. In both the detail and breadth of the writing, not to mention the photographic sweep, *Boston* is so rich that you're almost certain to close the cover occasionally to let your own sweet memories intermingle with the book's narrative.

It's easy to tell that this book was written by someone who has run Boston many times himself. You can't disguise passion. Hal Higdon has 40-some years of journalistic experience and dozens of books to his credit, but I'd wager he brought more emotion and enthusiasm to *Boston* than to all the others combined. He doesn't just recount the story of the Boston Marathon, he gets inside it. He sees it not just from the perspective of the most famous runners who have ever run Boston but also through the eyes of the unknown Boston Marathoners who have contributed as much to the race's lore as Clarence DeMar and Johnny Kelley.

Hal's *Boston* is a people's *Boston*, a public treasure as assuredly as Bunker Hill and Old North Church. You will want to "visit" it often. The Boston Marathon is a piece of living history that you embellish every time you run it or cheer its heroes from the sidelines.

—Amby Burfoot
EXECUTIVE EDITOR, *Runner's World* MAGAZINE

LEFT: Amby Burfoot won the Boston Marathon in 1968, the first American champion in 11 years.

THE BOSTON ATHLETIC ASSOCIATION (BAA) and its marathon have had more ups and downs than the course itself. Organized more than a century ago in 1887, the BAA was the product of the affluence, optimism and athleticism of the late nineteenth century. It was an exclusive men's club whose object was "to encourage all manly sports, and promote physical culture."

Within two years of its organization, the BAA opened its luxurious clubhouse around the corner from the current marathon finish line. Reflecting the mood of the era, a reporter observed, "A half-hour at the weights in a place like this, with a pleasant dining room. . . ample lounging rooms and good company is vastly more agreeable to contemplate than the same time spent in a bare and ill-smelling gymnasium."

BAA members were the backbone of the team that represented the United States at the 1896 Olympic Games in Athens. The long-distance race in those inaugural games inspired the creation of the BAA Marathon, originally called the American Marathon. The BAA's course was topographically similar to the Athens route and finished on the BAA's 220-yard track on Irvington Street near its clubhouse. The BAA Marathon was first held on Patriots' Day, Monday, April 19, 1897. It has been held annually since that date.

By August 1935 the Great Depression had swept away the BAA's many facilities and all of the events it organized except for the BAA Games (an indoor track meet last held in 1971) and the BAA Marathon. From the mid-1930s until the late 1970s the marathon was kept alive by the public's love of the event and the dedication, intensity and protectiveness of such individuals as Walter A. Brown. Then came the running boom, and in the mid-1980s salvation arrived in the form of sponsorship by John Hancock Financial Services and others.

The founders of the BAA would be proud of their most illustrious offspring, the BAA Boston Marathon. They would delight in the warmth with which it is universally regarded and would almost certainly come to enjoy its inclusiveness and diversity. They would also be pleased with its prestige and its history as told by Hal Higdon. The BAA welcomes the opportunity to endorse and recommend *Boston: A Century of Running* to all who love this great race.

—*Frank B. Porter, Jr.*
PRESIDENT, *Boston Athletic Association*

LEFT: Frank B. Porter, Jr., president of the Boston Athletic Association, has completed 18 consecutive Boston Marathons.

THE ORIGINAL STARTING LINE of the Boston Marathon, scratched in the dirt with the heel of Olympic sprint champion Tom Burke, exists only in memory. The dirt road has long since been paved. Metcalf's Mill, where 15 runners toed Burke's line on April 19, 1897, has also vanished.

When I visited the site recently, I looked for some plaque that might identify the first starting line. I found none—although Dick Fannon, of the Ashland Historical Society, assured me that one was planned for the 100th anniversary in 1996 of the Boston Athletic Association Marathon.

That was the race's official name: not the Boston Marathon, but the Boston Athletic Association Marathon, or the BAA Marathon. "I always called it that," insisted Will Cloney, the race's director for four decades between 1946 and 1984. "I always protected the marathon's official name."

Some runners would call the race The Boston, using the definitive article to confer upon it extra dignity. Dr. George Sheehan, who probably did as much as anyone to popularize Boston, spoke of it that way. "I ran The Boston 22 times," he told me shortly before his death in 1993.

But to most runners, as well as sportswriters, sidewalk spectators and sports fans everywhere for whom the 26-mile, 385-yard trek each Patriots' Day has achieved mystical and mythical proportions, it is simply Boston, as in "Do you plan to run Boston this year?"

Boston! The name is revered among runners. Ironically, though, only the last few miles leading to the finish line lie within the boundaries of Boston proper. Hopkinton, Ashland, Framingham, Natick, Wellesley, Newton, Brookline and Boston are the towns that lie along the route of America's most famous and the world's oldest marathon.

Technically, the Olympic Marathon is older by one year and nine days.

For it was that race from Marathon to Athens, Greece, in April 1896 that inspired BAA officials to stage their own marathon race the following April. But the Olympic Marathon is held only every fourth year, runs over different courses and has been interrupted by both world wars.

Remarkably, however, Boston has endured through war and peace. Although a relay of servicemen ran the course as a substitute race in 1918 and only 67 men started in the wartime year of 1945, the BAA Marathon has been run annually, without interruption, for 100 years.

Yet Boston can prove less than friendly. The hills, up and down, hammer at runners' muscles and test their reserves. Boston's weather in April is unpredictable: chilly one year, hot the next. And few major marathons have a starting line as narrow as Boston's.

For a time in the 1980s the BAA Marathon seemed adrift. Other races with million-dollar budgets began offering prize money to runners, luring them away from Boston. At first the BAA resisted this trend, hoping to rely on tradition to maintain its premier position among marathons. Eventually, however, race director Will Cloney's successor, Guy Morse, made important changes that brought the race to a higher level. After signing a long-term contract with John Hancock Financial Services, Boston became not only the oldest but also one of the richest marathons. The prize fund for the 100th race sets a record among world races. Also, a record number of runners will participate. The Boston Marathon seems secure for another 100 years.

Dr. Sheehan was right. It is The Boston!

—*Hal Higdon*

LEFT: Cosmas Ndeti ascended to the peak of marathon greatness with his three victories at Boston in 1993, 1994 and 1995.

S. Paine
(*Trainer*)

John Graham
(*Trainers Manager*)

F. H. Clark
(*High + Broad Jumps*)

Three Legends

Chapter One

1

Rejoice, we conquer!—*Pheidippides, Greek messenger*

REJOICE, WE CONQUER" was the dying cry of the Greek warrior-messenger, the legendary Pheidippides, as he rushed into

the marketplace of Athens with the news of the Greek victory over invading Persians in the Battle of Marathon in 490 B.C.

Pheidippides's run gave birth to a legend that inspired the long-distance running event.

This dramatic tale is only one of three intertwining legends that gave root to the marathons of today, including the

Boston Marathon. The others are the legend of King Pelops of Greece (who established the original Olympics) and the story of

Spiridon Loues, a Greek water carrier who performed splendidly at the revival of the ancient Olympic Games in 1896. Then,

inspired by a revival of the ancient Olympic Games, the Boston Athletic Association founded the Boston Marathon a year later

in 1897.

To truly understand the Boston Marathon means going back in time to the ancient Greek Olympics. In ancient times the

Olympics were contested not in Athens but in the Peloponnesus, the peninsula that forms the southern part of Greece. This

area owes its name to Pelops, an early Greek monarch, and thus, the story of the Boston Marathon begins with him.

❧

PAGE XIV: Boston Athletic Association members from the first Olympics. Inspired by the long-distance race at those Games, manager John Graham (seated, center) would direct the first Boston Marathon. LEFT: The Olympic stadium was built atop the remains of one from 330 B.C. The word stadium comes from the Greek *stadion*, a straightaway of about 192 meters. In the 1896 track, two long straightaways were linked by very tight turns.

Inspiration

LEFT: A fatal chariot race won by
Pelops, a Greek warrior competing for
the hand of the king's daughter, inspired
the early Olympic Games. CENTER:
Spiridon Loues, by his Olympic victory
in 1896, inspired the first Boston
Marathon. RIGHT: Spectators cheered
Loues as he finished.

Crafty Pelops, Founder of the First Olympics

Long before the birth of Christ, a man named Pelops sought the hand of Hippodamia, the beautiful daughter of King Oenomaus, whose kingdom included a fertile valley in southwestern Greece. Pine and olive trees grew within the valley, which was surrounded by high mountains. Through it ran the winding Alpheus River. The valley was known as Olympia.

The king decreed that to win Hippodamia a prospective husband had to escape with her in a chariot, pursued by the king with much faster horses. If King Oenomaus caught the escaping couple, he would kill the suitor with his spear. Before Pelops, 13 suitors had sought to win the princess and failed, the legend tells us.

But crafty Pelops bribed the royal charioteer to loosen a wheel on the king's chariot. During the chase the wheel came off and King Oenomaus died in the crash, which reportedly occurred at Olympia. Later, in honor of his victory over the king, Pelops instituted a religious and athletic celebration that became known as the Olympic Games, according to the legend.

The Earliest Olympics

Chariot races were not included in the early sporting contests held at Olympia, although eventually they would become part of the blend of events that became the Olympic Games. The first Olympic victory for which we have records is that of Coroebus, a cook from Elis who won a sprint race in 776 B.C. The symbol of victory in the early Games was a laurel wreath instead of today's gold medal. The top sculptors of the era carved statues of the Olympic champions, and thus, their names and deeds survive to the present day.

Archaeologists, however, suggest that from the evidence of ruins

MEMORIES ALONG THE COURSE

For many who lived along the Boston course, the marathon is interwoven with fond family memories. For Dorothy Deslongchamps in Natick, her first memory of the marathon dates from 1939, when she was four. She remembers it as a cold day. Dorothy's mother bundled her in warm clothes. Her father, Tom McGee, stood her on the rail of the porch to watch Tarzan Brown pass en route to victory.

Deslongchamps still lives in Natick in the same brick house and still watches the marathoners pass, although no longer with her late father. Her memories of the marathon blend with the stories of her father, a student of Greek language and history. Each year, he would repeat to his daughter the tale of the messenger who brought news to Athens of the Greek victory at the Battle of Marathon, the inspiration for the race that passed their front door.

"I somehow sensed that the marathon sprang from greatness to inspire greatness," says Deslongchamps.

As a child, Dorothy Deslongchamps watched from her porch as marathoners passed each Patriots' Day.

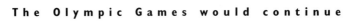

The Olympic Games would continue for more than 1,000 years.

Tradition

The heroic deeds of those who triumphed in the athletic arena (left) would inspire Greek artists, who pictured runners on amphora vases (center) or cast them in bronze (right).

found within the original enclosure for the Games, athletic competitions and religious celebrations were probably held at Olympia for several centuries before somebody recorded the name of Coroebus. Nevertheless, 776 B.C. became established among the ancient Greeks as beginning the First Olympiad. Each Olympiad—the period between the Games—lasted four years. The Olympics would continue through more than 1,000 years before the Roman emperor Theodosius I abolished the Games in A.D. 394. His reason: They had deteriorated into a spectacle rather than a sporting event. Too many chariot races.

"Rejoice, We Conquer!"

Next comes the legend of Pheidippides, a warrior-messenger (or *hemerodromos*) in the service of the Greek general Miltiades. In 490 B.C. Persian armies under the command of Darius sailed to invade Greece near the plain of Marathon, northeast of Athens. According to the legend, Miltiades first sent Pheidippides trotting to Sparta seeking reinforcements for his 10,000 troops, who were badly outnumbered by the Persians. The messenger received promises of help from the Spartans, then returned to fight the Battle of Marathon with his comrades. The Spartans never did provide reinforcements but Miltiades prevailed anyway, thwarting the invasion. According to the Greek historian Herodotus, 6,400 Persians died in the battle but only 192 Greeks were lost.

Joyously, Miltiades dispatched his messenger to Athens with news of the victory. In *The Story of the Olympic Games* John Kiernan and Arthur Daley present a dramatic description of this run:

"Though he had fought through the battle as a common soldier and endured the heat and the hardship of the day, Pheidippides tossed aside his shield, stripped himself of his armor and set off over the hills toward the distant city. It was about eight leagues (roughly 40 kilometers) from the plain of Marathon to the marketplace at Athens, but Pheidippides, spurred by the good news he was bringing, ran doggedly up and down the slopes and along the level stretches. As he went on, his lips became parched and his breath came in painful stabs. His feet were cut and bleeding. But the Acropolis loomed in the distance. Pheidippides plunged ahead. He entered the city streets. The elders of Athens heard a great shout and saw an exhausted runner staggering toward them. "Rejoice, we conquer!" gasped Pheidippides and, his message carried and his goal attained, he dropped to the ground and died."

Latter-day historians have doubted the veracity of the legend of Pheidippides, which didn't surface until Plutarch told the story in the first century A.D., more than 500 years after the Battle of Marathon. Author James F. Fixx attempted to authenticate the Pheidippides legend and concluded that, while the messenger sent by Miltiades to Sparta most likely bore that name, he was not the same messenger sent with news of the victory from Marathon to Athens. Still, Fixx considered the legend an agreeable, if unlikely, fiction.

Regardless of its origin, the story of the Greek messenger who died with news of the victory at Marathon on his lips had a romantic ring to it. It *should* have been true! The legend remained alive in the imaginations of the Greeks as well as those who revered the Classical era.

The First Modern Olympiad

Among those romantics who believed in the legend was Baron Pierre de Coubertin, a French nobleman who admired the strong athletic tradition that was linked to the educational system as in ancient Greece. To inspire his countrymen, Coubertin convened an International Athletic Congress in Paris on June 16, 1894. Of the 2,000 people who attended, primarily attracted by Coubertin's hospitality, most were unaware that

After winning the first
Olympic Marathon in
1896, Spiridon Loues
was acclaimed a hero by
his Greek countrymen
in a victory parade.

his motive for hosting the meeting was to revive the Olympic Games.

Originally, Coubertin planned that the first modern Olympiad would begin with a World's Fair scheduled for Paris in 1900. When the Greeks learned of Coubertin's Olympic revival plans, they insisted that the date be pushed four years earlier to 1896 and the Games first be held in the country of their birth.

Coubertin saw the logic in this link between old and new, even though Olympia lay in ruins. So he encouraged the Greeks to host the Olympic Games in the more populous Athens. Near the heart of that city were the remains of the Herodes Atticus stadium, dating back to 330 B.C. George Averoff, a wealthy Greek businessman living in Egypt, pledged funds to restore the stadium to its original glory. Rebuilt, this new Olympic stadium would provide seats for 70,000. During the Games an additional 50,000 would watch from the surrounding hillsides.

These spectators would witness at least one event never before contested, either in ancient Greece or in those modern days—a marathon. At the 1894 Paris Congress Professor Michael Breal, a classical literary scholar and friend of Coubertin, offered a silver cup as prize for a "Marathon race," commemorating the Battle of Marathon and the legend of the messenger who brought the news of victory to Athens. Coubertin apparently paid little attention to the offer at the time, but Greek organizers took Breal's suggestion more seriously. They began making plans for a footrace that would trace the route of the messenger, a distance of about 40 kilometers, or 25 miles.

Going the Distance

Nothing in the Olympic tradition suggested that the classical Greeks competed at distances anywhere near 40 kilometers. Their messengers certainly ran that far, and farther, but not their athletes. Early Olympic athletes ran a sprint race of about 192 meters known as a stadion. Later, grandstands where spectators could watch the Games were constructed beside the sprint straightaway. Thus, the origin of the word stadium.

As Olympiads passed, Games organizers added an up-and-back race in which runners ran to a post at the end of the straightaway then back, about 400 meters. The longest event was reportedly 24 stadion lengths (about three miles), which is the equivalent of the 5000 meters run in the Olympics today.

The ancient Games included an event in which warriors ran in armor for eight stadion lengths, or about a mile. These competitors carried a shield and wore a helmet and leg protectors—but nothing else since Olympic athletes traditionally competed nude. According to one tale, an early Olympian's belt slipped, causing his tunic to drop. After he won, others began running minus encumbering clothes. (This tale, too, probably owes more to legend than to fact.)

While amateur sportsmen in the nineteenth century rarely ran farther than a few miles in competition, professional athletes—both walkers and runners—frequently competed in events that sometimes lasted for days, even months. In 1867 Edward Payson Weston, sometimes referred to

WOMEN AT THE OLYMPICS

During the ancient Olympic Games women were refused entry not only as competitors but also as spectators. First of all, men competed in the nude. But, in general, women were considered a distraction. So women could come no closer than the far side of what is now the Ruphia River, nearly a mile away.

Until 1896, distance races—sometimes lasting days or
weeks—were not yet called marathons.

LEFT: At the 1896 Olympics in Athens, Greece, over 120,000 spectators watched the runners from Marathon finish in the stadium.

RIGHT: Wearing traditional garb, Spiridon Loues accepts the victory laurel in Athens.

as the man who invented walking, walked from Portland, Maine, to Chicago, Illinois (a distance of 1,226 miles), in 26 days. But nobody yet had coined the term *marathon* to describe these distance races. Until 1896, Marathon remained merely an obscure plain somewhere outside Athens, known only to those well-versed in the history of Greece.

The BAA Aims for Athens

Despite Coubertin's lofty goals, his revival of the ancient Olympic Games attracted relatively little attention at first, even among Europeans. Compared with what would come later, it was a minor event. Most Americans certainly did not yet take the Games seriously. A U.S. Olympic Committee was still far in the future, and we held no Olympic Trials. In fact, anybody able to pay their own way could become an Olympian. For the first modern Olympics only 13 Americans competed. Not too many athletes from other countries bothered to go to Greece either. After all, the jet plane had not yet been invented; travel by ship consumed several weeks.

As today, the centerpiece sport of the first modern Olympics was "athletics," which is called track and field in the United States. Toward the end of the nineteenth century, athletics was a sport practiced mostly in Great Britain or by those whose roots were English. This included the United States, or at least those cultured Americans who attended Eastern colleges or belonged to clubs such as the Boston Athletic Association, referred to more simply as the BAA.

In 1887 the BAA built its own nine-story clubhouse in Boston's Back Bay area, with racquet courts, a swimming pool, Turkish baths and a running track. BAA runners competed in track meets wearing singlets with the club insignia, featuring the head of a unicorn. In Greek lore the unicorn served as an attendant to the heralds, or royal messen-

gers. BAA members arriving at the clubhouse passed a bronze unicorn head statue in the lobby that contained a gas flame by which they lit their cigars. The club also had its own golf course, The Unicorn, named after its emblem. The unicorn remains central to the BAA logo today.

Coach and trainer for the BAA, John Graham was born in England in 1861 and later emigrated to the United States, where he taught athletics at Harvard University. After visiting Germany in the late 1880s for additional training in physical education, Graham became coach for the BAA.

When Graham learned of Coubertin's plans for an Olympic revival, he became intrigued with the idea of leading a BAA team to Athens. He discussed the idea with potential team sponsors as well as his athletes. The plan appealed to his runners. At an indoor meet in January 1896, Arthur Blake won a 1,000-yard race. Afterward, he was quoted as saying, "I'm too good for Boston. I ought to go over and run the marathon at Athens."

Oliver Ames, former governor of Massachusetts, and stockbroker Arthur Burnham helped raise money for a BAA team. In addition to Blake, the members included William Hoyt, a pole-vaulter; Thomas Burke, a sprinter; Ellery H. Clark, a high jumper; Sumner and John Paine, marksmen; and Gardner Williams, a swimmer. As coach, Graham accompanied them. The group departed on March 2, 1896, from New York City harbor, having been joined by several other athletes, including Robert Garrett, a shot-putter and captain of the Princeton track team. Garrett personally paid for several of his Princeton teammates to come along as well.

The U.S. Olympic team changed ships in Hamburg, Germany, and then stopped at Gibraltar, where they trained on playing fields used by British officers. On one sightseeing trip Blake trotted behind the carriages to train for the marathon.

Greeks Target the Marathon

Greek runners also practiced for the long-distance race, which promised their best chance for victory. At that time track and field held little popularity in Greece. Organizers of the Greek Olympic team reasoned that, while they might not be able to compete against the English-speaking athletes in the sprints, jumps and throws, they might well succeed in the newly created marathon race.

Greece held trials over the marathon route in the fall of 1895 to select and encourage competitors for the marathon. Among those chosen was a runner named Vanitekes, who had won several earlier runs. Practicing along the road between Marathon and Athens, Vanitekes smiled and nodded to his countrymen, who applauded his training efforts.

Placing fifth in an open trial, also earning a spot on the Greek Olympic team, was a 22-year-old peasant, Spiridon Loues. Loues was not an athlete in the traditional sense. He had developed a natural endurance delivering fresh water twice daily from his home village of Amarousion to Athens, a distance of nine miles. His training was his work, since he jogged beside his mule. Coubertin later would reveal that Loues spent two nights before the marathon on his knees praying in front of holy pictures. The day before the race, according to one source, he fasted. Still another story had him consuming an entire chicken for his pre-race meal. The legend of Spiridon Loues would continue to grow beyond these tales and become part of the history of the Boston Marathon.

The Legend of Loues

Twenty-five men toed the starting line near the village of Marathon on April 10, 1896, at 2:00 P.M. Four were foreigners to Greece, including the runners who placed first, second and third in the 1500 meters earlier in the Games. Edwin Flack, an Australian living in Great Britain, who competed for the London Athletic Club, had won the 1500 meters. Arthur Blake of the BAA had placed second, ahead of Albin Lermusiaux of France. The fourth non-Greek was a Hungarian named Gyula Kellner.

Lermusiaux was considered somewhat of a character by the Americans. On first meeting the Frenchman, one of the BAA athletes quizzed him about his events. Lermusiaux replied that he ran the 100-meter dash and the marathon. Asked to explain how he trained for such an odd combination, Lermusiaux replied, "One day, I run a little way very quick. The next day, I run a long way very slow."

Before the start, Lermusiaux stood sipping from a flask of brandy. A Colonel Papadiamantopoulos fired a starting pistol. The Frenchman dashed to the front, reportedly establishing a lead of 3 kilometers by the village of Pikermi, 15 kilometers into the race. (Three kilometers is nearly two miles, an unlikely margin at this stage, so his lead may have been exaggerated in race reports.) Flack trailed, with Blake and Kellner nearby, followed by three Greeks, including Georgios Lavrentis of Marousi. Spiridon Loues padded along somewhere back in the pack.

In this era before instant communications, horsemen dashed ahead to report results of the marathon to the crowd waiting in the Olympic stadium. The early reports looked bad for the Greeks, who had no color analyst to inform them that in marathons a steady pace wins the race.

Patience would prove particularly important on so demanding a course. The race began on the plain of Marathon—which means just that. Except for one hill, the first half of the original marathon was notably flat, teasing even experienced runners to push their paces beyond their means. Past 20 kilometers those impetuous runners pay for any early excesses as they ascend a series of hills. They crest the final hill just past 30 kilometers (about 20 miles) at a point called the wall by present-day marathoners. Beyond this point untrained marathoners experience new dimensions of pain. Finally, the last quarter of the race features a hammering descent through the suburbs of Athens before reaching the finish line in the Olympic stadium.

The non-Greeks leading the marathon were milers who had never before competed at such a long distance. Blake faltered first. At 23 kilometers he fell and failed to rise. Blood from broken blisters stained his shoes. Several Greeks also faltered and climbed into a hospital van trailing the field. Lermusiaux held the lead coming through the village of Karvati where several spectators ran from the crowd to offer him a victor's wreath as he passed beneath a flowered arch of triumph.

The Frenchman could hardly have felt triumphant. He sipped sugared wine as he ascended the mountains separating the plain of Marathon from Athens. As Lermusiaux struggled, Flack moved into the lead. Encouraged by his coach, who rode beside him on a bicycle, Lermusiaux repassed the Australian. Soon, however, Lermusiaux began to weave from one side of the road to the other. Coach and athlete collided. Lermusiaux fell. Yet he rose and continued.

As Flack regained the lead, a Greek runner emerged from the trailing pack. Spiridon Loues caught and passed Flack near 33 kilometers. Reportedly, Loues played tricks with runners he passed, slowing down to allow them to recatch him, then surging ahead to demoralize his rivals. His strategy worked on Flack. According to reports, Flack fell in a heap and was raving while being carried to the hospital van.

Two Greeks—Loues and Harilaos Vasilakos—continued in the lead, so close their shoulders once bumped. Eventually, Loues began to edge away from his countryman. A horseman darted ahead to bring news to the crowd at the stadium, including King Georgios and his two sons seated in the royal box. Cannons boomed announcing the approach of the marathoners. Along the streets girls threw flower petals before their feet. Boys darted from the crowd to sprint beside their new heroes.

Prince Constantinios and Prince Georgios descended from the royal box to greet the leader as he turned onto the track. Shouts arose from the crowd as Spiridon Loues came into view, threading his way between twin walls of people in the infield. Both princes jogged beside him as he ran the final steps to the finish line and almost carried him across the line. Pacing a runner in this manner was grounds for disqualification, but on that day nobody was about to lodge a protest. Spiridon Loues, winning in 2:58:50, became the first marathon champion in history.

Looking Ahead

After a long trip by ship from Athens and by train from New York City, the BAA athletes finally returned home on May 7, 1896. Reporters questioned them about the athletic competition and seemed particularly fascinated by the race from Marathon to Athens. Blake, who had dropped out of this first marathon, laughingly referred to it as the 23-mile straightaway.

Nevertheless, the marathon race had impressed BAA officials, including coach John Graham. Soon after returning to Boston, he and others within the club began making plans to contest a race at a similar distance.

TOP THREE FINISHERS IN THE FIRST MODERN OLYMPIC MARATHON IN 1896

1. SPIRIDON LOUES	Greece	2:58:50
2. HARILAOS VASILAKOS	Greece	3:06:03
3. GYULA KELLNER	Hungary	3:06:35

SOUVENIR of

THE · BOSTON · ATHLETIC · ASSOCIATION ·

A Superb Collection of
FORBES ART ALBERTYPES
Prepared Expressly For This Work
WITH DESCRIPTIVE ARTICLE BY EDWARD B. RANKIN OF THE BOSTON HERALD
Forbes Lith. Mfg. Co. Publishers
161 Devonshire St. Boston

McDermott's Run

Chapter Two

2

Never again. I doubt if I shall ever again run in a marathon race.

—*John J. McDermott*

As coach JOHN GRAHAM DISCUSSED plans for an American marathon with others in the Boston Athletic Association (BAA) in 1896, each piece gradually fell into place. To begin with, they decided to hold the race on Patriots' Day, which commemorates the Battle of Lexington on April 19, 1775.

The BAA already hosted a track-and-field meet on that holiday, using the Irvington Oval, a track near its Exeter Street clubhouse. The BAA Marathon could finish on that track, just as the Olympic Marathon had finished on the track at the stadium in Athens.

Determining the course was more difficult. In 1896, as today, Boston was linked to a series of smaller surrounding towns. A race that followed a course from Concord to Lexington to Boston would provide a logical and patriotic tie-in to Patriots' Day, but the distance would be only about half that run in Greece.

So where should they start the race? Graham began to survey possible routes and eventually worked his way back to the village of Ashland, which was strategically located approximately 24 miles to the northwest of Boston. The course paralleled

❦

PAGE 14: The clubhouse of the Boston Athletic Association was located on Exeter Street, across the street from the current Lenox Hotel. It was demolished in 1961 to be replaced by a new wing of the Boston Public Library. LEFT: John J. McDermott of New York City's Pastime Athletic Club won the Stamford to New York Marathon in 1896, and the following April he claimed victory at Boston.

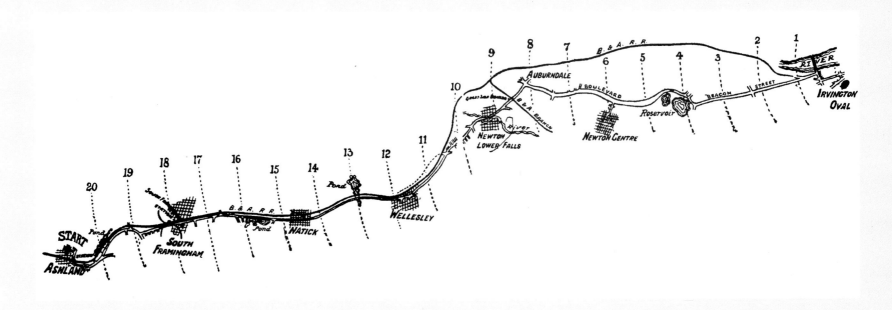

The first marathon course at Boston is described in the original instructions given to the runners by John Graham, coach of the Boston Athletic Association: "Start at Metcalf's Mill at Ashland, down Pleasant St., across the track to the trolley tracks, and then follow the trolley tracks through South Framingham, Natick, Wellesley, Newton Lower Falls, to the large signboards. Here are two roads, Beacon St. and Washington St. Take Washington St. on to the boulevard down to where the trolley tracks take a curve to the right. Follow the boulevard straight in to the old entrance to the reservoir, keep to the right until you strike Beacon St. Then it is a straight run to the junction of Beacon St. and Commonwealth Ave. to Exeter St. Turn right past the BAA to Irvington Ave. and over the bridge, first turn left in to the Irvington Oval and around the track once and finish."

the Boston and Albany Railroad, an electric line that started at South Station in downtown Boston and ran through Ashland. It offered an extra bonus in that runners and officials could reach the start by train, which also served to transport spectators to points along the course.

Setting the Course

BAA official Henry H. Holton rode a bicycle, with a wheel counter that measured revolutions, on roads beside the railroad tracks until he came to a point in Ashland opposite Metcalf's Mill. That would serve as the starting line for the first BAA Marathon.

As Graham and Holton designed this marathon course, they aimed to emulate the Olympic course topographically as well as in distance. The Olympic course between Marathon and Athens had combined flat stretches and hills. For the first half, that course had been relatively level then climbed a series of hills before descending into Athens. By design, Graham's route from Ashland through South Framingham, Natick, Wellesley, Newton and Brookline into Boston did the same. In fact, one of the BAA athletes who competed at the Olympics confirmed that the Boston route and roads "compare very favorably with those from Marathon to Athens."

Today, the length of the marathon course is an official distance—26 miles, 385 yards. But the original course, stated in the newspapers as 25 miles, could have been set as 40 kilometers (24.8 miles) or even as short as 24.5 miles. This lack of precision would surely rattle current-day course certifiers, who require that race courses be measured exactly— even a shortage of a few inches can invalidate records. In 1897, however, there was only one record—set by Spiridon Loues—and it was run on a course certainly measured without precision. After all, it was more important that the Olympic route go from Marathon to Athens rather than

cover a prescribed distance. And nobody knew exactly which route was run by the legendary Pheidippides.

Starting Out

As planned, the first Boston Marathon was run on Patriots' Day, April 19, 1897. The gathering point for these marathoners was the Central House, a hotel near the Ashland railroad station. On race morning a large crowd filled the hotel's small dining room for breakfast, including the athletes, who maintained a proper distance from each other. One reporter commented, "The six New York runners all dined at one table, while Boston, Cambridge and local men all occupied another."

Several runners had stayed overnight at the hotel. Others came up from Boston that morning, catching either the 7:00 or 9:12 train from South Station. Both trains were crowded with spectators, who planned to watch the start then return to Boston for the finish. Also boarding the early train with bicycles were 28 militiamen, including nine ambulance corpsmen, from Company B, 2nd Regiment, Massachusetts Volunteer Militia under the direction of Captain Walter E. Lombard. Lombard planned to ride ahead of the lead runners, requesting vehicles to move from the course and spectators to move back from the curbs. His militiamen would accompany the runners, providing lemons, water and wet handkerchiefs. The ambulancemen would provide medical aid if needed. Each entrant had a bicyclist assigned to him.

15 Men at the Start

For the first Boston Marathon only 17 runners signed up, all men. (Sixty-nine years would pass before a woman would appear at a Boston starting line.) Three failed to show and a last-minute entry brought the final field to 15.

Warming Up for Boston: The First New York Marathon

Like the Boston Athletic Association, the New York Knickerbocker Athletic Club (AC) was inspired by the Olympic Marathon race in Greece. Upon their return to this country, the New York club members made plans to include a marathon race of 25 miles in a track-and-field meet to be held September 19, 1896.

The course started in Stamford, Connecticut, and ended at William's Bridge at the southern tip of Manhattan. Running over soggy roads, through mud and slush, 30 men competed, including three New Yorkers who would join the first Boston race seven months later: John J. Kiernan of the St. Bartholomew AC, Hamilton Gray of the St. George AC and John J. McDermott of the Pastime AC.

Once they passed New Rochelle, McDermott took the lead and held it, but as the *New York Times* reported, "the miserable roads made it impossible for him to travel fast. Now and then he walked but Hamilton Gray seemed to be unable in the last part of the race to get any nearer to him than 200 yards."

Several bicyclists rode out from the oval to join the lead runners. As they approached the track, spectators began shouting, "They're here! They're coming!" Women screamed and waved handkerchiefs. Men dashed from their seats to trackside. McDermott won in 3:25:06.

Gray took second in 3:28:27. Kiernan failed to finish in the top ten.

New York, thus, was the site of the first American marathon, but the Knickerbocker AC failed to continue its sponsorship. The race died. In 1970 Fred Lebow founded a new marathon in Central Park. The current New York City Marathon, which now attracts over 25,000 entrants, is larger than the Boston Marathon—but not older.

The late entrant was Dick Grant, a student at Harvard University. Because of his late entry, Grant was the only runner not to have a bicyclist assigned to him. The Harvard track coach, J. G. Lathrop, tried to discourage Grant, who was a miler and had not trained to run such a long distance. Nevertheless, Grant insisted and inadvertently started a tradition among students from Harvard and other local universities of appearing race day only half-trained. Grant was handed the final race number: 18. He pinned it to the back of his crimson and white uniform.

Others did the same. Unlike later years when the fastest runners received the lowest numbers, no status was attached to wearing number 1 (which in later years would be awarded at press conferences to either the defending champion or the fastest runner in the field). At least in this first race, the BAA democratically issued numbers in the order that runners registered. Thus, A. T. Howe, representing the YMCA of Lowell, Massachusetts, wore the number 1.

Despite having won the earlier marathon in New York, John McDermott (described by the *Boston Record* as "a lithe, dark, curly-haired young man, 22 years of age") was given number 14. He pinned it to a Pastime Athletic Club (AC) shirt that sported a blue Brazilian cross.

A reporter from the *Boston Post* described the field: "McDermott and Gray looked as if they had trained carefully for this race and did not carry an ounce of superfluous flesh. Others looked as if they could spare a few pounds, including Dick Grant. Howe of Lowell was the smallest of the lot and was not expected to finish but he did, running to good style all the way."

Go!

Shortly before the scheduled noon start, athletes and their entourages walked and trotted three-quarters of a mile to Metcalf's Mill on Pleasant

Street. Graham had provided typewritten directions of the course to the runners, then, to make certain no runners became lost, he placed signs along the course to enable them "to find their way without slacking speed."

Most of the first Boston Marathon was run on unpaved roads, pavement being an artifact of the automotive age, which had just begun. The surface was far from smooth. A report in the *Boston Herald* stated "the going is fair from Ashland to Natick and improves coming in, the last half of the run being as good as most cinder tracks if the weather is at all decent."

The race had been scheduled to start at high noon, which would allow everybody along the course, including those waiting at the finish line, to know how long the marathoners had been running. But it was 12:15 P.M. before Olympic sprint champion Thomas E. Burke scraped his foot across the dirt road, marking the starting line. He called each of the contestants to the line by number. The road was so narrow that those 15 runners failed to fit in a single row.

At precisely 12:19 P.M., Burke gave the starting command, "Go!"

Harvard student Dick Grant and Hamilton Gray, a well-respected cross-country runner from New York City, moved quickly into the lead. McDermott stayed close. The others trailed in bunches of twos and threes, nobody more than 50 yards behind when they reached the village of Ashland.

A *Boston Globe* reporter, in a lengthy and colorful description of this first Boston Marathon, wrote: "The crowd at the Ashland station was good-natured and as it formed a line for the athletes to pass, the sleepy old town rang with the cheers of her lusty sons. As each passed he received a hearty greeting."

(continued on page 24)

RUNNERS IN THE FIRST BOSTON MARATHON

Entrant	Sponsor	City	Time
1. JOHN J. MCDERMOTT	Pastime Athletic Club	New York City	2:55:10
2. JOHN J. KIERNAN	St. Bartholomew AC	New York City	3:02:02
3. E. P. RHELL	unattached	Jamaica Plain, Mass.	3:06:02
4. HAMILTON GRAY	St. George AC	New York City	3:11:37
5. H. D. EGGLESTON	Pastime AC	New York City	3:17:50
6. J. MASON	Star AC	New York City	3:31:00
7. W. RYAN	South Boston Athletic Association	Boston	3:41:25
8. LAWRENCE BRIGNOLIA	Bradford Boat Club	Cambridge, Mass.	4:06:12
9. HARRY LEONARD	unattached	Melrose, Mass.	4:08:00
10. A. T. HOWE	Lowell YMCA	Lowell, Mass.	4:10:00
W. A. MITCHELL	Lowell YMCA	Lowell, Mass.	DNF
E. F. PETTEE	unattached	Boston	DNF
H. C. MORRILL	unattached	Dorchester, Mass.	DNF
J. E. ENRIGHT	Pastime AC	New York City	DNF
DICK GRANT	Harvard AA	Cambridge, Mass.	DNF

THE START

Before photography was commonplace in newspapers, artists provided renderings of events, like the first Boston Marathon.

LEFT: Boston Athletic Association club members could relax with a game of dominoes. **RIGHT**: The BAA clubhouse, at the corner of Boylston and Exeter Streets, symbolized nineteenth-century elegance.

The Spirit of the Unicorn: The Story of the BAA

The Boston Athletic Association (BAA) was founded in January 1887, a decade before the marathon that would bear its name. In establishing itself, the BAA patterned itself on social and athletic clubs founded about the same time in other major cities. Its patrons would be prosperous businessmen, looking for a place to lunch and a place to play.

Among its founders were such notables as Henry Parkman, Lawrence Tucker, Harrison Gray Otis, Charles P. Curtis, Jr., Thomas Nelson and A. Cortlandt Van Rensselaer. With 1,100 prospective members, they set dues at $30 a year, with an initiation fee of $40. A new clubhouse, built on the corner of Boylston and Exeter Streets in Boston's prestigious Back Bay area, was officially opened on December 29, 1888.

This clubhouse was a brick, multistory building, handsomely constructed with arched windows and turreted alcoves. "No new building in Boston has attracted so much attention as that recently opened by the Boston Athletic Association on Exeter Street," wrote a correspondent for the *American Architect and Building News*.

An upper floor housed a tennis court and a racquet court. One floor below that was a gymnasium with a running track. Along with a billiards room, a bowling alley and a swimming pool were Turkish baths and rooms where members could relax or obtain a shampoo and a haircut. "Before dressing, (the member) can receive a rubdown with alcohol, which will prevent his catching cold and will act like a cocktail before dinner," wrote the correspondent. The dining room seated 85. After their meals members could retire to lounging rooms to enjoy a cigar and a nap. Rooms were available for overnight stays. In the tradition of the era, the BAA only permitted women limited access on special occasions. Chosen as the symbol for the BAA was the unicorn, a mythical horned creature symbolic of purity.

In 1891 the BAA organized its first track-and-field competition. And on April 19, 1897, the first BAA Marathon was held.

The marathon would prove more durable than the clubhouse before whose doors it finished. The stock market crash of 1929 and the ensuing depression eroded the wealth of businessmen members. In 1935 the BAA filed for bankruptcy. Eventually, the BAA sold its clubhouse to Boston University. The clubhouse was finally demolished in 1961, replaced by an expanded Boston Public Library four years later. The marathon finish moved from Exeter Street around the corner onto Boylston Street.

As an organization, the BAA survived mainly through the efforts of Walter A. Brown, owner of the Boston Garden, and a handful of friends, who kept the former sportsmen's club alive as the sponsoring organization for the marathon and an indoor track meet. For a period during the 1970s the rising number of entrants in the marathon both revived the BAA and threatened to overwhelm the resources of its volunteer members. Support from John Hancock Financial Services, beginning with the 1986 race, ensured that the BAA Marathon would celebrate its centennial with a solid base of support.

The BAA now has a year-round staff in two offices: an organizational headquarters on Clarendon Street just blocks from the marathon finish line and a small office for processing race entries in Hopkinton near the marathon start. The opulent clubhouse is gone but the spirit of the BAA remains in the unicorn, pictured on their logo and on medals earned by fast finishers in the marathon today.

THE MUCH-MOVED STARTING LINE

"In all the hoopla around the 100th anniversary," says Dick Fannon, president of the Ashland Historical Society, "I hope they realize the Boston Marathon began in Ashland, not Hopkinton."

The site of that first start, Metcalf's Mill, is gone. Once used to manufacture shoe boxes, later an icehouse, the mill burned in the 1930s. All that remains—other than a memory—is a gaping hole almost hidden by overgrowth.

Even while the starting line remained in Ashland, it moved around. As the finish line shifted, the Ashland site was adjusted. In the marathon's third year the Boston Athletic Association (BAA) moved the finish to a point before its old clubhouse on Exeter Street, site of the current Boston Public Library. BAA official Henry H. Holton, who had measured the 1897 course, repositioned the start backward along Pleasant Street and onto High Street, where it crossed over the Boston and Albany railroad tracks. Thus, runners began the 1899 race in the middle of the railroad bridge. Though only 22 feet wide, the bridge easily accommodated the 17 starters that year.

But by 1907, 124 runners had entered the marathon, too many for the narrow starting area. Repairs that year closed the bridge, so the BAA moved the start again, onto Union Street at Steven's Corner.

In 1924 the course was lengthened to 26 miles, 385 yards. The start left Ashland forever, moving up the road and across the town border into Hopkinton. After several readjustments over the years, the marathon settled on the current starting point. A sign today on Hopkinton Green proclaims: "Welcome to Hopkinton. It all starts here."

But Ashland's Dick Fannon adds his own footnote: "But not in 1897."

The course turned left after crossing the Boston and Albany tracks near John Stone's Inn, built in 1832 but still serving patrons a century later as a restaurant. Runners passed the Ashland train station, which has since been remodeled and now serves as a doctor's office. The first Boston Marathoners ran with the Boston and Albany tracks on their left, as they would for most of the marathon's course. Within a short distance they reached Union Street, the main route between Hopkinton and Boston that is used for the marathon today.

Gray and Grant ran side by side through a long line of spectators that stretched from Ashland to South Framingham. The lead pair passed through that town in 23:00, having run about four miles. McDermott, running with Johnny J. Kiernan of the St. Bartholemew Athletic Club in New York City, allowed the distance between him and the leaders to stretch to nearly a quarter-mile. "The houses all along the line were filled with people," wrote the *Globe* reporter, "and many handkerchiefs and good wishes were wafted upon the beautiful April day as the men, with faces set, kept on."

At South Framingham the crowd was bigger and noisier. The day was sunny, the temperature 66 degrees. A brisk westerly wind blew, pushing the marathoners toward Boston. With today's paved roads, such a wind would be considered a blessing. In 1897, because the roads were dirt, dust filled the air around the lead runners. The trailing runners had it worse; they had to breathe the dust churned by the wheels of the bicyclists accompanying them. Not only that, but many spectators rode beside and behind the runners in horse-drawn carriages, motorcycles and every conceivable form of conveyance. Still, the 1897 marathoners were better off than those who ran decades later and were forced to breathe the exhaust fumes of automobiles carrying reporters. Not until 1947 would the BAA provide a press bus to keep reporters off the course.

"Rah for Harvard!"

Between South Framingham and Natick Grant and Gray remained in front. Though Grant ran unattended, Gray shared water canteens with him. Behind, McDermott surged up a hard hill to shake Kiernan—as well as several of the bicyclists pursuing. On the next flat the bicyclists caught up, but not Kiernan. At 1:06 P.M. Grant and Gray passed Natick Center, having run approximately seven miles in 46 or 47 minutes, somewhat faster than a 7-minute-mile pace. Several spectators, recognizing Grant, cheered "Grant! Grant! Rah for Harvard!" Two young girls jumped from the crowd in Natick and ran with Grant for 25 yards, shouting encouragement.

A quarter-mile behind was McDermott, with Kiernan a short gap behind him. McDermott's teammate from the Pastime AC, H. D. Eggleston, led a trail pack. The lead runners, as well as those behind, acknowledged the applause of the crowd by waving their hands. According to the *Evening Record*, "the people surged in from the sides of the road and left a very small space for the runners to get through."

Grant and Gray passed Wellesley at 1:33 P.M., suggesting a time of 1:19 for the 11 or so miles run, the same pace as before. McDermott, however, had begun to close the gap. Past Wellesley a long hill drops toward Newton Lower Falls. Here, McDermott finally caught the two leaders, rushing past on the downhill. After being passed, Gray lost heart and began to walk—though he soon started running again.

"Dick Grant gave chase," reported the *Boston Globe*, "and although nearly played out, he clung to the heels of the New York flyer. . . . It was a hot race for about a mile and the Harvard crack was applauded generously for his plucky but fruitless race. At the bottom of the hill and at the rise of the next hill, he staggered a few steps and quit running. He walked to the top of the hill just in time to see the little Pastime Athletic Club wonder disappearing around a turn in the road."

Grant spotted a street-watering cart. Signaling the driver to stop, Grant laid down, requesting that the water be turned on. Rising, he continued for a short distance to just before Hammond Street, but soon after that, he abandoned the race. Reportedly, his feet were badly blistered. J. E. Enright of New York quit near the same point and returned to Boston on a passing electric train.

Trouble along the Way

By Auburndale, the point where the course today makes a short right turn past a fire station and onto Commonwealth Avenue, McDermott's lead was estimated as "nearly a mile," certainly an exaggeration. Kiernan moved past Gray into second. The *Globe* reported: "The main part of the crowd now centered about McDermott and the attendants had to work hard to keep the road clear. He was running like clockwork. His legs seemed to rise and fall like a phantom Greek and his lithe body was bent just the least bit forward; his arms were at full length at his side and his face was set with determination.

"As he turned into the boulevard, he asked his attendant, Corporal Eddie Heinlein, to tell him when he had gone 20 miles. He breasted the long hill manfully, still maintaining his beautiful form, and he laughed at the wheelmen who were pounding their pedals in their endeavor to keep their machines in motion." But cresting the top of the Newton hills, near the entrance to a cemetery and about a quarter-mile from the reservoir entrance, McDermott was no longer laughing. He had run 20 miles, covering that distance in about 2:15, still under a 7-minute-mile pace. He now stopped to walk, continuing at that reduced pace for several hundred yards. Then he started running again. Several hundred

(continued on page 28)

The marathon starting gun fired by Walter F. Brown is a .38 caliber police revolver with a transducer attached that sends an electronic signal to the finish-line clock. When fired, it triggers a prerecorded and magnified howitzer explosion so that all runners on the starting line hear the shot. It is a long way from 1897 when Thomas E. Burke first used his heel to draw a line on the dirt and said, "Go!"

PATRONS OF THE BOSTON MARATHON: THE BROWN FAMILY

At noon each Patriots' Day Walter F. Brown fires the gun to start the Boston Marathon. In doing so, he continues a family tradition. Since 1905 a member of the Brown family has served as Boston's starter all but one year. More importantly, the Brown family—particularly George V. Brown and Walter A. Brown—provided the inspiration (and backing) that allowed the marathon and the Boston Athletic Association (BAA) to survive some lean years.

Born in 1880, George V. Brown attended Bryant and Stratton Business School and eventually came to work for George A. Billings, chairman of the BAA athletic committee, as his assistant and later as athletic director. Brown's duties included helping with the club's marathon, but it would not be until 1905 that a Brown became starter for the race.

Brown also officiated college football games and served as athletic director for Boston University. After the old Boston Arena burned, Brown convinced a wealthy BAA member, Henry G. Lapham, to finance its reconstruction. The Arena reopened in 1920 with Brown as its general manager. In addition to boxing matches, ice hockey games and figure skating events, he brought in two indoor track meets, one sponsored by the BAA. His early tenure with the BAA had been as an employee, but he now had the financial resources to become a member.

Tom Brown remembers attending the marathon each year with his father. "I used to go with him into Boston the day of the race," he recalls. I'd go to South Station, where it was my job to look for runners. I'd see someone walking around with a gym bag looking puzzled, and I'd ask if he was a marathon runner and get him on the train to Framingham."

The Roaring Twenties was a golden age for sports: the decade of Jack Dempsey, Babe Ruth, Bill Tilden and Clarence DeMar. The owners of New York's Madison Square Garden built an indoor stadium over Boston's North Station and began to siphon sports attractions away from the Arena, including the Boston Bruins of the National Hockey League. Lapham eventually acquired control of this second stadium, renaming it the Boston Garden and appointing George Brown as its general manager. George's son, Walter, worked with him as an assistant.

In 1937 George Brown suffered a heart attack and died. Walter A. Brown became the Garden manager. The BAA had ceased to exist as a private club, but it continued as nominal sponsor for the marathon and track meet. Walter, who assumed his father's duties as official starter in 1938, dedicated the track meet profits to the marathon. With small fields, it cost only a few thousand dollars for volunteers to organize the race each year.

In 1946 Brown and partner Lou Pieri organized a team in the newly founded National Basketball Association, calling it the Boston Celtics. Five years later, the Garden purchased control of the Boston Bruins, Walter becoming the team's president. He would be elected to both the NBA and NHL Hall of Fames.

George V. Brown, an early patron of the Boston Marathon.

Walter Brown served as president of the BAA between 1940 and his death in 1964. Afterward, Tom Brown served as starter for several years, and starting in 1991, Walter Brown's nephew, Walter F. Brown, took over the official starter's duties.

yards farther he stopped again. McDermott reached for his left leg, which had begun to cramp. By this time, a Sergeant West had joined Corporal Heinlein in escorting the leader. The two militiamen hopped off their bicycles, and Heinlein began massaging McDermott's leg. West offered a sip of brandy.

McDermott started again—then stopped. He straightened his leg. "Rub!" he instructed once more. Heinlein obliged and McDermott found himself able to resume running, soon passing through Cleveland Circle with approximately four miles remaining. He headed down Beacon Street past groups of people standing on the curb applauding.

Reaching St. Paul Street, McDermott walked one more time on his way to Carleton Street. Told by his escorts that another runner was approaching over the hill, McDermott began again. "He shut his teeth," reported the *Globe*, "set his face, and, leaning well forward, he dug his shoes into the hard Beacon Street surface and started on his last spurt."

McDermott approached Kenmore Square, up the short hill that now passes over the Massachusetts Turnpike. Crossing Massachusetts Avenue, he encountered a funeral procession blocking his way. The leader darted through the line of vehicles, causing two of the electric cars to stall.

Still leading, McDermott turned right onto Exeter Street, passing the BAA clubhouse. Reportedly, 500 people had assembled there to cheer the winner. Future marathons would finish at that point, across from the Lenox Hotel, but McDermott continued across Huntington and turned onto Irvington Street, then into the entrance to the Oval.

A Strong Finish

In the Oval the track meet had been going since 2:00 P.M. before a crowd estimated to be 3,500. At the time, John Graham described it as "the biggest crowd I ever saw here." In the handicap mile with 14 starters, A. W. Foote of Yale had just barely caught Harvard's J. F. Downey, who had been given a 40-yard lead. Their time was 4:48, considered fast for the track and the era but about what top marathoners today average per mile for 26 miles. Ellery Clark, a winner in Athens the previous April, placed second in three events: the discus, long jump and high hurdles. The 600-yard run had just finished with Yale's C. E. Ordway the winner in 1:14.8, when the sound of cheers from people on housetops and the streets outside began to get louder, signaling McDermott's approach.

"The cheering and yelling was deafening," reported the *Globe*. "Every available foot of standing room in the Oval was crowded. The fences were black with boys, young men and women. The policemen forgot their duty in the excitement, and the track was soon swarming with excited people, all wishing to grasp the hand of the victor of the first 'Marathon race' ever held in Massachusetts."

McDermott stumbled slightly moving down onto the track, then turned to the left to run a final clockwise lap. "McDermott! McDermott!" the crowd chanted. Several dozen athletes and spectators paced him on his final lap. Despite his struggle during the previous several miles, he finished looking strong. After winning, he was lifted to the shoulders of several people in the crowd.

A New Record

During a momentary lull the announcer shouted, "Two fifty-five and ten seconds—breaking the record." The record at that time was 2:58:50, set by Spiridon Loues in the 1896 Olympics. After acknowledging the cheers, McDermott headed back to the BAA clubhouse.

Kiernan finished second in 3:02:02, with E. P. Rhell of Jamaica Plain, Massachusetts, third in 3:06:02. Toward the end Kiernan was reduced to walking but would not yield his place to Rhell, who was behind him. Kiernan would walk until Rhell caught him, then would sprint ahead and walk again. Never anywhere near the front, Rhell had run steadily all day. Except for the three men who fell behind immediately, Rhell had run last all the way to Wellesley, nearly half the distance. In a classic example of good pacing, he then steadily advanced from seventh place to his eventual third. "He jogged right along all the way, just as you saw him here on the Oval," said his escort, Corporal Beaumont.

Gray, who had run in the lead with Grant for 14 miles until passed by McDermott, managed to finish fourth in 3:11:37. By the time Eggleston crossed the line in fifth in 3:17:50, the large crowd had begun to disperse. Five more would cross the line, the last three taking just over four hours. Finishing tenth and last was A. T. Howe in 4:10:00. The first six finishers received oak plaques with silver BAA shields, McDermott's being the largest but costing no more than $35 to comply with the Amateur Athletic Union's rules concerning prizes. The other four finishers received "souvenirs."

Always Fresh

Everybody seemed astounded at how good McDermott looked after running 25 miles. Sergeant West told a reporter from the *Evening Record*, "That little fellow is a wonder. I never saw anything like it. He was always fresh. Never for an instant in all that long distance did he give the faintest evidence of exhaustion. Why, he was the most unconcerned fellow I ever saw. He talked all the way coming in—asked us our names, asked who was behind him and how far. In fact, he appeared to be just as fresh as a daisy all the way in, and he is now. Look at him."

The *Globe* reporter also bragged about the early finishers, "Had it been necessary for them to run five miles more, they could have done it."

(To which the tens of thousands who would finish Boston over the next century might respond, "Have you ever tried it?")

In the BAA clubhouse McDermott spoke with reporters: "Yes, I feel pretty tired in my legs. My body is all right but my feet are pretty sore, of course. My toes are blistered and the skin has peeled off the bottom of my feet."

Before starting the race, McDermott had weighed 123.5 pounds. He lost 9 pounds during the run. He had suffered several stitches in his left side but overcame them. He praised the bicycle escorts and said that nobody had interfered with the runners at any stage of the race. He felt that Grant had run a remarkable race for someone untrained for the distance. He credited Graham for both the organization of the race and the course selection. "He could not have had a better course made to order," said the gracious winner.

"This probably will be my last long race," McDermott claimed. His reaction was typical of so many marathoners yet to come. Decades later Olympic champion Frank Shorter would remark, "You can't begin to think of your next marathon until you've forgotten your last one." Regardless, McDermott would return to Boston the following year and run the course 13 minutes faster yet place fourth.

Although McDermott might not have been ready to consider another marathon, the reporters who had followed this first journey from Ashland to Boston already had begun to look to the next one. "The BAA's Marathon runs have been inaugurated," enthused the *Boston Journal*. "Posterity will—as the runs are held year by year—point to this which was the beginning." But even the most enthusiastic reporter could not have guessed what the next 100 years might bring.

Dust and Mayhem

Chapter Three

3

The BAA Marathon race on Tuesday will eclipse all former runs in

the matter of entries.... At least one hundred athletes will have

entered before the final closing.—*The Boston Globe, 1903*

TRADITIONS STARTED EARLY in the Boston Athletic Association Marathon. From the beginning, those watching the marathon far outnumbered those running in it. In fact, in Boston's second year, although only 25 men entered the race, thousands of spectators lined the roads between Ashland and the Irvington Oval, waiting for a glimpse of passing runners.

How many thousands watched the marathon in these early years is open to question. The *Boston Globe* would report 25,000 people watching in 1900. Their estimate for 1902 grew to 100,000. By the marathon's seventh running in 1903, at a time when Boston's population was just over 500,000, the paper reported, "Near 200,000 saw the race or finish." Had the mass of spectators increased that rapidly or was it merely the *Globe*'s perception of that mass? Nobody can say for sure.

Regardless of the ability of reporters to estimate crowd size, Boston's ability to attract spectators unquestionably began with Year One. "The Boston Marathon was special for the Morrill family from the beginning," remembers Mary E. Morrill, who lives on West Central Street in Natick along the marathon course. "My husband's family watched the race from the first, in 1897, when his mother walked two miles from her home in South Natick to Lincoln Square to see it. By 1900 she was

PAGE 30: Those starting the 1912 marathon stared out over a sea of mud. Mud didn't slow Mike Ryan that day. He set a course and world record of 2:21:18 for the 25-mile distance. LEFT: As years passed, the roads linking Hopkinton and Boston, such as the one leading into Framingham during the 1936 marathon, were paved, eliminating mud and dust as a problem. Instead, marathoners breathed automobile exhaust.

Nowhere were the weary contestants viewed more
expectantly than at Wellesley College.

Spectacle

LEFT: Only 165, including six former Boston Marathon winners, started the race in 1940. The crowds would come later. RIGHT: Although the number of runners entered each Patriots' Day rarely reached more than 200 during the Boston Marathon's first seven decades, race fans by the tens and hundreds of thousands appeared beside the course to view the spectacle. The women of Wellesley College were out on the curb from Year One.

34

married and living on Elm Street near the marathon course.

"Every year, the Morrill clan of 40 cousins gathered at the end of the street for the marathon," says Morrill. "Since my husband and I moved into our present home in 1946, we have been able to sit on our front steps and watch the runners. The only time my husband ever missed the race, until he died in 1989, was the day we were married in 1940."

Shrieking Spectators

Most onlookers watched from the population centers that still serve as landmarks along the race route: Ashland, South Framingham, Natick and beyond. On the open stretches between these towns, fewer people gathered (as is somewhat true today). But once the marathoners approached the town centers, they found sidewalks lined with cheering people, who often pressed into the street, shrinking the marathon course to a narrow corridor.

"There was an immense crowd at the starting point in Ashland," wrote a *Boston Herald* reporter in 1898. That same year, a *Globe* reporter described the scene at Natick Center: "A wall of humanity lined both sides of the road." In 1900 the same paper reported: "The streets were lined with people in South Framingham, and the runners were followed by hundreds of wheelmen and carriages to the outskirts of town." And two years later: "Every foot of the course from the reservoir to Coolidge Corner, both sides of the boulevard, were black with shrieking spectators, and Brookline's aristocracy leaned out of windows and waved lace handkerchiefs in the April breeze."

The Women of Wellesley

The tradition of women from Wellesley College cheering the runners also began early. Harvard's Dick Grant had attracted attention while passing the all-women's school in the first year. With Grant not running in 1898, fewer Wellesley students appeared by the side of the road. When Grant returned the following year, interest near this halfway point picked up.

"The rivals were heartily cheered all along the route, but nowhere were the fagged out contestants applauded more liberally than at the home of Wellesley College," gushed the *Globe* reporter in 1899. "Of course, when the (Harvard) colors and familiar face of 'Dick' Grant were discovered, the bevy of pretty girls all gowned in fashionable and vari-colored gowns, but with crimson predominating, arose as one, and standing on the very edge of the street, clapped hands and shouted to the Harvard man that he had the best wishes of the entire town."

And in 1902, the same paper described the "pretty college girls at Wellesley" assembling along the highway to "flaunt their dainty kerchiefs and class colors in the faces of the heaving, panting leaders."

Much later in this century, those "pretty college girls" were participating in the marathon themselves and expressing a different way of thinking. In fact, in 1994 a woman runner from Wellesley ran the marathon in a T-shirt that proclaimed, "Wellesley is not a girls' college without men; it's a womens' college without boys." And the response was deafening as she passed the college.

The Horseless Carriage and the Iron Horse

During the turn of the century, college girls may have been plentiful, but few automobiles were on the roads. The initial appearance of an automobile on American streets was in Springfield, Massachusetts, on September 21, 1893. And the first car race was held in Chicago on November 28, 1895. Six motorized machines entered that 52.4-mile event but only two finished. The winner averaged 7.5 miles per hour—slower

LEFT: Outfits worn by the 1902 marathoners bespeak a raiment of another era (no Spandex). **RIGHT:** Between the official attendants from the Massachusetts Volunteer Militia and those out for a holiday jaunt, bicyclists often outnumbered runners on the road, as they did during the 1899 Boston Marathon. That soon would change.

than John J. McDermott's pace when he won the first Boston Marathon! In the coming years cars would play a bigger part in the Boston drama.

Early spectators trailed the runners on any conveyance available. "Carriages, fancy traps, a few motor wagons and equestrians followed the fast disappearing plodders as far as Natick," reported the *Boston Globe* in 1898. "The clanging of gongs and the constant ringing of bells was hideous, but a good deal of fun was furnished. Collisions were frequent and the gallant members of Company B of the 2nd Regiment (ambulance corpsmen), Massachusetts Volunteer Militia, had their hands full to stay the progress of the energetic and inquisitive youth who insisted on riding alongside a runner and whispering words of encouragement or shouting advice to the weary men who were doggedly plodding along."

Others used the railroad line paralleling the race course to see the marathoners at one or two places en route before hurrying back to town. "A large party from this city went to Ashland to witness the start," reported the *Globe* in 1900, "after which they took the electrics to South Framingham and an express train to town, which was reached in season to allow them to dine and then witness the finish."

Pedal Pushers

Overall, though, the vehicle of choice for those who accompanied the marathoners was the bicycle, particularly for the Massachusetts militiamen under the command of Captain Walter E. Lombard. Dressed in their regulation blue uniforms, they appeared at South Station in Boston each Patriots' Day during the early years to catch the 9:15 train with athletes and officials. Each runner, thus, had an accompanying cyclist to offer aid, ranging from liquids to a rubdown for cramping muscles. (This form of support is known in English-speaking nations as sec-

onding, which continues to some extent in South Africa today.)

Some marathoners also had trainers or coaches trailing in their wakes. This support crew proved vital to the success of many runners. In the 1900 race Canadian William Sheering collapsed toward the end. His attendants immediately swarmed over him.

Reported the *Globe*: "After a couple of minutes of hard rubbing and the application of restoratives, (Sheering) made an effort to rise but sank down to the turf again. His attendants gently lifted him to his feet, said a few encouraging words, and, with their assistance, he hobbled along for a short distance, then walked freely and finally broke into a slow run, much to the delight of his trainer." Sheering finished second, running in 2:41:31 that year, part of a Canadian sweep of the first three medals.

Officials at early Boston Marathons encouraged—or at least condoned—levels of support that in later races would be judged illegal. At the 1908 Olympic Marathon Italy's Dorando Pietri was disqualified after being aided across the line by officials. American Johnny Hayes, who had placed second at Boston that same year, received the gold medal.

The Grand Cavalcade

By 1903 the number of runners entering Boston had surpassed 100, too many for Captain Lombard's militiamen to effectively support. Henry H. Holton, the BAA official in charge of the race that year, issued a plea for additional bicycle escorts, promising that the club would provide transportation to Ashland as well as a meal at the finish line. Soon, however, because of practical considerations, attendants on bicycles would disappear.

The automobile was fast growing in popularity and by the century's second decade had begun to replace carriages and bicycles as the mode of

The wide street was black with humanity, who surged forward to catch a glimpse of the probable winners. —*The Boston Globe*

LEFT: Cyclists patiently wait for a glimpse of runners passing through Natick. RIGHT: Minutes after the 1932 start, marathoners spread out between spectators on both sides. Traffic was less a problem then and race fans often could jump in their cars, or catch a train, and see their heroes several times along the course—and still make the finish.

transportation for many Americans. In keeping with this trend, the *Globe* began to provide its reporters covering the race with an open-air vehicle decorated with a pennant saying Boston Globe. For several years the paper published photographs of its reporters and their cars. In 1902 the paper carried this account of the race: "With each succeeding mile, the grand cavalcade of automobiles, bicycles and teams grew larger and the roads became more dusty, but the three leaders plugged along determinedly. Into South Framingham sped the foremost. The wide street was black with humanity, who surged forward to catch a glimpse of the probable winners. With the aid of the *Globe*'s Crestmobile, adroitly handled by Dudley Marks, the chauffeur, the South Framingham police were enabled to clear a pathway through the deep throng."

The newspaper's chauffeur received credit, but ironically, none of its reporters were recognized. Unlike today, no bylines appeared on stories. Thus, those early chroniclers of the Boston Marathon in the *Globe* and Boston's numerous other dailies remain unknown.

Bylines Emerge with Jerry Nason

One reporter who would not remain anonymous for long was Jerry Nason, who covered the marathon for the *Globe* from the 1930s through the 1980s, a period when bylines on feature articles became more common. Nason missed the first dozen years of the race only because he had not yet been born. On April 14, 1909, Jerry Nason was born in a hospital in Newton, located on the marathon course. He was five days old when the marathon was run that year. Nason later would claim that a nurse picked him up from his cradle and held him up to the window while the marathoners were passing.

Later, as a boy, Nason and his friends would ride their bikes from Newton to Ashland to see the start and accompany some of the back runners, who did not have attendants. The youngsters would carry their packs, hoping they were trained well enough to finish. In an interview with Joe Falls, Nason described his earliest memories of the race: "Years ago they didn't have macadam roads until you reached Boston. The race started out in the country and the roads were muddy; they were filled with rocks and they had mud ruts in them from the wintertime. That's why these fellows had to wear such heavy, thick-soled shoes. You could hear them coming down the street. It sounded like wet fish being slapped on a table. It was a big handicap to them, but if they didn't have those heavy shoes, they'd be turning their ankles or bruising their feet so they couldn't run at all."

A Race within a Race

Nason also talked to Falls about the problems automobiles posed to the runners: "The Marathon was covered by the six Boston newspapers, and each newspaper had its own car on the course. Each paper had a writer in the car and maybe two photographers. There were 2 official cars, so that made 8 in all. And I'm not even counting the wire services, the AP, UP and International News Service. They had their own cars, too, so that there were maybe 10 or 12 cars out there surrounding the runners. We'd all be concentrating on the leaders, and we'd be jockeying back and forth to get in position to get the best photos. . . . We kept cutting in and out and back and forth. It was like a race within a race. It was like Indianapolis in slow motion. We'd be yelling at the other cars, 'Get out of the way!' and they'd be yelling back at us. All the while, mind you, nobody is thinking of the poor runners, who were being caught up in the fumes from these cars and all but being asphyxiated."

In 1947, after Will Cloney took over management of the race, he banned automobiles from the course and forced reporters into a single

THE MARATHON THAT WASN'T

Although the Boston Athletic Association (BAA) celebrates a centennial in 1996, that race has not always been a marathon. In the war year of 1918 the marathon was replaced by a relay race for servicemen. Starting at Steven's Corner on the Hopkinton Road, 14 teams of ten men each ran the 25 miles to the BAA clubhouse on Exeter Street, with each runner covering about 2½ miles.

Few of the servicemen seemed ready to run even that far. They wore dress uniforms and boots instead of running suits. "It was a most unusual sight to see the runners plodding along fully clothed and with apparently never a thought of saving themselves for the long, hard miles ahead," reported Lawrence J. Sweeney of the *Boston Globe*. "They were out to run only 2½ miles each and they knew it and gave everything they had in that distance." Sweeney noted that many runners crumpled to the ground at the end of their relay legs.

Clarence DeMar, Boston's winner in 1911, was stationed with the U.S. Army in France, so he did not run. Canadian Jimmy Duffy, the winner of Boston in 1914, had been killed fighting in France the following year. Few participants had any running experience. Among the 140 competitors, apparently only Al Harrop of Fall River, Massachusetts, had run the Boston Marathon, placing seventh in 1911 in 2:32:31.

Few spectators watched the relay, which began at 10:30 instead of noon. Nevertheless, the BAA did preserve the continuity of its annual event. The Camp Devens Divisional team won in 2:24:53, more than three minutes slower than Mike Ryan's course record (2:21:18) from 1912. All 14 teams finished. The following year, with World War I over, the BAA reinstated its marathon race.

Because of World War I, in 1918 a relay race that covered the 25-mile marathon course was held for servicemen. The winning team's time was over three minutes slower than Mike Ryan's 1912 course record.

40

press bus. Ironically, Cloney, a former reporter for the *Herald*, had covered the marathon by car in the 1930s.

A Rough Course

The problem with vehicles on the course, even bicycles, was not so much that they impeded the runners, but more that so many wheels churning the dirt surface raised huge clouds of dust. The softest part of the course was the four miles leading into South Framingham (what today is simply part of Framingham). In 1898, seeking a more level path, one runner had moved to a concrete sidewalk coming through that town and almost escaped the notice of officials checking numbers.

Louis Liebgold of the New Jersey Athletic Club fell victim to the rough course that same year at Newton Lower Falls. Crossing some streetcar tracks, Liebgold caught the heel of his shoe in a rail and ripped the heel off. He also wrenched his ankle. His handler helped him to the nearby fire station where Liebgold changed clothes, eventually catching a train back to Boston from the Woodlawn station nearby. Liebgold had been running tenth in the race at the time.

The infamous Rosie Ruiz was not the first cheater at Boston.

THE FIRST IMPOSTORS

Before Rosie Ruiz, there was Howard Pearce—and Freddy Merchant. Ruiz was the woman named winner of the 1980 race before the Boston Athletic Association (BAA) realized she had run only the last mile.

Although Howard A. Pearce of New Bedford, Massachusetts, started the Boston Marathon in 1909, he quit at eight miles and accepted a ride to near the finish. Stepping onto the course behind the lead car in the final mile on Commonwealth Avenue, he started to run again. Officials, including John Graham and George Brown, slowed the car and asked him to stop. Pearce continued to the applause of the crowd, but police halted him before he could cross the line ahead of the real leader, Henri Renaud of Nashua, New Hampshire. Pearce pleaded innocent. He claimed that, as a novice, he merely was jogging to the clubhouse to retrieve his clothes. The New England Amateur Athletic Union was not impressed; they suspended him.

Eight years later A. F. "Freddy" Merchant chose a similar route to infamy. Ironically, Merchant ran for the BAA and was a legitimate contender, having placed 11th in 1915. For the first 16 miles, Merchant ran near the lead, but he crumpled in the hills. Having run nearly 24 miles, he climbed into an automobile. He stepped out several blocks before the finish and crossed the line in 5th place.

The 6th-place finisher, Hans Schuster, protested. A bicyclist accompanying Merchant insisted he had run the entire way, but a Boy Scout attendant, also on a bicycle, claimed seeing Merchant climb into the car. A motorcycle policeman saw him re-enter the race. Nor was there any record of Merchant on the official checksheets at either Coolidge Corner or Audubon Circle. The BAA disqualified Merchant. And 63 years later came Rosie Ruiz.

Onondaga Indian Tom Longboat was an exceptional runner, but is best remembered for beating the train during his 1907 victory. "I heard it behind me and had to chuckle when I thought of the others getting shut off," he said.

Brignolia and Prince Kick Up Their Heels

The following year, Lawrence Brignolia had a big lead over the second-place runner, Dick Grant from Harvard, when he passed through Coolidge Corner, a few miles from the finish line. Near St. Mary's Street Brignolia stumbled on a loose stone and slipped to the ground. The *Globe* reported: "He tried to rise but he was seized by his trainers and carried to the grass at the side of the road and compelled to rest five minutes, while he was vigorously rubbed all over. From that point in it was little but a jaunt as he walked and ran the remaining distance."

Up to that point, Brignolia had an 11-minute lead and seemed certain to break the course record. He finished in just under three hours, only three minutes in front of Grant, who had also fallen once during the race. A blacksmith from Cambridge, Massachusetts, and a single-scull oarsman, Brignolia weighed 173 pounds and is the heaviest person to win the Boston Marathon.

The *Globe* also reported that Brignolia had been followed the length of his run by a dog named Prince. No explanation was offered as to how the newspaper obtained the name of the dog, unless it belonged to Brignolia or one of his handlers. Brignolia had started the first race in 1897 with only a month's training and failed to finish. He was in good shape from his rowing and his blacksmithing but suffered cramps because he ate immediately before the start. For 1899 he trained more consistently and avoided a last-minute meal.

"Senseless by the Wayside"

Those not felled by the rough course often were toppled by their own lack of training. Some entered the race after little more than a month's running. Others overestimated their own abilities. The *Boston Post* reported what happened to G. Roy Starkey in the 1898 race: "Every few yards he fell to the ground from exhaustion. . . . Game to the end, he attempted to finish but fell senseless by the wayside."

Runners grabbed liquids where they could. After passing through Wellesley Center in 1899, two runners named Hallen and Kelly spotted a watering trough for horses by the roadside and sprayed themselves with the water. Some residents along the course used garden hoses to moisten the street and hold down the dust. Thirsty competitors begged water from the same residents with hoses, as they would in later years. By 1911 those in charge of the race used sprinkler trucks moving ahead of the runners to attempt to minimize dust.

In the Winner's Circle

Except for Canadian Jack Caffery, who won in both 1900 and 1901, no single runner dominated the race during its early years. Through the first decade of the twentieth century no other winner repeated as champion. The names of most of these early heroes have almost been forgotten: Mellor, Lorden, Spring, Lorz, Ford, Morrissey, Renaud and Cameron. Only the name of Tom Longboat stands out and not entirely because he won the race.

Longboat was an Onondaga Indian from Canada. A talented runner, he was the race favorite in 1907. Ten runners, including Longboat, re-

mained near the front as the field passed through Framingham at a spirited pace. Several other top runners chose a more conservative pace, hoping to catch the leaders later. Those lagging included Robert Fowler, John Hayes and Tom Hicks, who won the marathon in the 1904 Olympics.

But in Framingham, after the lead groups crossed over a railroad track, a slow-moving freight train cut across the road, blocking the trailing runners. "I heard it behind me and had to chuckle when I thought of the others getting shut off," Longboat told reporters later. He won in a course record of 2:24:24. Fowler finished three minutes behind in 2nd with Hayes 3rd and Hicks 13th. Given the margin of victory, Longboat probably didn't need the freight train's help.

Longboat never returned to run Boston. The following year, he turned professional to compete for money in match races. One race at Madison Square Garden was against Italy's Dorando Pietri, who was famous for his collapse at the 1908 Olympics, allowing American John Hayes to win. Longboat beat Pietri in their indoor match in 2:45:05, earning $3,750. Reportedly, the Onondaga Indian won $17,000 in prize money during his career, a sizable sum in that era. He later was wounded fighting for Canada in World War I.

Among the early winners of the Boston Athletic Association Marathon, only Longboat achieved fame and fortune. Despite winning marathons in New York and Boston in 1896 and 1897, McDermott soon vanished from the sports pages. Little is known about McDermott's later days other than he returned to Boston in its second year and placed fourth. While several Olympic champions (Hayes, Hicks and Sheering) ran Boston during this period, they never won. By the end of the first decade, however, there appeared at the starting line in Ashland a runner who would provide Boston with its first dominant presence.

DeMar

Chapter Four

4

Do most of us want life on the same calm level as a geometrical

problem? Certainly, we want our pleasures more varied

with mountains and valleys of emotional joy, and marathoning

furnishes just that.—*Clarence DeMar*

Just a few nights before the BAA in 1911, in my sleep I dreamt distinctly that I had won the big race," wrote Clarence DeMar. "Of course, I know such things are just a coincidence, but I was glad of the encouragement. One or two runners thought I might win and just one newspaper, the old *Boston Journal*, had an item in Bob Dunbar's column, saying, 'Watch DeMar, he might win in fast time.' "

Clarence H. DeMar did win the 1911 race—and his time was fast. He ran 2:21:39, slashing nearly three minutes off Tom Longboat's record from 1907. DeMar wrote about his first Boston triumph: "For this victory I received a large bronze 'chariot of victory' with a special gold medal for breaking the record. And of course, there was plenty of publicity and ballyhoo, which was very stimulating and amusing for a while."

Eventually, DeMar decided he no longer found publicity and ballyhoo quite so amusing. A private, acerbic individual, DeMar embraced solitude even while chasing glory. Newspaper reporters seeking interviews often were told to get lost.

PAGE 44: Clarence DeMar triumphs in the 1930 Boston Marathon, winner for the seventh time at age 41. His singlet identifies him as a member of the Melrose American Legion post; a Legionnaire waves a flag in his honor. The marathon then finished on Exeter Street in front of the Boston Athletic Association clubhouse, across from the Hotel Lenox. **LEFT**: DeMar accepts his seventh-winning award from Governor Frank G. Allen of Massachusetts. Nobody has ever come close to equaling DeMar's achievement—and probably none ever will.

I'll keep on running as long as my
legs will carry me. —Clarence DeMar

LEFT: Many current runners believe crowds appeared after the running boom in the 1970s, but as this overhead shot of Clarence DeMar's 1927 victory proves, Boston always supported its marathon. CENTER: Chuck Mellor (68) beat Clarence DeMar (1) by only 37 seconds in the 1925 race. RIGHT: DeMar in 1933 would place eighth in 2:43:18 at age 44, remarkable for that era.

Fellow runners offering congratulations were treated brusquely. He disliked the cheers of the crowd, considering it distracting. He once even slugged a spectator who got in his way during a race.

After a hard-won victory during the day, he would be back at work at his printing job at night, ignoring those who might offer him congratulations. Despite a college education, he preferred the blue collar job of compositor, sometimes setting type for the same newspapers that displayed his pictures on their front pages. Nevertheless, DeMar would dominate the Boston Marathon by his prowess and his presence for much of its first half-century.

A Long Career

When fans of running debate who was America's greatest marathoner, they begin with Clarence DeMar. He won Boston a record seven times, his first victory in 1911 coming at age 22. After bypassing the race for most of that decade, he logged five wins between 1922 and 1928. Then, he won again at age 41 in 1930.

"I'll keep on running as long as my legs will carry me," DeMar said after win number seven—and proved true to his word, doing his 33rd and final Boston in 1954 at age 65. He ran his last race (a 15-K in which he placed 14th) in 1957, only a year before his death from cancer.

He also won numerous other marathons and long-distance races and placed third at the 1924 Olympic Games. Throughout his life his greatest joys and triumphs were centered on his running achievements.

Just Go Faster

DeMar won no awards for style. A reporter from the *New York Times* once described him as running "with a shuffling gait as if the next stride would be his last. His face was screwed into wrinkles, his knees were stiff

in action, and he threw his arms out like no other runner." DeMar didn't disagree. "I never was a graceful runner," he admitted, "but then, I never have thought an athletic event should be a beauty show!"

DeMar expressed those sentiments in a remarkable autobiography published in 1937, *Marathon: The Clarence DeMar Story*. A lean volume of 92 pages that wastes as few words as DeMar wasted steps in a footrace, it provides an honest portrait of a man confident, though not boastful, of his own abilities and disdainful of those who might change his ways. He wrote: "My whole attitude is that whether one shall run on his heels or his toes is hardly worth discussing. The main thing in distance running is endurance and the ability to get there as quickly as possible."

He added elsewhere: "A sense of proportion is necessary in case of minor aches of distress or blisters. If there is distress, why not endure it as a minor thing compared to the great fame that is to be yours at the finish? That, of course, does not mean for anyone to force himself against internal pain which might be serious. Always slow up for a pain in the side, until it goes. But for a blister or an abrasion or a sore muscle, just go faster to get the distress over with quicker!"

Moving from an Early Age

He might have been describing the stresses of life as well as those encountered in a marathon. His formative years were spent in relative poverty, separated from his family. Born in Madisonville, Ohio, a suburb of Cincinnati, DeMar had five younger brothers and sisters. His father came from a large family; in fact, a baseball team of DeMars once played an exhibition game against the Cincinnati Reds, losing by the score of 2 to 1.

When he started his studies at age seven, DeMar discovered he enjoyed jogging, rather than walking, to school. His father died about that time. To help his mother support the family, young Clarence began to

LEFT: The start of the Boston Marathon in 1928. **RIGHT:** Olympic Marathoners from 1924 adopt knotted handkerchiefs to protect their heads from the sun. Bronze medalist Clarence DeMar is third from the left.

sell small items—pins, needles—in neighboring communities, sometimes walking 10 or 20 miles on his trips. Thus was laid the base for his endurance.

Though demonstrating little sprinting ability at Sunday school picnic races, DeMar claimed to have once done "fairly well" in a mile race for schoolboys at age 14. Throughout his career he competed infrequently in track races but later ran a 4:47 mile, an achievement of which he was apparently quite proud since it is one of the few statistics he offers in his sparse autobiography.

When DeMar was ten, his mother moved the family to Warwick, Massachusetts. Her eldest son continued his practice of walking around the neighborhood selling items. He also hiked frequently through the woods, once to the top of nearby Mount Grace. Winters, he practiced ice-skating. Later in life DeMar became active as a Scoutmaster, sharing his love of the outdoors.

A Fierce Independence

Stretched for money, DeMar's mother eventually was forced to split the family. She placed Clarence in a home called the Farm School (later the Farm and Trades School) on Thompson's Island in Boston Harbor. Unhappy, DeMar once tried to escape by water but was captured after he had swum a mile. "The failure of the effort to escape," wrote DeMar, "caused me to crawl into my shell tighter than ever and take to storybooks and study."

Graduated from the school at age 16, he went to work for a fruit farmer in Vermont, pitching hay and cutting corn, earning $10 to $20 a month. He attended Maple Lawn Academy and later the University of Vermont, paying his way with chores at the University's experimental farm. He also worked beating rugs and in print shops.

DeMar's early struggles taught him a fierce independence. He disliked any regimentation, which included gym classes. At Vermont he trotted between his chores and passed physical education without attending any classes. During his sophomore year he began to consider the idea of some day running a marathon and perhaps participating in the Olympic Games. "From the first," he would write, "I decided that whatever else I might do, I would be a marathon runner."

Running to Work

At the beginning of his junior year, DeMar decided to try cross-country. He placed well in several meets but left college midyear to rejoin his mother in Melrose, Massachusetts. Now 21, he was old enough to support the family. This he did by working in a print shop.

Although DeMar eventually earned an associate's degree from Harvard University and a master's degree from Boston University in night school, he would continue to work as a compositor in various print shops for the rest of his business career, usually training for his races by running to and from work, carrying a dry shirt with him.

At one point in his life, when he worked in downtown Boston, DeMar would run from North Station to his job at 117 Franklin Street. "That was nearly a mile and I could do it in six minutes in traffic with my clothes on," DeMar proudly noted.

DeMar started to compete for the North Dorchester Athletic Association but disliked coaches. He almost never trained with other runners, preferring to run alone. Once, while running, DeMar was offered a dime for carfare. Another time, a farmer yelled, "Hey, if you want some exercise come over and work. Do something sensible." While passing through West Everett, he heard a man call for him to stop. DeMar obliged and the man told him, "A year from now you'll be dead running like that."

The main thing in distance running is endurance and the ability to get there as quickly as possible.—Clarence DeMar

AS 11 YEARS AGO, DE MAR WINS MARATHON IN RECORD TIME

Globe April 20, 1922

Melrose Flyer, Running Wonderful Race, Speeds Through Dense Crowds, Reaching Finish Line in 2 Hrs 18 Min 10 Sec—Henigan Brothers Set Pace in Early Stages

PAIR WHO FOUGHT THE GOOD FIGHT AND FINISHED CLOSEST TO VICTORIOUS DE MAR

Zuna Sees Great Mark Set 1921 Wiped Out, and Is Able To Get Only Eighth

POSITION OF FIRST EIGHT MEN TO FINISH AT VARIOUS POINTS ON LONG MARATHON ROUTE

Endurance

LEFT: Winners of the Boston Marathon received a diamond-studded medal (center). Those finishing behind got simpler medals. **RIGHT:** The *Boston Globe* trumpets Clarence DeMar's victory in 1922. As a compositor, he often set type on his own headlines.

Dreaded Distractions

DeMar seemed to suffer benignly the taunts of strangers during workouts, perhaps because that was when he was happiest. He felt less kindly toward those who interfered with his concentration during races.

"The one thing I dreaded was interruption or distraction of any kind," he said. "Any word or deed aimed at getting my attention would be like throwing a monkey wrench into a finely geared piece of machinery. Just a personal word like 'Step on it there' or 'Get going, Clarence' and I felt furious."

Grazed by a car during the 1922 Boston Marathon, DeMar aimed a blow at the driver but was disappointed to only hit a passenger in the rear seat. During the *Los Angeles Times* Marathon in 1930, a man in a car dumped a pail full of water over DeMar, causing the angered runner to grumble that it took three miles to squash all the water out of his shoes. In 1935 at Boston a drunk staggered into DeMar's path wanting to shake hands. DeMar punched him in the chin.

He thrilled in his first year of running at seeing his name in the newspaper, but DeMar eventually became annoyed with publicity. On the starting line of a memorial race honoring a late runner, DeMar turned to another Boston legend, John A. Kelley, and grumbled, "Don't ever let

Clarence DeMar didn't take kindly to photographers—or anyone—interfering with his race plans, but he posed for this shot before the 1928 Boston Marathon.

CLARENCE DEMAR'S TRAINING

Long before Joe Henderson popularized LSD (long slow distance) as a form of training, Clarence DeMar practiced that approach. He gained his early knowledge about running from a ten-cent book on distance running published by Spalding (the sporting goods company). He trained regularly at the leisurely pace of 7:30 to 8:30 a mile, running 7 to 14 miles a day, sometimes more. In the two months before one Boston, he averaged 100 miles a week. On days when he didn't run to and from work, he'd travel by bicycle.

To gauge his fitness and bolster his confidence, DeMar often ran long trials. Several weeks before first running Boston in 1910, he went to Wellesley Square and ran as fast as he could along the course to the finish, covering the hilly 14 miles in 1:18, faster than a 6-minute-mile pace. Then he jogged home to Melrose, a half-dozen miles more. Earlier that winter, he had run a marathon-length workout on a course that wound through Reading and Andover. "I did the 26 miles in about three hours without much exertion and so, felt very confident," reported DeMar.

Because of his work schedule, he often was forced to run in the dark. But that didn't bother DeMar. He would circle a 5-mile loop around Spot Pond near his home two or three times after work. Nor did cold weather offer an excuse to stint his training. One year when the 44-mile Providence-to-Boston race was postponed by a snowstorm, DeMar took the train to Providence anyway and jogged back "for the fun of practice." The following weekend, he won the actual race and that spring again won Boston.

Clarence DeMar married in 1929 at the age of 40. Though his friends warned that marriage would ruin him as a runner, he proved them wrong. Here, he runs with his two young children in 1935.

them name a memorial race after me." Yet, toward the end of his career, when DeMar no longer was a front-runner, he accepted more gratefully the accolades of the crowd, confessing that a number of times he felt tears of appreciation come to his eyes because of well-wishes directed at him.

Breakfast of Champions

It would be more than a half-century before runners began to talk about "carbo-loading," but DeMar had begun to pay early attention to his diet. After his first Boston victory in 1911, he received a letter from a doctor from Battle Creek, Michigan, named J. H. Kellogg, a medical researcher whose brother founded the famous cereal company.

"Dr. Kellogg wrote me a lot about calories, proteins, carbohydrates and fats and the advantages of abstaining from meat," said DeMar. Before the Brockton Marathon that summer, DeMar followed Dr. Kellogg's directions to eat one dozen oranges, a quarter-pound of pine nuts and one pound of high-grade caramels. The runner found it took him most of the morning to eat this pre-race meal. He won the marathon but eventually quit the vegetarian regimen, figuring it did little to improve his performance and was inconvenient.

Nevertheless, DeMar did watch what he ate. He believed in fruits and vegetables and liked those vegetables lightly cooked. He drank ample amounts of milk. In preparing for Boston in 1936, DeMar stopped at a store to purchase oranges and prunes to chew on during the evening and the next morning.

Up early, he ate a breakfast of cereal, toast, eggs and oranges three hours before the race, then went for a stroll. But prior to a 20-miler he won on another occasion, DeMar admitted his meal at work the night before was a cheese sandwich and a piece of apple pie. Of course, the 20-miler was not as important to him as the Boston Marathon.

Legends

LEFT: The start in Clarence DeMar's time was near Lucky Rock, up the road from the Tebeau Farm, which is now the Weston Nurseries.

CENTER: At age 44 in 1933 DeMar was past his prime—but he still finished eighth in 2:43:18. **RIGHT:** Before becoming race director in 1947, Will Cloney (second from left) rode in a press car. One of Cloney's first decisions was to ban such vehicles and make reporters ride a bus.

56

Amateur Standing

Had DeMar's seven Boston victories come in the era of pedestrianism a half-century before or in the era of prize money a half-century later, they might have made him a wealthy man. But he followed the code of the amateur athlete, unable to accept more than token prizes, although he sometimes stretched the rules. Returning from the 1924 Olympic Games, he switched the steamship ticket he received as a member of the U.S. team to steerage in order to save the difference in fares.

That same year, he permitted his name and photograph to be used in an advertisement promoting a dress shoe manufacturer. Whether or not he received payment, he maintained his amateur standing.

In one of his first races, a 10-mile handicap race in February 1910, he was pleased to win a silver tea set. He was not so happy a month later at the Cathedral Race to place ninth when there were only eight prizes. After he became a celebrity, he wrote reports of his victories for the *Boston Globe*, accepting $100 payments that he then donated to the Scout troop he served as Scoutmaster to maintain his amateur standing.

A Quiet Man

DeMar was as frugal with words as with money, describing himself as "one who doesn't talk too much." Nor did he boast excessively of his victories. Summing up his first win at Boston in 1911, he wrote: "I just ran with a determination that made me confident of doing the job. At 19 miles I took the lead from Festus Madden and won by a half-mile in 2:21:39.6, taking about three minutes off Tom Longboat's record. My sore knee had stayed just the same throughout the race and was no worse after it."

Many interpreted what may have been merely a basic shyness as unfriendliness. Bob Campbell, a coach and an Amateur Athletic Union of-

ficial from West Roxbury who ran against DeMar in the 1930s, remembers him as "rude." Once during that decade, Campbell won a 10-miler in Braintree. After crossing the finish line, DeMar approached Campbell, who was changing in the dressing room, and barked, "Who won?"

"Campbell," replied the victor.

"Are you Campbell?" DeMar asked. When Campbell conceded he was, DeMar turned and stalked away without offering congratulations.

Arnie Briggs, a runner from Syracuse, New York, however, believed DeMar's alleged unfriendliness was from his being hard of hearing. "A lot of runners found Clarence difficult to approach," remembers Briggs. "It was partly because he couldn't hear them. I found that if you stood where Clarence could see you and talked in a loud and clear voice, he could be quite friendly."

The Perils of Marriage

DeMar's interests other than running were teaching Sunday school and serving as Scoutmaster of Troop Five in Melrose. On one occasion, his future wife, Margaret Ilsley, recruited him to teach a class of blacks at a Methodist mission. He also enjoyed hiking.

And he believed in the benefits of a good night's sleep, particularly during periods of heavy training. "With the exception of one or two nights a week, I think it is necessary to spend nine or ten hours in bed each night with eight or nine hours of sleep," instructed DeMar.

DeMar did not marry Ilsley until 1929, after he had passed 40. His fellow marathoners warned that marriage would interfere with his running career; he was delighted to confound them by winning Boston again the following year.

DeMar said of his sport: "Running has several advantages as a pastime. It is economical in cost of equipment and in the space required and the time is optimal; it is not dangerous to life or limb, and it usually improves health."

A Sabbatical from Running

Doctors who examined DeMar early in his running career did not necessarily agree with that last statement. A physician in Roxbury told him before his first attempt at Boston that he had a heart murmur and should not run more than a year or two. Doctors at the 1911 marathon heard the same murmur and advised DeMar that this should be his last race, and that he should drop out if tired. (After DeMar's victory one of the doctors expressed surprise at how well he had run.)

Legend, thus, states that DeMar's absence from Boston for most of the next decade was because of fears for his health, but that was not entirely true. He ran the Brockton Marathon later in 1911 and only skipped Boston in 1912 because he already had been selected for the Olympic team and wanted to point for that race in Stockholm. "I felt that Boston was only a step," said DeMar, "and I still longed to win an Olympic Marathon."

At Stockholm, in his first of three Olympic appearances, DeMar ran poorly, placing only 12th in a time that (adjusting for differences in distance) was 20 minutes slower than his Boston performance the year before. He blamed his disappointing showing on what he considered to be nagging interference by the Olympic coaches. In truth, lingering fatigue from the long steamship ride coupled with overtraining (since he refused to modify his high mileage routine in the days before the race) may have been more of a factor.

During his late twenties, in what should have been the prime of his career, DeMar did little racing. He explained this sabbatical as being for religious and business reasons, as much as medical. "My time and in-

terest was so absorbed in Scouting that I hardly thought of running."

Only one year during his absence, 1915, did DeMar bother to watch the marathon. He was studying at the Boston Public Library, a block from the Exeter Street finish, and spent 15 minutes watching the winners finish. Earlier that day, however, he had competed in a handicap 10-mile race in Jamaica Plain, Massachusetts, placing ninth but with a fast time that pleased him. DeMar ran Boston in 1917, placing third, but skipped the race the next four years.

Back to Boston

Clarence DeMar returned full-time to the Boston Athletic Association (BAA) Marathon in 1922 with a performance that kicked off a string of three consecutive victories. From that point through his final Boston in 1954, he missed running the race only occasionally. In those years, he reported from the press bus.

In 1922 DeMar came from behind to catch front-runner Jimmy Henigan near Auburndale. The two traded the lead through the Newton hills; on the downhill past Boston College, DeMar surged ahead and Henigan dropped out. DeMar won with a course record 2:18:10. "I expected to win the race," DeMar wrote later. Finishing second was Willie Ritola, an immigrant from Finland who would win three gold medals (3000 meter steeplechase, 5000 meters and 10,000 meters) competing for his birth country at the 1924 and 1928 Olympics.

DeMar dueled with Whitey Michelson of New York in 1923. Michelson surged ahead up the Newton hills while DeMar placidly bided his time. Michelson walked the final hill. DeMar took the lead at Boston College, survived a collision with a bicycle that caused one shoe to come partially off and won in 2:23:37, more than a minute ahead of Frank Zuna, the 1921 champion.

With the 1924 race an Olympic Trial, DeMar not only wanted to win, he wanted a fast time to impress the Olympic selectors. After he took the lead at Natick, a fan told him, "Hurry up!" Characteristically, DeMar told the fan to mind his own business. Canadian Billy Churchill challenged DeMar at Wellesley, but DeMar moved back into the lead. Cheered by a dozen students in identical dress at the women's college, DeMar actually waved. Lengthening his lead, he won in 2:29:40, a record on the course that now conformed to the official Olympic distance of 26 miles, 385 yards. Chicago's Charles Mellor placed second but returned to Boston the following year for a 37-second victory over DeMar.

In between, DeMar placed 3rd in the marathon at the Olympic Games in Paris. Finland's Albin Stenroos won the race. DeMar was disappointed not to have won the gold medal but pleased at his performance. The second-best American in Paris finished 16th. Nearly a half-century would pass before another American marathoner (Frank Shorter in 1972) won a medal at the Games.

Stenroos ran Boston in 1926 but finished second to Canadian Johnny Miles, with DeMar third. The Canadian's winning time of 2:25:40 seemed so unbelievably fast for the era that BAA officials remeasured the course. They found it to be 176 yards short.

DeMar won Boston in 1927 and in 1928. Thus, in ten starts between 1910 and 1928, he had won America's most prestigious race six times. His third try for an Olympic gold medal in 1928, however, ended in failure. He placed 27th, but at age 40 conceded that he might be getting too old to keep pace with the improving runners on the international scene.

DeMar's Competition

Other than Canadian runners, few foreigners ran the Boston Marathon during its first half-century. Many of those who did—Stenroos of Finland or the 1913 winner, Fritz Carlson of Sweden—actually had emigrated to the United States. The journey from Europe by ship was too long for most. Asians and Africans would not begin running Boston until airplanes shrank travel time.

While DeMar was spared having to meet fast foreigners in Boston who might have cut his string of victories, those foreigners were spared from his winning their races. Considering DeMar's bronze medal at age 36, he certainly would have held his own at home and abroad, even against increased competition.

Regardless of how long it took runners to travel to Boston, the BAA refused to offer them any expense money and would continue this no-assistance policy into the 1980s. In 1929 when Miles won the marathon again, DeMar finished uncharacteristically far back, ten minutes behind the leader in ninth place. He won his seventh and final victory at Boston in 1930, taking the lead at Wellesley Square near the halfway point and never relinquishing it.

Placing seventh that year was a man born in Scotland who had apprenticed as a carpenter but could earn only three dollars a week in his home country. At his father's urging, he emigrated to the United States in 1924. His name was John Duncan Semple. The Scotsman preferred to call himself Johnny, but became better known by his nickname Jock.

In 1930 Jock Semple hitchhiked to Boston from Philadelphia, finished the marathon in 2:44:29 and hitchhiked back to learn he had been fired from his job repairing streetcars. Soon after, Semple moved to Boston and obtained a job as a locker-room attendant at the Lynn YMCA. In two decades of running Boston through 1950, he would place in the top ten six times but never better than seventh place. Yet, Jock Semple eventually would leave his own mark on the Boston Marathon.

LEFT: Racing footwear has come a long way since the shoes Johnny Miles wore in his 1926 Boston Marathon victory. **RIGHT**: Canadian Miles's victory set a course record, but the course was remeasured and found to be 176 yards short. He would return to win again in 1929.

JOHNNY MILES: BOSTON'S OLDEST LIVING CHAMPION

Preparing for the 1926 Boston Marathon, Johnny Miles used to run along the electric streetcar tracks in Sydney Mines, Nova Scotia. During the cold Canadian winters it was the only road kept clear of snow. Miles had worked in the mines to support his family, starting when he was only 11, while his father fought in World War I.

Running eventually allowed Miles to escape the mines. Born October 30, 1905, John Christopher Miles started running at age 17 because a friend suggested they could win a prize. In his second race, a 3-miler, a merchant offered a 98-pound bag of flour for the first runner past his door. Miles surged early to win the flour then held on to also earn a trophy for third.

Several years later his father offered to take Miles to the Boston Marathon if he won a 10-mile race in Halifax. Having won that race, Miles ran a 26-mile time trial one month before Boston up and down the streetcar tracks. "I ran in a snowstorm," Miles recalls. His father timed him in 2:40.

In Boston Miles and his parents stayed in a boardinghouse. Several days before the race his father drove him to Hopkinton. Miles walked and jogged the course so he wouldn't get lost while leading.

"It was late afternoon by the time I finished," Miles recalls. "I felt terrible. I thought, 'Do I have to run this whole distance?' But I had a bath and a rubdown and felt a whole lot better."

On race day his mother made him a steak sandwich. About 90 minutes before the start, Miles sat beside the road for his pre-race meal. "While I was eating the sandwich," says Miles, "these two fellows passed. One was Clarence DeMar, the other was Albin Stenroos from Finland." DeMar already had won Boston four times; Stenroos was the 1924 Olympic champion. Miles carried a newspaper clipping picturing the Finn in his wallet.

"Those are the fellows you want to run against," Miles had been told by his father. "Don't let them get ahead of you!"

In the race, Miles positioned himself behind the pair. After five miles Stenroos began to move away from DeMar. Miles hesitated, thinking it wise to stick with the veteran champion, but as Stenroos stretched his lead, the youngster decided to catch him.

Miles remembers the race well: "I ran with Stenroos for about ten miles. At any time I could have put my hand on his back. I stayed behind until we reached the Newton hills. As we were going up this one hill, he seemed to slow. I pulled alongside and looked at his face. His eyes looked like he was blind. I thought, 'This is the time to pass.' When I got ahead, I was scared to look back. I kept going until the race was over and I was the winner."

Miles ran 2:25:40, faster than any Boston winner until 1947. Back in Sydney Mines, Miles received a ride home by fire engine as thousands cheered.

Miles returned to run Boston four more times, winning again in 1929. He also ran two Olympic Marathons but without success. Over the years, he continued to stay active, walking, playing golf, jogging and lifting weights. In 1995 at the age of 90 he still looked remarkably fit.

His two winning medals from Boston are gold with a diamond inlaid in each and say American Marathon. When Johnny Miles won the first of those medals in 1926, he was, at age 20, one of Boston's youngest champions. At age 90 he remained its oldest living champion, a still remarkable man.

Clarence DeMar, seven-time Boston Marathon winner, strides to another Boston finish. He continued running the marathon into his sixties. Spectators would wait for DeMar to pass, and only then go home.

Winning a Seventh Time

Just short of his 42nd birthday, DeMar won his seventh Boston Marathon. This was long before the term *masters* had been coined to designate athletes over age 40. (At one point, the BAA actually had prohibited runners over that age from entering its race.) As a "master," DeMar would win seven marathons open to all comers, including four in 1930.

Despite his dominance of the American long-distance running scene, DeMar never won the Sullivan Award, the top honor bestowed by the Amateur Athletic Union. Several times he placed in the top ten. In 1930 only golfer Bobby Jones placed ahead of DeMar in votes.

In his autobiography, *Marathon*, DeMar offered what could serve as his epitaph: "I can truly say that, aside from Olympic junkets, the game had been worth it. Some people are born writers, that is, they may be good or bad writers, but they were born with something that makes them want to write. Some people are born competitors and need the stimulus of athletic competition. These people may have started out as baseball players and in later years transferred their efforts to golf. I happened to stick with one sport. I still enjoy the long grind of the marathon."

CLARENCE DEMAR'S BOSTON MARATHON RECORD

Year	Place	Time	Age
1910	2	2:29:52	21
1911	1	2:21:39*	22
1912–16	DID NOT START		
1917	3	2:31:05	28
1918–21	DID NOT START		
1922	1	2:18:10*	33
1923	1	2:23:37	34
1924	1	2:29:40†	35
1925	2	2:33:37	36
1926	3	2:32:15	37
1927	1	2:40:22‡	38
1928	1	2:37:07‡	39
1929	9	2:43:47	40
1930	1	2:34:48	41
1931	5	2:46:45	42
1932	18	2:46:15	43
1933	8	2:43:18	44
1934	16	2:56:52	45
1935	18	2:58:27	46
1936	16	2:48:08	47
1937	14	2:53:00	48
1938	7	2:43:30	49
1939	30	2:51:27	50
1940	27	2:55:32	51
1941	20	3:05:37	52
1942	24	2:58:14	53
1943	17	2:57:58	54
1944–45	DID NOT START		
1946	32	3:09:55	57
1947	NO RECORD		58
1948	51	3:37:25	59
1949	49	3:28:42	60
1950	41	3:28:13	61
1951	67	3:37:41	62
1952	DID NOT START		
1953	81	3:36:23	64
1954	78	3:58:34	65

* *Record for the early course, about 25 miles long*
† *Record for the course lengthened to 26 miles, 385 yards but apparently 176 yards short*
‡ *Record for the remeasured full-distance course*

A Certain Greatness

Chapter Five 5

Running is a way of life for me, just like brushing my teeth.

If I don't run for a few days, I feel as if something's been stolen

from me.—*John A. Kelley*

John Adelbert Kelley rose at 6:00 on the morning of April 19, 1935. Not yet married, he was living at home with his parents in the town of Arlington, Massachusetts, a northwestern suburb of Boston. His mother prepared him a breakfast that morning that included steak. Because Patriots' Day in 1935 was also Good Friday, Kelley obtained a special dispensation from a priest so he could eat his usual pre-marathon meal.

Carrying a bag that contained several chicken sandwiches in addition to his running gear, Kelley took a streetcar to Harvard Square and transferred to the subway headed toward South Station in downtown Boston. The final car on the 8:30 train was reserved for runners heading to the start of the Boston Athletic Association (BAA) Marathon. Arriving in Framingham, they disembarked and boarded buses to be transported the remaining distance to the Tebeau farm in Hopkinton that served as gathering point for runners and organizers of the race.

Each Patriots' Day, the BAA talked the Tebeau family into moving out of their farmhouse so officials could pass out numbers and runners could have a place to change. Some of the runners who came from out of town stayed overnight.

❦

PAGE 64: John A. Kelley (the Elder) hugs John J. Kelley (the Younger) after the latter's victory in 1957. Young John was the first Boston Athletic Association runner to win the race his club sponsored. LEFT: In 1936 Old John sang and played the piano for his mother and three sisters. Kelley had finished only fifth, but he was always happy to oblige the press. Years later, he would entertain a new era of runners with his renditions of "Young at Heart."

Runners referred to the farm as the Marathon Inn.

"We took all the furniture out of the first floor," recalled Will Cloney, who covered the marathon for the *Boston Herald* and later served as its race director. "It was a madhouse."

The weather that marathon day was cool, ideal for running but not for waiting outside. Most of the runners lingered inside along with reporters, who sought last-minute interviews with potential winners. They looked for Clarence DeMar but didn't spot him.

To avoid the pre-race activities—which he considered distracting—DeMar usually stayed across the road with a family named the Halleys. He'd appear the morning of the race to take the necessary physical examination and pick up his number, then disappear until just before the start.

In his autobiography DeMar described the scene at the Tebeau farm at a typical race. DeMar talked about wandering through the farmhouse and spotting every runner of note he could think of. "More noticeable than the runners," DeMar wrote, "was the stench of rubdown, with a mixture of alcohol, witch hazel, wintergreen and lesser known substances. And what a mess for someone to clean up, with newspapers, bottles and boxes scattered everywhere." DeMar thought the BAA got a terrific bargain in contracting to use Tebeau's farmhouse for only $50.

The Favorite

DeMar spoke of Johnny Kelley as sitting "cramped up in a corner, like a fourth-rater, looking thin and determined." DeMar considered it curious that Kelley had not thought to hire a room in the neighborhood. Not wishing to break his golden rule of silence before competition, DeMar said nothing to the other runner.

DeMar, however, recognized in this younger man a certain greatness. At that time most New England road runners used a 20-mile run sponsored in March by the North Medford Club as their Boston Marathon tune-up. The course wove through the Massachusetts towns of Somerville, Stoneham, Malden and Medford. Kelley won the race in 1934, marking him as a marathon favorite. After that race DeMar had approached Kelley and shook his hand, predicting: "Within three years, you'll win Boston!"

Kelley came close that year. He placed second, four minutes behind Dave Komonen, a Finn who lived in Canada. As a result of that placing, Kelley in 1935 wore the number 2 pinned to the front of his singlet. Low numbers were now considered a mark of status among runners. They signified either a runner's previous year's placing or a belief among the organizers that he might place well this year. Occasionally, a runner sporting a high number would run with the front-runners but usually not for long.

Kelley was dressed all in white. A stripe along the bottom of his shorts and a shamrock over his left breast offered the only adornment to his uniform. He even wore white running shoes.

As defending champion, Komonen was given the number 1, but he seemed to have no expectations of victory in 1935. The Finn clasped Kelley's hand just before the start and announced, "You win! You win!" Both Clarence DeMar and Komonen seemed confident that Johnny Kelley would win the Boston Marathon, and it was now up to him to fulfill their predictions.

Kelley, however, did not relish the role of favorite. It made him nervous. As the minutes ticked away to the noon starting time, he longed only for that moment when he would be free to run. That is what he did best: run. All else didn't matter.

"Track Was My Cup of Tea"

At 5 feet 6 inches and 121 pounds, Kelley possessed the natural build of a distance runner. But he enjoyed all sports when growing up. "I tried football," he recalls, "but almost got killed. I liked skating but didn't care to play hockey. Baseball was fun, but track was my cup of tea."

Kelley ran the mile in 4:40 while at Arlington High School but later would have trouble translating that speed to the long distances run in road races. He ran his first marathon in March 1928 in Rhode Island, from Pawtucket to Woonsocket, fading at the end and finishing in 3:17:00. In his first attempt at Boston the following month he went only 22 miles, slowing to a walk at Coolidge Corner. A man with a car offered him a ride to the finish. Kelley swallowed his pride and got in.

Kelley would not return to the starting line in Hopkinton for three more years. Instead, he established himself at distances from five to ten miles. Still, it was impossible for a road runner in New England to ignore the BAA Marathon. Kelley had first watched that race with his father at age 13. It was 1921 and he saw Frank Zuna win. "A policeman let me sneak under the rope so I could watch the runners up close," he recalls.

After his first try at Boston, Kelley returned to a position on the sidewalk, watching in the last mile with his brother Jimmy. A half-century later Kelley still could remember Canadian Johnny Miles winning in 1929 with a face almost as red as the maple leaf on his uniform. The next year, he saw DeMar win his seventh and final victory. The year after that, Jimmy Henigan won on a hot day, even though forced to walk the last few miles. Kelley remembered Henigan walking past him looking parched. "Jimmy later told me one of the motorcycle cops announced there was a runner right behind him. Jimmy said he almost froze on the spot but started running again. He finished more than two minutes ahead."

This was the height of the depression. Jobs were scarce. Kelley

KELLEY'S MARATHON TRAINING

John A. Kelley remembers the training marathoners did in the era between World Wars I and II. They ran long runs—but not as often as today's runners—and did interval training on cinder tracks, calling their alternate fast and slow laps ins and outs. And they felt no qualms about taking off for days—or even months!

During his early years Kelley trained only three or four times a week. After Thanksgiving most runners quit running until January. "Then we'd start training for Boston," Kelley explains.

"Years ago, we just ran anything. There was no set program, no schedule. We just ran to enjoy it. I averaged 35 to 40 miles a week. Clarence DeMar once told me that you have to do 20-milers when training for the marathon, but the trick is not to do too many of them."

Most of Kelley's weekday workouts consisted of runs anywhere from five to nine miles with trips to the track once or twice a week. He would run longer only when preparing for Boston. His work schedule with Boston Edison Electric Company eventually required him to work through one weekend with three days off the following weekend. "I'd come home Thursday night and have a big meal, but do no running. Friday, I'd do my long run of 2 to 2½ hours. Saturday, I'd take it easy, maybe two or three miles. Sunday, I'd run 1 hour and 20 minutes, then take Monday off. I'd run hard every other weekend. The schedule worked fine for me."

In 1947 a pair of Finnish runners arrived to run Boston. "They told me, before you begin your workout, walk at a fast pace for 300 to 400 yards, then jog at an easy pace and build up into the fast part of your workout." Kelley successfully adopted that pattern to his later training. He continues doing it today.

Les Pawson, shown here winning Boston in 1938, was one of John A. Kelley's toughest rivals. Pawson also won the Boston Marathon in 1933 and 1941.

bounced from one odd job to another, but most often was unemployed. At the time, his parents were not supportive of his running. They felt he should be out looking for work. "Running was something to do" is how Kelley explains his obsession. "Running was fun. It helped kill time." He eventually obtained a job as a florist's assistant in the greenhouses of the G. O. Anderson Florist Shop in Arlington.

Winning Respect

Kelley soon realized that you could win every 5- and 10-mile race they held in New England, but nobody respected you unless you ran the BAA Marathon. That's the race that reporters took time off from their baseball beats to cover. That's the race that the people came to see. They stood on street corners and camped on lawns to cheer the marathoners as they passed. Kelley decided he would rather be cheered than do the cheering.

In 1932 Kelley entered his second Boston. He was 24. He put Vaseline on his feet and wore heavy socks. He ran with the leaders, but by the halfway point in Wellesley his feet began to blister badly. He dropped out of the race won that year by Paul deBruyn, a German immigrant who shoveled coal for a living in a New York City hotel. (deBruyn competed for Germany in the 1932 and 1936 Olympics but eventually became an American citizen and served in the U.S. Navy during World War II.)

Kelley ran Boston again in 1933 despite having the flu. He finished in 3:03:56, placing 37th. That year, Les Pawson of Rhode Island won the first of his three Boston Marathon victories. Pawson and Kelley became close friends. "John was a real scrappy runner," Pawson recalled just before his death in 1993. "Winning was very important to John. He wanted to win every race." Kelley sometimes traveled to Rhode Island to train with Pawson.

Kelley entered Boston as one of the favorites in 1934. He ran with Dave Komonen until they crested the final hill just before Boston College (named Heartbreak Hill two years later). Crowds had narrowed the course to a slender corridor at that point. Reportedly, Komonen shouted, "Rata auki!" That was Finnish for "Clear the way!"

The break point had been reached. Komonen edged away on the downhill stretch leading to Cleveland Circle, the same area where DeMar several times had dropped his rivals. When Komonen surged, Kelley could not stay with him. His feet badly blistered, he limped to the finish line four minutes behind the Finnish runner, clinging to second place.

The following year, Kelley spent $7.50 for custom-made shoes made from white kid leather that weighed only 5½ ounces. Seeking every edge possible, he also participated in tests at the Harvard Fatigue Laboratory, receiving $1 an hour. While there he asked the scientists how he might overcome the fatigue that struck him like a curse during the closing miles of marathons. The scientists recommended that he consume glucose tablets during the race for extra energy.

One Victory Out of the Way

Kelley arrived at the starting line on Patriots' Day with his custom-made shoes and 15 glucose tablets tucked in a pouch inside his shorts. For luck, he also carried a handkerchief from a favorite aunt.

Tony Paskell took the early lead. Kelley followed closely in a pack with Komonen and several others. As they passed Wellesley College, Kelley moved to the front. Komonen remained close for about a mile but stopped soon after passing the halfway point near Wellesley Square. Pat Dengis, a toolmaker in an airplane factory near Baltimore, had run as far back as 13th through Framingham but now moved up to challenge

(continued on page 75)

Some of John A.
Kelley's memorabilia
from over 60
years of running.

SHOES OF OUR FOREFATHERS

"The poorest running shoes manufactured today would be far better than anything we had years ago," claims John A. Kelley. But not all early racers were badly shod. Ronald MacDonald wore bicycle racing shoes while winning in 1898. A *Boston Globe* reporter noted that his feet were "in excellent shape, not a cut or abrasion being evident." Lawrence Brignolia won in 1899 in shoes with "light leather uppers, lacing nearly to the toes, light leather soles and rubber heels."

Although by the 1920s some marathoners wore custom-made shoes, not all runners chose footwear wisely. In 1927 Johnny Miles defended his title in sneakers razor-trimmed by his father to remove excess weight. Miles's feet began blistering by mile three; by mile seven, he quit. Chicago's Joie Ray appeared in 1928 as one of the favorites, but finished third, his socks bloody.

In Kelley's second attempt at Boston in 1932 he ran with the leaders through Wellesley, but stopped because of blisters. For 1934 Kelley chose a pair of indoor high-jump shoes, slitting them with a razor blade because they were too tight. He limped home second, his feet again badly blistered.

Before the 1935 race, Clarence DeMar and Jock Semple told Kelley about an Englishman named Samuel T. A. Ritchins who custom made running shoes, called S.T.A.R. Streamlines, after Ritchins's initials. Made of white kid leather to reflect the heat, they also were perforated for ventilation. Kelley purchased a pair for $7.50 and won Boston. One year, eight of the first ten Boston finishers wore S.T.A.R. Streamlines.

By the 1950s many runners were wearing Converse shoes made with separate rubber soles and heels. Then, toward the end of the decade, the German shoe companies Adidas and Puma began to crowd American companies out of the market. One shoe from this era favored by New England runners was made by the New Balance Company. It had ripple soles to provide cushioning.

Fred Wilt, a two-time Olympian from Lafayette, Indiana, finished tenth at Boston in 1956, slowed by blistered feet. By the early 1960s Wilt had found a Japanese source for the athletes he trained, including several who ran Boston. The Japanese company was Onitsuka.

In 1964 a former University of Oregon half-miler visited Japan to obtain the rights to distribute Onitsuka shoes in the United States. His name was Phil Knight. He renamed them Tiger shoes, selling them out of the trunk of his car. Eight years later, when the Japanese attempted to limit Knight's franchise, he founded a new company: Nike.

Knight succeeded because a new generation of road runners sought shoes that could carry them blister-free from Hopkinton to Boylston Street. As running boomed, shoe company profits soared, allowing more investment in research and development.

Today's runners no longer must wear custom-made shoes; we are better shod than our forefathers.

These shoes used by a Boston Marathoner in the 1930s were actually track shoes, modified by having the spikes removed.

LEFT: In his fifth attempt at Boston, John A. Kelley finally won in 1935. He ran again to victory at Boston in 1945. **RIGHT:** Les Pawson (left) and Kelley (right) were close friends and often trained together. For over a dozen years at Boston, though, they remained fierce rivals.

Kelley. No sooner did Dengis pass Kelley, however, than he suffered stomach cramps. Kelley regained the lead. The pair remained together through the town of Wellesley Hills, then Kelley began to edge ahead on the downhill stretch leading to Newton Lower Falls, the low point on the course near 16 miles.

Making the turn onto Commonwealth Avenue and climbing the Newton hills, Kelley then stretched his lead to 300 yards. Seemingly, he had the race won, but the glucose tablets he had been ingesting during the race began to sicken him. He had taken the tablets without benefit of much water to dilute them. The high sugar content upset his stomach and made him nauseated. At Kenmore Square, with barely a mile remaining, he stopped and bent double. Relentlessly, Dengis drew closer. Kelley began running but stopped again. He vomited the glucose tablets. So much for science, thought Kelley. Relieved, he continued toward the finish line feeling "like I could run all the way to South Boston."

Kelley's winning time was 2:32:07. Dengis trailed by two minutes. DeMar finished 18th that day in just under three hours and paused long enough to congratulate the winner—and himself for predicting that Kelley would triumph within three years. "Well, we got your victory out of the way," said DeMar.

Though beaten, Dengis seemed cheerful. He accepted a kiss from his wife and told reporters that he was ready to run the race again. Dengis joked about his conqueror: "Would you imagine this, a florist runs 26 miles for a laurel wreath!"

Reporters from the *Boston American* drove Kelley to a nearby restaurant. A plate of chicken was placed before him, but (dispensation or not) his father objected to his son having his picture taken eating chicken on Good Friday. The chicken was replaced with a plate of haddock. Kelley's father said that his son's victory was the happiest moment of his life.

Kelley rode home to Arlington in a town police car with sirens screaming. The Arlington Fire Department rang the fire bell 39 times, it being the 39th Boston Marathon. Neighbors came by the house to offer congratulations. Governor James M. Curley telegrammed congratulations. Even in Boston, however, a marathoner's fame is only good for 24 hours. Saturday morning Kelley was back at work at Anderson's Florist Shop, preparing lilies for Easter.

A Friendly Tap

One year later, in 1936, Kelley appeared at Lucky Rock in Hopkinton wearing the number 1 that identified him as the defending champion. But a Narragansett Indian who went by the name of Tarzan Brown showed him no respect. Brown's given name actually was Ellison. His boyhood friends gave him the nickname Tarzan because he loved to climb trees and yell like the character Johnny Weissmuller played in the movies.

In the previous year Tarzan Brown had run the last five miles barefoot after his shoes came apart. He placed 13th. This year Brown jumped to an early lead, breaking all of the checkpoint records as he opened a lead that reportedly reached 900 yards by the Newton hills. Kelley ran conservatively then mounted a charge through the hills that brought him even with Brown on the fourth and final hill. Brown seemed beaten. Passing his rival, Kelley gave him a tap on the shoulder, a friendly tap such as you might offer a beaten opponent.

But Brown was not beaten. Apparently, he had been coasting through the hills, waiting to see if anyone would catch him. Whether or not Kelley's tap inspired Brown (as reporters believed), he quickly regained the lead, fought off another bid by Kelley, then began to pull away. William McMahon of Worcester caught and passed Kelley. So drained were these leaders that at one point in the closing miles all three were walking.

Champions

LEFT: Three Boston Marathon champions crossed paths at the 1943 Yonkers Marathon. Canada's Gerard Cote runs in front, John A. Kelley

behind. The man handing water to the runners is Paul deBruyn, the Boston winner from 1932. RIGHT: Had he been born a half-century later,

Ellison "Tarzan" Brown would have earned more than a laurel wreath for winning Boston twice.

Brown almost staggered into the path of a car. Someone doused him with a bucket of water. Revived, he started running again, walked once more but finished in 2:33:40, two minutes ahead of McMahon. Kelley helplessly watched two more runners go by him in the last mile, pushing him back to fifth. His time was 2:38:49. "I used very poor judgment," he says about his charge through the hills after Tarzan Brown.

Learning from Mistakes

Decades later, Kelley would reflect on the 1936 race as one he might have won if he had approached it more intelligently. Maybe, but he was 28 and still learning the marathoner's trade.

Each year for the next decade Kelley would dominate the Boston Marathon by his presence near the front of the race. Including his second place from 1934, he would finish runner-up on seven occasions. He would participate in the Olympic Games in 1936 and 1948. (He also made the team in 1940 when the Games were canceled because of World War II and certainly might have been an Olympian if the war had not continued through 1944.) And there would be one more Boston victory.

Would Kelley have been more respected as a runner had his list of Boston Marathon championships reached four? Or seven? Or more? It's hard to imagine a higher level of respect than that achieved by John A. Kelley during the decades that followed.

Tricks of an Ancient Marathoner

Kelley settled into a regular training routine. He soon left his position as a florist's assistant for a better-paying job as a maintenance man with the Boston Edison Electric Company. The job, which he held for 36 years, involved hard labor; he was on his feet all day. Kelley didn't complain. He rationalized that the job made him stronger. "I think it

HOW HEARTBREAK HILL GOT ITS NAME

Heartbreak Hill was named after the 1936 race, in which Ellison "Tarzan" Brown and John A. Kelley battled on the final Newton hill. Kelley caught the fast-starting Brown and confidently patted him on the shoulder as he passed him. Kelley thought Brown beaten, but the other runner accelerated, went on to win and Kelley faded to fifth. In his report on the race *Boston Globe* reporter Jerry Nason described Kelley losing the race on "Heartbreak Hill." The name stuck.

In running Boston many other runners would have problems on that hill, partly because of its position so late in the race and partly because it comes as the climactic hill on a very hilly course. And, of course, Heartbreak Hill has a certain poetic ring to it.

Yet, not all are humbled by it. When Joan Benoit asked another runner about the location of Heartbreak Hill en route to her first Boston victory in 1979, she was told, "Lady, you just passed it!"

Many runners have ascended Heartbreak Hill since Johnny Kelley lost the lead to "Tarzan" Brown on that hill during the 1936 marathon.

They cheered Johnny Kelley by name and told him it was all downhill from there.

Bridesmaid

LEFT: Canada's Gerard Cote won Boston four times. He usually celebrated with a post-race cigar—an act that would offend many runners today. Johnny Kelley placed second to Cote three times. CENTER: Eventual winner Walter Young (49) from Verdun, Quebec, watches John A. Kelley cool himself as they pass the Framingham checkpoint in 1937. Kelley finished second. RIGHT: Greece's Stylianos Kyriakides (77) eventually won in 1946, with Kelley coming in second.

toughened me up, climbing and walking and stooping." But it also drained his strength and made training more difficult. "When I began my run at night, I was tired but after a mile the tiredness went away."

Nevertheless, he rarely ran more than 60 miles a week, barely half the mileage of runners generations later whose full-time occupation would be running, and running alone. Kelley's personal record of 2:30:00, achieved at Boston in 1943 at the age of 35, must be considered in that context.

Unlike Kelley, Canadian Walter Young didn't hesitate to train long miles. Young averaged more than 100 weekly miles in training, doing frequent runs of two and three hours. During the winter, he also competed in snowshoe races. He arrived in Boston one month before the marathon in 1937 to train specifically for the race under the direction of Pete Gavuzzi, a veteran of C. C. Pyle's coast-to-coast Bunion Derbies.

In 75-degree heat Young and Kelley traded the lead that year. Kelley pushed the Newton hills and took a 100-yard lead but was passed at 23 miles. Young won in 2:33:20 with Kelley six minutes behind. Dehydrated, Kelley had lost eight pounds in the race. There was little water on the Boston course for marathoners, partly because the runners didn't think they needed it. At that time, drinking water was considered a sign of weakness by many.

In 1938 Kelley ran with Les Pawson through 17 miles before dropping off the pace. Passed by Pat Dengis in the last mile, Kelley finished third. Tarzan Brown won again in 1939, Kelley fading to 13th. Then, during a seven-year span between 1940 and 1946, Kelley placed second five times. Three of those losses, in 1940, 1943 and 1944, were to Canada's Gerard Cote (who would win a fourth time in 1948). Cote liked to light a cigar to celebrate victory, but his training routine included 100-mile weeks and long runs up to 35 miles. Like his countryman Walter Young, he also snowshoed during the winter.

Life at Home

Kelley trained hard, but he didn't allow his running to interfere with either his work or his regular life. He first married in 1940 at the age of 32, but his wife, Mary, died of cancer two years later. "Running helped me get through a bad period," says Kelley. Although he remarried, his second marriage lasted only a half-dozen years. "My second wife, Barbara, and I just weren't compatible," admits Kelley.

He had more luck with his third marriage, to Laura Harlow. She had been a year behind him at Arlington High School, but they had not been friends. They finally met when he decided to attend the movies two days before the 1953 marathon. By chance, he sat next to Laura.

"Aren't you Johnny Kelley?" she asked. Two years later they were married. Although he would have liked children, they never had any. For 40 years Laura and Johnny were close companions, devoted to each other. When Johnny ran his 61st and final Boston Marathon in 1992, Laura was waiting at the finish line to embrace him. Laura died early in 1995, just before the 99th running of the Boston Marathon. "I wish she could be here for the 100th," says Johnny.

"The Smartest Race I Ever Ran"

Because of the war, only 90 runners entered the 1945 marathon and only 67 started. It was the smallest field since 1903. Among those missing was Gerard Cote, serving with the Canadian Army in Great Britain.

Cote's commanders had sponsored his trip to Boston in 1943 and to the Yonkers Marathon, which he also won. They rejoiced in his victories, but other Canadians considered it unpatriotic for Cote to be winning championships while their friends and relatives were dying on battlefields. The army refused him permission to run Boston in 1944, but he

(continued on page 83)

John A. Kelley's Boston Marathon Record

Year	Place	Time	Age	Year	Place	Time	Age
1928	DID NOT FINISH	—	20	1966	57	2:56:10	58
1932	DID NOT FINISH	—	24	1967	135	2:58:13	59
1933	37	3:03:56	25	1968	DID NOT START		
1934	2	2:36:50	26	1969	186	3:05:02	61
1935	1	2:32:07	27	1970	163	3:03:00	62
1936	5	2:38:49	28	1971	977	3:45:47	63
1937	2	2:39:02	29	1972	890	3:35:12	64
1938	3	2:37:34	30	1973	1,105	3:35:02	65
1939	13	2:41:03	31	1974	1,266	3:24:10	66
1940	2	2:32:03	32	1975	1,633	3:22:48	67
1941	2	2:31:26	33	1976	1,524	3:28:00	68
1942	5	2:37:55	34	1977	1,892	3:32:12	69
1943	2	2:30:00	35	1978	3,729	3:42:36	70
1944	2	2:32:03	36	1979	3,577	3:45:12	71
1945	1	2:30:40	37	1980	3,444	3:35:21	72
1946	2	2:31:27	38	1981	5,074	4:01:25	73
1947	13	2:40:00	39	1982	*	4:01:30	74
1948	4	2:37:50	40	1983	*	4:23:22	75
1949	4	2:38:07	41	1984	*	SUB-5:00	76
1950	5	2:43:45	42	1985	*	4:31	77
1951	6	2:39:09	43	1986	*	4:27	78
1952	12	3:04:59	44	1987	4,490	4:19:56	79
1953	7	2:32:46	45	1988	*	4:26:36	80
1954	16	2:50:25	46	1989	*	5:05:15	81
1955	24	2:45:22	47	1990	*	5:05	82
1956	DID NOT FINISH	—	48	1991	*	5:42:54	83
1957	13	2:53:00	49	1992	*	5:58:00	84
1958	9	2:52:12	50				
1959	23	2:47:52	51				
1960	19	2:44:39	52				
1961	17	2:44:53	53				
1962	25	2:44:36	54				
1963	84	3:14:11	55				
1964	48	2:49:14	56				
1965	59	2:48:32	57				

Beginning in 1993, Kelley stopped running the full-distance marathon and ran only the last seven miles from his statue at the base of the third Newton hill to the finish line. In 1995 he served as Grand Marshal and did not run.

* Kelley's places are generally not available after 1981 because he was finishing far back in the crowded field. Several of his times with missing seconds appear to be estimates.

Michael Dukakis ran
the Boston Marathon
in 1951. In 1988, he
would run for Pres-
ident. He didn't win
either race, but com-
peted well in both.

DUKE: THE WOULD-BE PRESIDENT RUNS BOSTON

Michael Dukakis vividly remembers the 1946 Boston Marathon, won by Stylianos Kyriakides. "For the Greek community, that was a very big moment. Kyriakides had run Boston in 1938, the first marathon I ever watched. He returned in 1946."

Dukakis, who lived in Brookline, watched the race from Kenmore Square. "We were torn because we loved Johnny Kelley, but we also wanted Kyriakides to win," recalls Dukakis. "This was before transistor radios, so we had no idea who was ahead. Soon, we heard clapping, then we saw motorcycles approaching. 'Who is it?' everyone asked. And the word began to sweep through the crowd: 'It's Kelley and the Greek!' By the time Kyriakides passed us, he had opened a 25-yard lead. Every Greek child had heard the legend of Pheidippides, so we were delighted when a Greek runner won Boston."

Five years later Dukakis, a senior at Brookline High School, and a friend, Reed Wiseman, decided to run the Boston Marathon.

They started at a comfortable 6:50 pace, fast enough for a time just under three hours. Soon after turning into the Newton hills, Dukakis began to suffer cramps. "It wasn't my legs," he says, "it was my chest. I told Reed to go ahead. With about two miles to go, the cramps went away, and I actually finished fairly strong." Dukakis ran the marathon in 3:31, placing 57th, 10 places ahead of Clarence DeMar.

Dukakis served several terms as Governor of Massachusetts. "Some of my proudest moments as governor were presenting the laurel wreaths to the winners of the Boston Marathon." Boston Mayor Ray Flynn usually ran Boston during that period. "I'd get a call from Ray each April challenging me to run. I'd tell him I'd accept the challenge as soon as he got his time under 3:31."

Clarence DeMar ran his last Boston Marathon at age 65.
At that age Johnny Kelley was still warming up.

Spirit

LEFT: In 1984 John A. Kelley ran his 53rd Boston Marathon. CENTER: A statue in Newton on the marathon course shows John A. Kelley winning in

1935 at age 27 and finishing at age 83 in 1991. The statue by sculptor Rich Munro was dedicated in 1993. RIGHT: Johnny and wife, Laura, at home.

took leave and won again. To prevent that from happening in 1945, they sent Cote overseas.

Clayton Farrar of the Coast Guard Academy took an early lead, followed by Baltimore's Don Heinicke, Charles Robbins of the Navy and Lloyd Bairstow of the Coast Guard. Farrar pushed the pace, but faltered in the Newton hills where he was caught and passed by Bairstow.

Kelley started slowly, reportedly trailing by half a mile at one point. At Auburndale, just before the start of the Newton hills, he had moved up to fifth place, still three minutes behind. Kelley ran paying attention only to his body's signals and not his opponents ahead and behind. At age 37 he finally had mastered the tricks of the ancient marathoner. He maintained a steady pace through the Newton hills, not yet ready to attack.

By the time he crested the fourth and final hill—Heartbreak, named after his 1936 disappointment—Kelley had shaved a minute off Bairstow's lead but did not yet know that, nor could he see the leader because of turns and rises and spectators crowding into the street on both sides. They cheered him by name and told him he was catching the leader and it was all downhill from there and he had only five miles to go, but he dared not believe them.

With the last major hills on the course behind him, Kelley began to stretch out on the descent past Boston College. Coming through Cleveland Circle and onto Beacon Street, he had a view down the long straight street. Finally, he could look ahead and gauge the remaining distance separating him and the leader.

"I paced it absolutely perfect," said Kelley afterward. "I could see Bairstow up ahead, and it took the longest time for him to come back to me but gradually I could see him coming back, slowly, slowly, slowly. With two and a half miles to go—at Coolidge Corner—I went by him."

Kelley would add, "It was the smartest race I ever ran." Despite the relatively small field, Kelley's winning time of 2:30:40 was only 40 seconds off his career best, the fastest time in the world that wartime year and the seventh fastest time on the full-distance Boston course.

An Impressive Record

Kelley returned in 1946 to defend his title, placing second behind Greece's Stylianos Kyriakides, the first of the foreign athletes who would dominate the Boston Marathon for the next quarter-century. It was Kelley's seventh second place to go along with his two victories. Equally impressive, he placed 18 times in the top ten, six of those top ten finishes coming after the age of 40, one after 50.

Clarence DeMar ran his last Boston Marathon at age 65. At that age Kelley was still warming up. In 1992 at the age of 84 Kelley started his 61st Boston Marathon. For this final marathon he finished in 5:58:00. Since he had dropped out three times at Boston, that was Kelley's 58th time finishing the race. Most observers of the distance-running scene believe that Kelley's record number of starts at Boston may never be equaled, certainly never by a runner who includes two firsts and seven seconds among his finishes.

In 1993 a statue was erected near the start of the third hill in Newton, not Heartbreak Hill, but the one that serves as a prelude to it. The statue portrays two figures crossing the finish line with clasped hands: Kelley as he looked winning in 1935 and as he looked in his final Boston in 1992. Beginning in 1993, Kelley stopped running the full-distance marathon, running instead the seven miles from statue to finish line.

Kelley the Younger

Among those impressed with the accomplishments of John Adelbert Kelley was another Boston Marathon champion—another Kelley, in

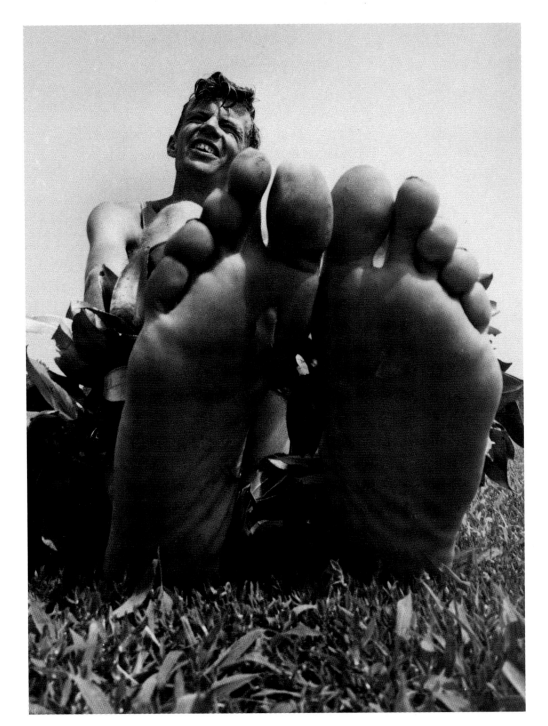

Newspaper photographers, who covered baseball and football the other 364 days of the year, often were fascinated by the agony of runners' feet. Young John Kelley obliges them. When else but on Patriots' Day could a marathoner get his picture in the paper?

fact—who would say of him: "His first marathon was in 1928. Think about it. That was only three years after F. Scott Fitzgerald had published *The Great Gatsby*. Hoover had not yet begun his term as president. Prohibition was still in force. Enrico Fermi had not yet split the atom. Think of what has happened since the beginning of his marathon career, all these things that seem so remote to modern consciousness. Only someone as old as I am has that historical point of reference."

The Kelley speaking was by 1994 then in his midsixties, a quarter-century younger than the man about whom he spoke with such reverence. He had been born in New London, Connecticut, on December 24, 1930. His full name was John Joseph Kelley, and he would win Boston once, place second on five other occasions and compete in two Olympic Marathons—a record strikingly similar to that of John Adelbert Kelley.

Those who ran against the two Kelleys sometimes referred to them as Young John and Old John, or more politely as Kelley the Younger and Kelley the Elder. They were not related and they reached their competitive peaks during different eras, but the coincidence of their similar names and talents would irretrievably link them in the history of the Boston Marathon.

"I kept having to tell reporters that he wasn't my son," says Old John. Young John adds: "A lot of people assumed when I came along that we must have been related." Despite his accomplishments (including eight consecutive victories in the Yonkers Marathon), Kelley the Younger found himself permanently relegated to standing in the shadow of Kelley the Elder.

Runner's Legs

The two Kelleys first met at a race in Littleton, Massachusetts, on Labor Day in 1947. Young John was then a junior in high school, 16 years old, when his friend George Terry spotted a listing for a 10-mile handicap race in Littleton in the calendar section of *The Amateur Athlete*. The pair plotted a trip that included an early-morning bus ride from New London to Boston, changing buses in Newport, Rhode Island, then transferring to a coal-burning train to Littleton, about 20 miles northwest of Boston. Learning about the trip, Young John's father (who also was named John) decided to accompany them, using as his excuse, "Maybe we'll get a chance to meet Johnny Kelley."

Coincidentally, the Littleton race celebrated the 40th birthday of Kelley the Elder, who then lived nearby in West Acton. Recalls Young John: "The entire town was out with Johnny Kelley stickers and pennants. Johnny was the scratch man. They gave George and me a 7½-minute head start. It was a blistering hot day, 90 degrees with equal humidity. I wore low-cut Keds. My feet were pulps of steak by five miles. George and I had forged into the lead by then but by seven miles I was sitting on the curb not even able to walk. George won the first-place prize. Old John took the time prize. I was the odd man out, lying on the ground, sobbing, disconsolate, saying, 'I'll never do this again, I hate running.' "

After the awards ceremony Young John's father brought Old John over to meet him. "You'll be all right, kid," said Kelley the Elder. "You've got runner's legs."

Kelley the Younger states, "That one remark kept me in this sport for the rest of my life."

Not to Be Deterred

Even at this early age Young John was aware that there was a Boston Marathon, but his first road race experience convinced him that he was not ready for that long of a distance. Two years later, in 1949, Kelley's friend George Terry convinced him to try Boston. Terry was working in

Protector

LEFT: Jock Semple's favorites could avoid the crowds by dressing in a side room at the Hopkinton gym. Olympian Alex Breckenridge and Young John Kelley get ready before the 1963 race. RIGHT: At the finish line, Jock would be waiting with a blanket and a word of encouragement, whether you won or lost. Here, he stands with Young John after his 1957 triumph.

a grocery store prior to going into the Army. Kelley was a senior at Bulkeley High School in New London. After a successful cross-county season during the fall, he had been troubled by a knee injury in the spring.

Kelley recalls: "There was a warning printed on the Boston entry blank—'To attempt this race without sufficient preparation would be most harmful to any runner'—but somehow that message failed to deter me." Nor was Young John deterred by his high school coach, who warned that running long distances would aggravate his knee injury. The minimum age for entry at Boston was 19; Kelley was 18 but Jock Semple, trainer for the BAA, knew him from summer road races and accepted his entry anyway.

Kelley the Younger recalls his first Boston: "We stayed at a seedy hotel, the Irvington Rooms for Men, near Copley Square. Rooms were 75 cents a night. The next morning we awoke, imbued with the romance of being in Boston. It was like being on the plain of Marathon. For breakfast we had double stacks of pancakes and thick chocolate milk shakes at Hayes-Bickford's on Boylston Street. We figured most was best.

"In the race, I was cooked at 13 miles. By the time I got to Wellesley, I knew I probably wouldn't finish. I limped through the Newton hills. After passing Boston College I looked ahead and saw the city spread out before me. Except for one visit to Yankee Stadium, I had never been to a big city before. I was overwhelmed by its enormity.

"I sat down on a curbstone to reflect upon my condition. The sun was starting to sink. It was getting cooler. I didn't even know the way to the finish. At that point, a newsboy came over the hill hawking the *Boston Record*. It was the marathon edition with the headline 'Swede wins BAA,' and here I am still in the race—but out of it." Within a few minutes Young John received a ride to the finish and learned his friend George

Terry had finished 23rd with a time just under three hours. Kelley's first attempt at Boston would not be indicative of his future success.

A Conflict with Coaches

When Kelley's track coach learned that he had run the Boston Marathon, he was furious. To teach him a lesson, he made Kelley run in a track meet the next day. Young John struggled through a mile in 4:59, losing to a runner he normally would have beaten. "It was one of the most agonizing experiences in my life," Kelley recalls. Later that season, he ran 4:36, placing second in the state meet. Six weeks of rest during the summer cured his knee injury. That fall, he enrolled at Boston University on an athletic scholarship.

Kelley's new coach was Doug Raymond, whose main love was indoor track meets. Kelley showed promise at first, winning the freshman title at the New England cross-country championships but cramped at the ICAAAA meet in Van Cortland Park, New York, dropping out. He ran poorly in that same meet as a sophomore (head cold) and junior (mononucleosis).

Eventually, he would run a 4:17 mile indoors and anchor some successful 2-mile relay teams, but Kelley frustrated Raymond, who felt his flighty athlete spent too much time training on the roads with members of the BAA. When Kelley was beaten his senior year by Northeastern's Ed Shea at the New England cross-country championships, Raymond decided not to accompany Kelley to the ICAAAA meet. He gave Kelley his ticket and told him to go with his new wife, Jessie. "Doug thought I was like the Red Sox," says Kelley. "I always blew up in the clutch."

Kelley responded by winning the ICAAAA meet, edging John Joe Barry, an Irishman attending Villanova University. That encouraged Raymond to take Kelley to the National Collegiate Athletic Association

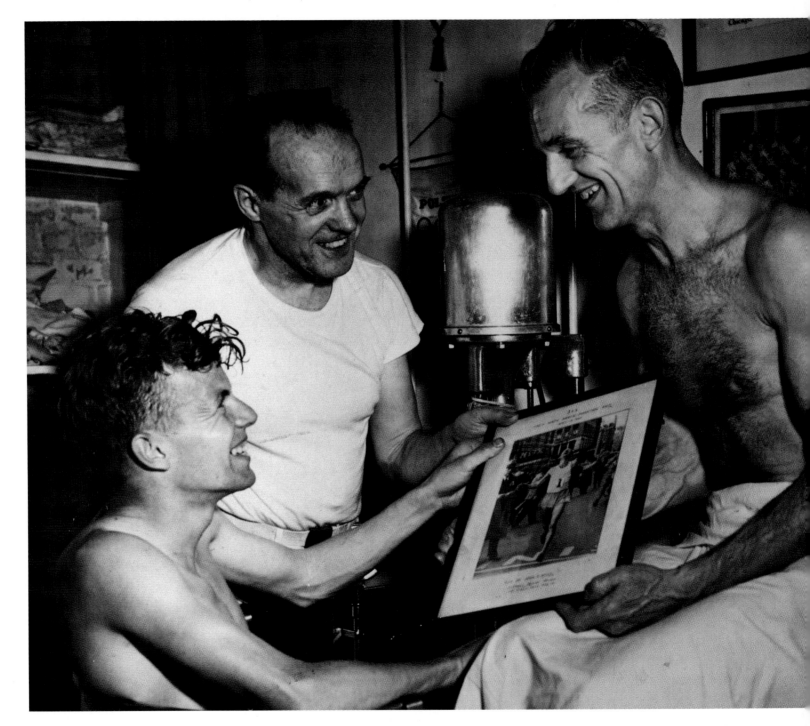

The two Kelleys, John J. (left) and John A. (right), often obtained pre-race massages from Jock Semple (center). In this 1957 photo, John J. had just won the Boston Marathon, and here they look at a picture of John A.'s victory 12 years earlier.

championships in East Lansing, Michigan. Kelley ran the best race of his collegiate career, finishing second, 120 yards behind Wes Santee, an Olympian from Kansas University and America's top miler.

Semple Befriends Kelley

Being able to compete at a level with Santee impressed Kelley, but he felt more at home hanging around Jock Semple's training room at the old Boston Arena, next to Symphony Hall. Semple had served in the U.S. Navy during World War II, training recruits while stationed at Samson Naval Base in Geneva, New York. Later, he was transferred to the South Pacific. While in Saipan he read an article in a Boston newspaper about ex-athletes who obtained jobs in sports. That got Semple thinking. Bill Kennedy, a bricklayer who had won Boston in 1917 and continued running the race into the 1940s, suggested to Semple that he become a physical therapist.

Returning to Boston, Semple spoke to Walter A. Brown, president of the BAA and owner of the Boston Garden. Brown had just founded the Boston Celtics as a companion tenant in the Garden with the Boston Bruins. Brown figured he could use an extra trainer. Through Brown's assistance Semple obtained a job as a carpenter at Boston University and attended physiotherapy classes. He also guarded doors during basketball and hockey games.

Eventually, Semple became a trainer, usually working with visiting teams. He also gave massages, working out of a tiny room in one corner of a mammoth floor that was used to store equipment, including checkpoint signs for the marathon.

Jock Semple's main love remained that marathon, and the runners who ran it and other New England road races. He organized a running team for the BAA to compete in races. Semple befriended Young John as

JOE COLLEGE RUNS THE MARATHON

John J. Kelley was among the first of the college-educated runners who would bring change to the Boston Marathon. In the decades before World War II most marathoners worked as blue-collar laborers. In the decade after the war the G.I. Bill made education more accessible for many Americans, not just runners. Those most talented could obtain college scholarships to run track.

More and more of these college track runners continued their careers on the road. Because of a booming young population there was a large demand for teachers. Many aspiring marathoners in the 1950s and 1960s chose this profession.

One advantage of being a teacher was that classes usually ended at 3:00 P.M. Although you might need to prepare lesson plans in the evening, you could train in the late afternoon when it was still daylight. Bill Kennedy was a bricklayer when he won the Boston Marathon in 1917, but the day when a blue-collar worker could compete with college-trained athletes was about to pass.

With the advent of college scholarships to run track, the Boston Marathon saw a dramatic increase in college-trained competitors during the 1950s and 1960s.

How the Course Shrank

In 1956 Finland's Antti Viskari set a course record, running Boston in 2:14:14. Viskari was among those who were shocked at the time. "I'm not that fast," he conceded. Officials remeasured the course and found it 1,183 yards short!

Where had that distance gone? Boston Marathon historian Tom Derderian speculates that road construction over a period of years (but mainly after 1951) straightened turns and shrank the course. "All the Boston Marathons between 1951 and 1956 were short, but not all by the same amount."

Course inaccuracies at Boston may well have robbed Kelley the Younger of his only sub-2:20 marathons. His invalidated times probably would have been a minute or two under 2:20 on an accurate course. In 1957 Boston Athletic Association officials moved the starting line near Hopkinton Green. Later measurements, however, suggested that between 1957 and 1965 the course may have been 80 yards too long! Derderian estimates that would add 15 seconds to the time of a runner moving at a 5-minute-mile pace.

That, of course, is hindsight. Those few runners who ran Boston in the 1950s were less focused on time than on position. Later runners who rarely won a trophy, understandably, became more interested in time. Today, course measurement and certification is a precise science that guarantees that a marathon be 26 miles, 385 yards long, no more, no less. But you still have to run from Hopkinton to Boston.

he had befriended others, talented and untalented.

"I met all these great runners from the road," Kelley recalls. "They knew what runners discovered later in the 1960s: that long slow distance was the key to training. College coaches were more speed oriented. They put people on the track and pushed buttons on their stopwatches. Being on scholarship, I was condemned to run track, but I didn't like it. For me, going out on the weekends with Jock's runners and doing 20 to 25 miles around Jamaica Pond was fun. I looked forward to it all week."

Semple cautioned Kelley not to do anything to endanger his scholarship. Nevertheless, in his senior year, Kelley confronted Coach Raymond with his plans to run the 1953 Boston Marathon. By then, Raymond realized his runner never would challenge Wes Santee on the track. He agreed to let Kelley run—but not wearing a BAA jersey. He had to represent Boston University. Kelley the Younger placed fifth in 2:28:19, 4 minutes and two places ahead of Kelley the Elder.

A New Crowd Favorite

For the next decade at least, Young John would replace Old John as crowd favorite on the route from Hopkinton to Boston. He finished seventh in 1954. The following year, serving in the U.S. Army, he missed the race. Discharged, he returned to Connecticut and obtained a job teaching remedial reading at Fitch Junior High School in Groton. He also coached the high school cross-country team, which won the state title within two years. Later, one of his high school runners (Amby Burfoot) would win the Boston Marathon. Burfoot, in turn, would play an important role in inspiring a third Connecticut runner (Bill Rodgers) to victory.

In 1956 at Boston, Kelley the Younger ran a stunning 2:14:33, placing second to Finland's Antti Viskari, who set a course record with 2:14:14, although the course was later found to be short.

Kelley the Younger enjoyed the celebrity that came with having run so fast, but he was more interested in victory. He set his sights on winning Boston in 1957.

Well-Protected

Young John and his wife, Jessie, stayed overnight in Arlington at the home of Laura Harlow, Old John's fiancée at the time. Old John recognized his young namesake's nervousness. It reminded him of himself two decades before. Old John, thus, became Young John's protector. He would see his namesake through this moment of crisis. He would protect him from those who might mindlessly rob Young John of his energy. That energy, Old John knew, needed to be carefully preserved for the next day's race.

Most of the Boston reporters knew where to contact Old John; many may have known Young John was staying with him. When the phone rang Old John jumped to answer it. He would screen incoming calls. Nobody would get through to Young John that evening. If Old John determined that the person calling for information on the marathon was uninformed, he would hang up quickly. "Kid," Old John told Young John, "you quickly learn that in life the worst combination is ignorance and arrogance."

Usually troubled by pre-race jitters, Young John slept with the peace of the well-protected. At 6:20 A.M. he heard a tap at his door. "Kid, you ready?" Breakfast consisted of grapefruit, toast, scrambled eggs, bacon and coffee. At precisely 8:30 they departed by car for Hopkinton. "Johnny was a ritualistic man," Young John recalls. "He knew which back roads to take to avoid traffic."

"Passing Hopkinton State Forest, we pulled over and cut the engine. Laura reached into her bag and pulled out a jar of honey shaped like a bear. Johnny stuck a spoon in the honey and passed it to me. You did not dare violate this procedure getting ready for a race. It worked for Johnny and for me, too, that day."

In 1957 140 runners started Boston, about average for the decade. They picked up their numbers, obtained their physical examinations and changed into race uniforms in the Hopkinton High School gymnasium. With the starting line moved back that year to Hopkinton Green, runners would no longer gather at the Marathon Inn or start at Lucky Rock. There was ample room in the bleachers for all to sit. Most of the runners, even those from out of town, knew the other entrants because they encountered each other at other races.

Waiting for the Call

Aldo Scandurra, Ted Suito and Mike O'Hara were among the names of Boston regulars during the 1950s. Not expected to challenge for the top prizes, they nevertheless were dedicated runners—midpackers—who took their sport seriously. They greeted each other as friends and chatted easily, seeking to use camaraderie to defuse the tension of the coming competition. Newcomers were quickly spotted, eventually to be welcomed into this exclusive club whose main entry requirement was a willingness to punish yourself for 26 miles, 385 yards.

A side dressing room was reserved for the faster runners, many of them by then foreign. Keizo Yamada of Japan had won in 1953; Veikko Karvonen of Finland was the 1954 champion. There was also Nobuyoshi Sadanaga of Japan and Olavi Manninen of Finland plus two runners from Korea, C. Lim and S. Han. Canada's Gordon Dickson was considered a challenger. The Kelleys were admitted into this elite circle along with a few other favored members of the BAA. The BAA's Jock Semple usually guarded the entrance to this dressing room.

Pacesetters

LEFT: John J. Kelley finished second in 1956 to Antti Viskari, the pair posting stunning 2:14 times. The Finn later claimed the course must have

been short. He was right. **CENTER:** Writer Don Kardong once asked a spectator who was leading? The response: "Some cop on a motorcycle."

In this case, the pacesetter was a dog. **RIGHT:** Kelley congratulates Aurele Vandendriessche after finishing second again in 1963. Similar to his

namesake, Young John finished second on five occasions.

After going to work for Walter Brown, Jock Semple had become increasingly involved in race organization, assisting race director Will Cloney. Cloney handled logistics; Semple fielded entry blanks and dealt with the athletes, particularly on race day.

At 11:00 A.M. Semple would announce to runners in the gymnasium that they should throw their bags into trucks for transport to Boston. Hopkinton High School was located on the south end of town. Leaving the gym, runners walked or jogged approximately a mile along Hayden Rowe to Hopkinton Green in the center of town. ("Green" is the New England equivalent of a town square.)

Hopkinton Green was one block square, no buildings and only grass. On the east end of the square officials used snow fencing to erect a compound into which runners reported. An official from the BAA stood at the narrow opening to the compound checking numbers of those entering. Once inside, runners milled or stood around waiting for the call to go to the starting line, which usually occurred five to ten minutes before the noon start.

No Bad Omens

"This was a very nervous time," Kelley recalls, "because you could see all of your competition." Young John was relieved when the gun finally sounded, allowing him to do that for which he had trained: win the Boston Marathon.

"I was really a psychoneurotic runner, almost superstitious. I'd look for omens and signs but that day nothing disturbed me. I was not concerned about whether a black cat crossed my path or whether a white dog might be taken as success or failure."

Kelley ran a stoic race. "It was a controlled race," Kelley would say. "I ran well within myself. I saw Jock at three miles and told him I felt good. He was on the press bus following the lead pack. Karvonen was running up front. He was a man to be reckoned with. George Terry ran a more controlled race than he had in 1956 but fell apart and eventually dropped out.

"After George faltered I was running mostly with people who could not speak the language. We could do nothing more than exchange looks. I ran with Rudy Mendez of the New York Pioneer Club. We were friends and helped each other through Wellesley. Then I found myself alone in the lead with Karvonen. We had broken the field. I couldn't hear them behind us.

"Karvonen was the man who had hammered England's Jim Peters, the world record holder, at Boston in 1954—which was unnerving. But heading up from Newton Lower Falls I felt good. I looked for little signs. I looked at Karvonen's neck because he was a half-stride ahead. He was sweating profusely. I thought, he's working harder than me.

"Karvonen did seem determined. He looked completely riveted to his task. I knew I had to deal with the hills and deal with Karvonen. Just before the last hill up to Boston College, on the flat where it levels off near the Newton Town Hall, I decided to give it a shot and see what happened. See if I could spook him. I threw in a mile ten seconds faster than we had been running. I tightened the pace, and he didn't go with me. By the time I got to Boston College, I couldn't hear him anymore. I thought maybe it worked, but I was not sure and couldn't look around. When you look around, that's an indication of weakness—you're giving your opponent confidence."

At that moment, the press bus appeared beside Kelley. Semple shouted, "You've got 200 yards." Kelley said to himself, "Don't screw it up. Hold it where it is. Don't do anything dramatic. Hold your pace. If somebody comes up on you, hold them off."

John J. Kelley (2) and author Hal Higdon (129) lead Boston in 1959, just ahead of Canada's Gordon Dickson (17) and Finland's Eino Oksanen (behind Dickson). Oksanen, Kelley and Dickson finished 1-2-3. Higdon dropped out, but kept coming back for more.

A Perfect Day

At Kenmore Square with one mile to go Kelley could hear nothing but the roar of the crowd. They shouted to him, "There's nobody in sight!" He thought, "Even if they're wrong, I'm still strong enough to win." Until that point in the race he had not been willing to concede himself victory.

Later, Young John would reflect on that race: "The races you remember are those you did well in, where everything works. A perfect day. Temperature about 55 degrees. A light wind off the right shoulder. Sunny but some cumulus clouds. Great running weather.

"From Kenmore Square in, I truly enjoyed my day. Later, Walter Brown made a lot of the fact that I was the first BAA runner to win the BAA Marathon, but I hadn't thought of that yet. I thought, 'This day is perfect and I've run this race perfectly. Jesus, I'm going to enjoy this marathon.' The last stretch was all roses. Had I been John A. Kelley, I would have been blowing kisses to the crowd, but I just ran through to the finish line."

John J. Kelley crossed the finish line for his career's sweetest victory. He was the first American winner since John A. Kelley won a dozen years before in 1945, and it would be 11 years more before another American won Boston. Young John's time of 2:20:05 established a record on the newly lengthened course.

Told years later that the course had been 80 yards long and probably cost him an extra 15 seconds, Kelley laughed and said, "I want those 15 seconds taken off my record." But he had made a mark as a runner that would last as long as people remembered the Boston Marathon.

Run for Your Life

Chapter Six

6

...to take part in a Marathon race is to risk serious and permanent injury to health, with immediate death a danger... exercise should always be purely subordinate to the business and pleasure of life.—*The New York Times, 1909*

Running long distances was considered hazardous in Boston's early years. You might suffer a heart attack and die! As early as 1899 each runner at Boston was examined by five physicians before being allowed to run the race. The doctors also checked the runners after finishing and found them "little the worse for the run except, of course, for the severe strain upon the muscular system."

The pre-marathon physical examination thus became a ritual that runners at Boston would endure for seven more decades. Through the first half of this century Amateur Athletic Union (AAU) regulations required physical examinations of athletes engaging in endurance events longer than six miles. The exams were conducted for the runners' protection—but also for the protection of the race organizers, who feared they might get sued for negligently permitting unfit people to compete in their races.

Not all runners welcomed this medical scrutiny. In 1958 overcautious physicians rejected three top runners, including Ted Corbitt, a marathoner on the 1952 U.S. Olympic team. Corbitt did have a suspicious-sounding heart murmur, but it affected neither his health nor his ability to run races.

❦

PAGE 96: Water, the elixir of life, helps John A. Kelley keep going in 1963. LEFT: Many runners avidly followed the writing and the footsteps of philosopher/guru George A. Sheehan, M.D. Here he pauses to reflect on yet another hot Boston.

One of the first physicians to run Boston, Dr. Charles Robbins loved the role of front-runner. Here, in the 1955 race, Robbins leads third-place finisher Nick Costes through Wellesley (he eventually finished 37th).

Nervous about medical exams, his heart rate sometimes jumped to as high as 140 beats a minute when a physician pressed a stethoscope against his chest. That prompted examining physicians—a Dr. Cohen and a Dr. Kelly—to deny Corbitt the right to run that year's race. They also rejected two other runners, Al Confalone and John Lafferty. Ironically, Confalone and Lafferty competed for the sponsoring Boston Athletic Association (BAA).

The three ran anyway with Corbitt crossing the line sixth, Confalone seventh and Lafferty ninth. Forced to run without numbers, they unfortunately failed to receive credit for their finishes. Corbitt was waiting to shower when the two physicians approached to re-examine his heart. Dr. Cohen listened, said nothing and walked away. Dr. Kelly listened and smiled.

"What's happening?" Corbitt asked.

"It's getting faster," said Dr. Kelly.

In succeeding years Corbitt would arrive at Boston with several letters from different physicians attesting to his health and nervously wait to see if he was going to be rejected. No physician made that mistake again.

Within a few years the Road Runners Club of America helped lobby the AAU to eliminate the obligatory physical examination. With the increase in numbers of runners and races throughout the 1960s, these exams became logistically impractical. The doctors didn't like them any more than the runners; they'd rather treat sick people than healthy people. By the 1970s runners were required merely to certify their own fitness when they filed their entry forms.

Running: An Egalitarian Sport

Until that decade, few physicians ran marathons—or ran much at all. Most doctors occupied themselves with their busy practices. They worked long hours. They had little time for frivolous pursuits—except maybe golf on days off.

The link between running and good health had not yet been clearly established. Most marathoners who ran at Boston during its first half-century were working men, who ran for other reasons. Either they were good enough to win trophies and prizes or they enjoyed the social milieu that running provided. Running was an egalitarian sport, although most of its early practitioners were blue-collar workers. They labored eight to ten hours a day in physically demanding jobs and trained at night or on weekends.

John J. McDermott, Boston's first winner, for example, had been a lithographer. The 1899 champion, Larry Brignolia, worked as a blacksmith. The 1917 champion, Bill Kennedy, was a bricklayer. Joe Smith, winner in 1942, delivered milk. Whether or not they considered it beneath their dignity, doctors rarely ran road races.

Medics Turned Racers

One exception was Charles Robbins, M.D., a psychiatrist on the staff of Connecticut Valley Hospital in Middletown. Robbins was born in Manchester, Connecticut, on September 13, 1920. While a student at the University of Connecticut he placed third in the 1941 National Collegiate Athletic Association cross-country championships. He graduated in January 1942. "I had heard about the Boston Marathon," recalls Dr. Robbins, "so I thought I would run it once, then retire like everybody else."

Through the winter, Robbins increased his training distances. Prior to the marathon, he ran several warm-up races, the first a 20-mile run sponsored by the North Medford Club. Robbins bolted into the lead but quickly faded and finished in 13th place.

In the next race, a 10-miler, he repeated the pattern of starting fast and then fading. Dr. Robbins remembers chatting with Les Pawson, a mill-hand, who won the Boston Marathon three times. Pawson told him, "Charlie, why bother with long distance? You've got speed."

At Boston in 1942 Robbins ran near the leaders but again faded, finishing 18th (out of 145 entrants) in 2:51:55. Robbins had caught the marathon bug. He went to work as a chemist for United Aircraft Company and returned to Boston the following year. Lacking his previous fitness, he started conservatively. His time of 2:52:10 was almost identical to what he ran in 1942, but he finished feeling more comfortable and improved his place to 13th. Finishing one place and seven seconds ahead of him was Jock Semple, future trainer of the BAA.

By 1944 Robbins was in the U.S. Navy, stationed at Samson Naval Base in Geneva, New York. Semple also served at Samson, supervising the base athletic program. He recruited Robbins for his Navy team, providing time for him to train. Robbins placed third at Boston that year in 2:38:31. He also cracked the top ten at Boston in 1945 and 1946.

After World War II Robbins briefly returned to work at United before enrolling in New York Medical School. In 1948 he needed to obtain permission from his embryology professor to skip an exam and run that year's Boston Marathon. "The other students thought I'd never get permission," laughs Dr. Robbins, "but the professor once had run the mile for the University of Wisconsin. He told me to go."

Though his top-ten finishes were behind him, Dr. Robbins often would surge to the front through the early miles before fading. In 1955 he ran in the lead then barely broke three hours. In 1961 at the age of 40 he ran his 20th consecutive Boston Marathon, finishing 83rd in 3:46:04. That was his last appearance at Boston. But Dr. Robbins continued to run into the 1990s, racing occasionally, most often in the Manchester Run, a 5-mile race held on Thanksgiving Day in the town where he was born.

The New Era Dawns

If Dr. Robbins was one exception to the rule that physicians never ran road races, another was Warren Guild, M.D. Dr. Guild never placed among Boston's top ten but was good enough to train occasionally on weekends with John A. Kelley, the elder. Dr. Guild practiced at Peter Bent Brigham Hospital, near the Harvard Medical School. As students arrived in the fall of 1961, Dr. Guild already had begun to anticipate running his seventh Boston Marathon the following spring.

One new student arriving on campus was an Air Force physician assigned to do post-graduate work in preventive medicine at the Harvard School of Public Health. Born March 4, 1931, in Oklahoma City, this doctor had once been a talented middle-distance runner. He won the state high school mile championship in 1949 with a time of 4:30.8 and also made all-state in basketball. He attended the University of Oklahoma on an athletic scholarship, where he lowered his mile time to 4:18. He ran on winning 2-mile and 4-mile relay teams at the Texas and Drake Relays but graduated one year early to pursue a medical career.

The Air Force physician's name was Kenneth H. Cooper, M.D. He would achieve later fame as author of the best-selling book *Aerobics.*

Dr. Cooper recalls: "Attending medical school I had allowed myself to get sadly out of shape. I weighed 204 pounds. I was totally inactive." After graduation he entered the service and was sent to San Antonio to work in the U.S. Air Force's Manned Orbiting Laboratory program. This motivated Dr. Cooper to start running again. Within six months he trimmed down to 165 pounds. He ran regularly on his lunch hour with 15 to 20 other runners. Showing an early affinity for attending to the health of others, Dr. Cooper supervised construction of a shower on the back of the laboratory. His running group soon became known as Cooper's Poopers.

"Doc, I'm Going to Jog on In"

After two years in San Antonio the Air Force sent Dr. Cooper to Harvard. While Dr. Cooper attended classes, his wife, Millie, worked at Peter Bent Brigham Hospital. "That's when I met Warren Guild, who introduced me to Johnny Kelley," recalls Dr. Cooper.

One Saturday, the two doctors met Kelley, the renowned Boston Marathoner, for a 10-mile workout around the Fresh Pond reservoir, a favorite training area for runners living near Cambridge. Dr. Cooper already had begun thinking about running the Boston Marathon the following spring.

Kelley, who was then 54, and Dr. Guild, who was in his midforties, ran at what for them was a comfortable pace, chatting as they circled the reservoir four times. Dr. Cooper, age 30, did his best to stay close to the two older road runners. With a mile left in the workout Kelley turned to him and said, "Doc, if you don't mind, I'm going to jog on in."

The Air Force physician recalls Kelley accelerating like a jet pilot who had switched on the afterburner, finishing the last mile in nearly 5:00 and leaving him and Dr. Guild in his turbulent wake.

Afterward, Kelley offered his new running companion some advice: "Doc, you'll never run a marathon if you run entirely on your toes."

The Father of Aerobics Decides to Run

Nevertheless, Dr. Cooper was determined to run Boston, even though it meant training in the dark at 5:00 A.M. Freezing rain and snow failed to daunt him. He and his wife lived in a garden apartment in Waltham. Dr. Cooper remembers one time returning to the apartment after an early-morning run, the clothing around his face covered with frost. A newsboy on the corner said to another, "Hey look, here it comes again."

To avoid the dark and cold, he tried training indoors at a gymnasium at the Harvard Medical School, on one occasion running 250 laps around a basketball court. "For three days I couldn't walk," recalls Dr. Cooper.

He sought the advice of Dr. Guild, who suggested riding a bicycle to strengthen his quadriceps muscles for Heartbreak Hill. The apartment where the Coopers lived was a dozen miles from where Ken attended classes and Millie worked. Many days, after a 10-mile run in the morning, Dr. Cooper would bicycle to class. Whether or not it helped his running, he found he could at least beat his wife through the traffic to work.

Dr. Guild recommended that 18 miles be his longest workout before the marathon. Dr. Cooper also ran several road races, including a 10-miler from Lexington to Cambridge. "The police stopped traffic for the lead runners," smiles the onetime Oklahoma state champ. "I finished so far behind, I had to wait for red lights to change."

"My Husband's Still on the Course"

In the 1962 marathon Dr. Cooper ran comfortably through the first 18 miles—the limit of his longest training run—but the hills in Newton proved his undoing. The day was chilly and damp. Several hours into the race it began to drizzle. Dr. Cooper had taken no fluids. He slowed. He began to walk. The bus that picked up dropouts hovered nearby. Dr. Cooper shook off several requests to board. He recalls: "Pride wouldn't let me board the bus—but if Millie had appeared driving a car, I would have accepted a ride immediately!"

Another runner walking nearby suggested that if he suck on an orange, it might help. Dr. Cooper took not one orange but three. "I bit a hole in the skin and sucked out the juice," he says, recalling that epicurean moment. "I couldn't believe how much better I felt!" On Beacon Street with several miles to go, he began jogging again.

Belgian Aurele Vanden-
driessche accepts con-
gratulations from the
crowd in 1963 following
the first of his two vic-
tories.

Finland's Eino Oksanen had long since won the race in 2:23:48, his third victory in four years. Kelley the Younger was fourth. Kelley the Elder finished 25th in 2:44:36. With the race clock ticking toward four hours and with 98 runners across the line, the chilled finish officials started to pack up their gear to go home.

Millie Cooper pleaded with them to stay. "My husband's still on the course. You've got to record his finishing time." The officials might have been inclined to ignore her plea but, just then, Dr. Cooper turned the corner onto Exeter Street. After having walked much of the way since mile 18, he was back on his toes sprinting, looking like an anchor runner at the Drake Relays. He finished 99th, his time just under four hours.

"I was surprised how fast I could sprint at the end," recalls Dr. Cooper. "I thought, 'Where has this been all the time?' I cried when I crossed the line. Millie was there to support me. I was so happy to finish."

Dr. Cooper recalls Millie helping him into the Lenox Hotel across from the finish line, where he sought help from a lone podiatrist ministering to runners. The podiatrist looked at Dr. Cooper's feet and asked, "Son, when did you get those blisters?" As a physician Dr. Cooper was embarrassed to admit that the blisters had started back in Framingham, barely six miles into the race.

The podiatrist shook his head and said, "Son, you don't need a foot doctor, you need a head doctor."

Dr. Cooper vowed to train harder the following year and conquer Boston. As he increased his training and improved his fitness, he suffered several injuries. He sought counsel during training runs with Johnny Kelley: "What do you do when you have injuries? Do you stop running?" Kelley responded, "Doc, if I stopped running when I had problems, I never would run."

(continued on page 108)

Scribes

LEFT: Dr. Ken Cooper ran Boston twice in the 1960s. Several years later he started a fitness revolution with his book *Aerobics*. **CENTER:** Dr. George A. Sheehan ran Boston 22 times and authored eight books based on his running philosophy. **RIGHT:** Erich Segal ran Boston before he wrote *Love Story*.

DRINKING ON THE RUN

In marathon history 1968 would prove a watershed year, not so much because of the runners, but because of a scientist who sought to study them. David L. Costill, Ph.D., head of the Human Performance Laboratory at Ball State University in Muncie, Indiana, decided to use the 1968 Boston Marathon as a test site to study the effects of fluid intake (or lack of it) on athletic performance.

Among his subjects was Amby Burfoot, then a student at Wesleyan University. That winter, Dr. Costill and graduate assistant Ed Winrow drove to Detroit to watch Burfoot run the National Collegiate Athletic Association indoor championships. Burfoot failed to place. Afterward, they took him to Muncie for extensive treadmill tests. Although they found Burfoot to be lean and fit, of the six in Dr. Costill's study who planned to run Boston that April, the scientist predicted Burfoot would finish fifth. One quality that Burfoot possessed, however, was an ability to tolerate high internal temperatures, as much as 105.3°F. "That's extremely high," says Dr. Costill. "If your temperature reaches 106, you probably won't finish. Much higher and you can die."

Not all runners tolerate heat as well. As they lose fluids through sweating, dehydration compromises their performance. Dr. Costill reasoned that if runners took more fluids during competition, they might perform better. Conditions at Boston in 1968 proved perfect for a study on dehydration. The temperature was 73 degrees, humidity 68 percent. A headwind slowed runners further. More a problem was the lack of cloud cover. Burfoot's most vivid memory of the weather is "bright blue sky and sun, sun, sun!"

Little water was available along the course at that time. Runners grabbed what they could from spectators beside the road. Dr. Costill hoped to supply some fluids to the half-dozen in his study, but found the logistics too formidable.

Burfoot didn't care. "I ran the race dry," he recalls. "The first 13 miles it seemed like we were jogging. Then I decided to throw in a surge to drop a few people, and only Bill Clark went with me."

Clark dropped back after the hills, but Burfoot soon began cramping (probably from dehydration). Though he slowed, neither Clark nor anyone else caught him on that hot day. Burfoot won in 2:22:17. The others in Dr. Costill's study ran subpar performances. Average weight loss for the group was 7.4 pounds, largely from sweating.

Dr. Costill reasoned that if runners drank more fluids while running, they could lower their body temperatures and improve their times. Inviting the group back to his laboratory that summer for a two-hour treadmill run, he proved that continuous fluid intake lowered body temperatures by several degrees. At the Olympic Trials in Alamosa, Colorado, in August, however, officials refused to allow Dr. Costill to offer fluids to runners before ten kilometers. The international rules at that time prohibited it!

After Dr. Costill published the results of his study, those rules were changed. Major marathons now provide water stops every few miles. Elite athletes use water bottles to make certain they drink enough.

Now that he is executive editor of *Runner's World*, Amby Burfoot frequently writes of the importance of fluid intake. Although he admits, "I still hate drinking while I run," he knew enough to drink plenty along the way when he ran Boston in 1993 to commemorate the 25th anniversary of his 1968 win. On a warm day, he finished well, and with no dehydration problems.

In the 1963 race Dr. Cooper stayed on a three-hour pace through 21 miles but once past Heartbreak Hill started to slow. "I'm too large-boned," concedes Dr. Cooper. "I wasn't designed to be a marathoner." He finished in 3:24:20, a half-hour improvement from the year before but lost three places, finishing 102nd out of 183 finishers.

That was Ken Cooper's last marathon. He returned to San Antonio but continued running in 10-K races. In 1969 he participated in a 40-mile walk, choosing to run the distance in a time over six hours.

Running and Being

Another physician who would profoundly influence runners, particularly in the way they viewed their running experiences, arrived at the starting line of Boston in 1964, the year after Dr. Cooper returned to Texas. He, too, was a former track athlete, having run a 4:19 mile in 1939 while at Manhattan College. He was the eldest of 14 children, born November 5, 1918, and was reared in the Park Slopes section of Brooklyn. He and his wife, the former Mary Jane Fleming, would have 12 children.

After graduating from Long Island College of Medicine (now the State University of New York Medical College), he interned for three years in the Navy, then established a practice in cardiology in Red Bank, New Jersey. His name was George A. Sheehan, M.D.

While Dr. Cooper systematized an exercise regimen designed to preserve the bodies of those who chose to exercise, Dr. Sheehan found his niche concentrating on the minds that controlled those bodies. If Cooper could be classified a physiologist/physician, Sheehan was the philosopher/physician. The former titled his seminal book *Aerobics*; the latter called his *Running and Being*. In determining why people should exercise, Dr. Cooper would cite scientists such as Balke, Robinson and Paffenbarger; Dr. Sheehan quoted poets such as Emerson, Yeats and Blake.

"Like Thoreau, I occupy my body with delight," wrote Dr. Sheehan. He described the marathon as "William James's moral equivalent of war." One reporter attending a lecture given by Dr. Sheehan counted 40 references to poets and philosophers—all offered without benefit of notes. Dr. Sheehan, however, viewed deprecatingly his philosopher status and told about struggling past the 23-mile point at the New York City Marathon one year only to hear someone call from the crowd, "Dr. Sheehan, what would Emerson have said now?"

That delighted him, and he also enjoyed the comment of a friend who put his Boston celebrity status into perspective: "George, three blocks away from Boylston Street, you're just another skinny Irishman."

Drawn to the Roads Like a Moth to a Candle

It wasn't until midway through his life that Dr. Sheehan gained his following on Boylston Street, the finish line for the Boston Marathon. After settling in Red Bank, Dr. Sheehan spent nearly two decades as a physician.

An occasional squash and tennis player, Dr. Sheehan was 44 in 1963 when he attended a track meet to watch two of his sons (George III and Tim) run. Dr. Sheehan watched them race and thought, "I wonder how I can do compared to them?" He started running almost immediately.

He trimmed his weight from 160 pounds to the 136 he had weighed in college. He set as his goal breaking 5:00 for the mile and eventually ran 4:47.1 in 1969 at age 50, setting a series of world and American single-age records at that distance for the next half-dozen years. But though his talents seemed best suited to the track, Dr. Sheehan was attracted—like a moth to a candle—to the road, where he could direct his competitive spirit inward.

At first, Dr. Sheehan scoffed at long-distance runners, believing that anyone who ran farther than five miles was crazy. "The second race I ever

THE BIRTH OF A RUNNING MAGAZINE

Through the 1960s *Track & Field News*, founded by Bert and Cordner Nelson, was the most visible American running publication. Its main focus, however, was track rather than road running. Browning Ross's *Long Distance Log*, a newsletter for distance runners, concentrated almost entirely on race results. No publication offered runners information on how to train, or covered running as a lifestyle rather than as merely a sport. None recognized that the Boston Marathon exerted a magic draw for its readers.

In 1966 a high school cross-country runner from Kansas decided to fill that gap. Bob Anderson started a newsletter, *Distance Running News*, publishing two issues in the first year. Anderson's publication found a ready audience. Many early subscribers were those who first had been attracted to running as an activity after reading Ken Cooper's book *Aerobics*. Boston was just beginning to attract large numbers of runners, and circulation grew rapidly.

Bob Anderson was more suited to being an entrepreneur than an editor or writer. One of his early contributors, Joe Henderson, was also a staff reporter for *Track & Field News*, living in California. In 1969 Anderson asked Henderson to move to the Midwest and edit *Distance Running News*. But Henderson wouldn't leave California, so Anderson moved his one-man operation west in January 1970, opened an office in Mountain View, California, and renamed his burgeoning publication *Runner's World*.

By the March issue of that year, Henderson had recruited George A. Sheehan, M.D., to write two regular monthly columns: one offering medical advice, the other his philosophical musings. Dr. Sheehan frequently focused his attention on the Boston Marathon. During the formative years of the magazine Dr. Sheehan received no payment for his writings in the underfinanced magazine. It was mainly a labor of love for him and for many others who contributed to the publication. Nouveau runners first bought the magazine to learn how to train for 10-K races, but they quickly encountered the philosophy of Dr. Sheehan. He became their Thoreau.

Within the 1970s, *Runner's World* readership grew from a few thousand to almost a half-million. It soon was challenged by a second magazine, *The Runner*, started by New York publisher George Hirsch, a friend of Dr. Sheehan. Hirsch soon convinced Dr. Sheehan to switch to *The Runner*.

In 1985 Anderson sold his magazine to Rodale Press and no longer is associated with it. In 1987 Rodale also acquired *The Runner*, merging the two magazines and retaining Hirsch as publisher. *Runner's World* today remains the world's most influential running publication.

Dr. George A. Sheehan achieved a fame greater than all but a few Boston Marathon winners.

ran," he recalled, "a fellow came in and there was blood coming out of his shoe. I said to myself, 'See what happens if you run more than five miles, you start bleeding.' "

Hitting the Wall

Yet, within the year, Dr. Sheehan discovered himself—almost against his will—running a marathon in Philadelphia. "I ran with Aldo Scandurra, whom I had beaten in a 20-miler, and was cruising along thinking, 'This is a snap. Not only am I going to finish but I am going to break three hours.' And I got to the 17-mile mark and I stopped! Right like that. That was the end."

Afterward, he approached Adolf Gruber, an Austrian marathoner who competed in American road races. Dr. Sheehan asked, "Adolf, what happened? I was feeling fine and all of a sudden I stopped."

"You went out too fast," barked Gruber. "Be last at five miles. That way you'll finish."

Feeling World Class

Dr. Sheehan continued the story: "My first Boston, I'm running with Bill Castle, who was a teacher. He said to me, 'The last four marathons I've walked in. I'm not going to do it today. The trick is what Gruber said, to go slow. We are going to go so slow that no one will even want to run with us.' So we ran and did just that."

There were 369 entrants in 1964, a record number and the first hint of the coming boom for both running and the Boston Marathon. Dr. Sheehan continued: "Coming into Boston, there was somebody on the sidewalk counting off numbers. We were now in the top 100. We had passed more than half the field doing nothing. Bill said to me, 'You're still full of running. Go ahead.' I said, 'I've run the whole way with you.

I'm going to stay with you.' I finished 95th or something. Somebody told me years later, 'If you placed that high now, you'd be world class.' I said, 'I was.' Bill and I were world class that day."

George Sheehan's time in his first Boston Marathon went unrecorded by officials, who had not wanted to wait in the cold to time runners so slow as to finish over three hours. He remembered it as being about 3:10. Dr. Sheehan would run Boston 22 consecutive years and would also participate in many other marathons, probably more than 100 total, but somehow never achieved his goal of breaking three hours. Ironically, he achieved his fastest time of 3:01:00 when he was over 60.

A Theater for Heroic Acts

Dr. Sheehan felt that the lure of the marathon for runners and its popularity as a spectator sport arose from a basic drive toward heroism. "Every marathon becomes a theater for heroic acts," he wrote. He believed that The Boston (as he always referred to it) particularly had the quality of real greatness, stating:

"It is a course that may be triumphed over but never defeated. To challenge the Boston course, you must be at your peak. Accept your limitations and, with thought and care, you will have a creditable race. But go for broke and prepare to be broken."

Dr. Sheehan told runners who attended his lectures that he learned something in each marathon. Before the New York City Marathon one year, a runner asked him, "What are you going to learn this year?"

"I don't know," Dr. Sheehan replied whimsically. "I haven't run yet."

Run on a Shoestring

His philosophical approach to running—and being—attracted many runners to Dr. George Sheehan when he began writing about their sport.

His first writing assignment was in 1968. He wrote about attending the Olympic Games in Mexico City that fall for his local newspaper, the *Red Bank Register*. There he met Joe Henderson, who at that time worked as a staff reporter for *Track & Field News*.

Henderson had won Iowa state high school championships for the mile in 1960 and 1961 and attended Drake University on a track scholarship, but like Dr. Sheehan, Joe was attracted to the roads. He ran the Boston Marathon in 1967, placing 98th in 2:49:48. In Mexico City Henderson and Dr. Sheehan crashed the Olympic Village to talk to some of the athletes. The pair quickly discovered that they shared a mutual love of running. Two years later Henderson invited Dr. Sheehan to become a columnist for a new magazine he edited, *Runner's World*.

While *Runner's World* became the arena for Dr. Sheehan's thoughts, Boston became the arena for his actions. By the time The Boston had grown in size to near 10,000, he had become its main celebrity, even more so than the much swifter runners who led the race.

Dr. Sheehan recalled how it had been in the beginning: "We had our heroes. We'd walk into the gym at Hopkinton and say, 'There's John Kelley. There's so and so.' But they were approachable. You could walk up and talk to them. Everybody knew each other back then. Even Erich Segal, who had just written *Love Story*, was just another guy in a Harvard singlet. A couple of the *Sports Illustrated* editors—Andy Crichton and Walt Bingham—started running the race around then. We got dressed midcourt between the two bleachers. The marathon was a big thing, but it didn't seem that big to us. It was still run on a shoestring."

Sheehan Describes Boston

"You walked to Hopkinton Green, and they put you in a bull pen where you had to wait until they let you go to the starting line. There were no refreshments on the course. Anything you got for survival came from the crowd. I remember a sign in Framingham at the railroad station that said '19⅞ miles to go,' which was ridiculous. You could spend the rest of the marathon trying to figure out what your time was from there.

"Even later, when the BAA began providing refreshments, there would never be enough for those of us in the back of the pack. You would be running through Framingham and Natick picking up empty juice bottles trying to find something to drink. At that point, I was inclined to drink water—nothing else. So if they gave you orange juice, I'd pour it on me. By the time I got to Boston, I'd be a sticky mess from the juice. They also gave you orange slices and ice. I would decide to get a cup, and I'd gradually get the biggest cup I could. Then, when you went by the hoses, you'd fill it up—and that was how we survived.

"But you'd get into Boston and look at the 'Pru' Building, and once

A SUDDEN TWINGE

A marathoner once finished with a broken leg. Eugene Gaston, M.D., a surgeon from Framingham, achieved fame among his peers by diagnosing the problem from a distance as the runner limped through the finishing chute. Dr. Gaston spotted the bulge caused by a fractured femur. The runner, who finished under 3:00, recalled feeling a sudden twinge in the leg coming down one of the Newton hills but thought the pain no more than what he expected toward the end of a marathon.

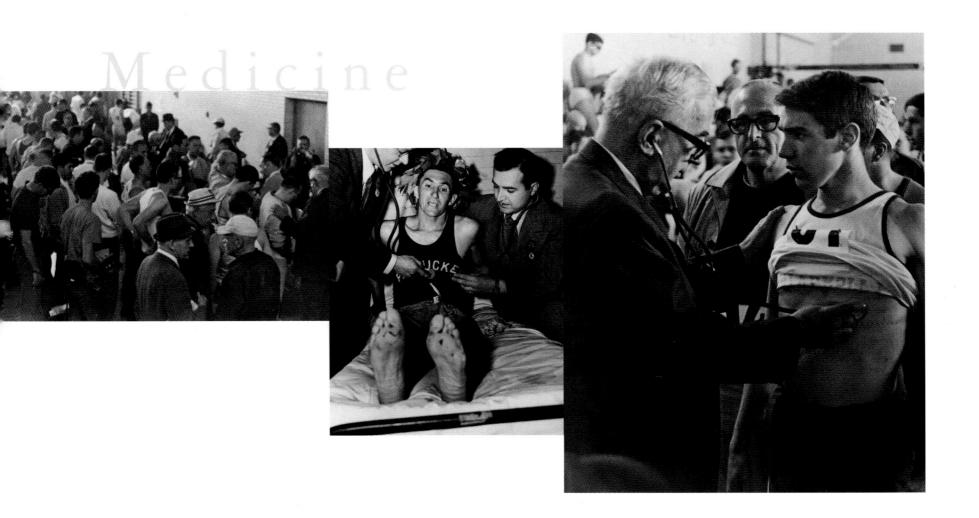

Physical examinations were a Boston tradition, beginning with the first race. Amateur Athletic Union rules also required them for races longer than six miles. With increasing numbers of entrants, beginning in the 1960s, the rules were modified and physicals were discontinued.

more you're not going to break three hours. I had the potential to run that fast in The Boston. I ran 3:01 or 3:02 there, but I never put in the time. I always said, 'You could run marathons on 30 to 35 miles a week.' You can but you can't run your best marathon on 30 to 35 miles a week.

"At one time Nina Kuscsik (1972 Boston winner) and I were pretty even, then she decided she was going to do better and started to train twice a day. Nina dropped her time five or six minutes and finished ahead of me. I figured if I ever put in the time I would come down five to six minutes, too, but I didn't think it was worth it. I wasn't that interested. It would have been nice, but it would have been like a onetime thrill to break three hours—then what next?"

Dr. Sheehan smiled at the thought. "What else would be left in life after you broke three hours in the marathon?"

Another Peak Experience

When later asked to describe his most memorable Boston, Dr. Sheehan chose one in which he had failed to finish, one of the hot years in the early 1980s. "I came down the hill from Boston College, and I was running on nothing. My muscles were gone, so I was just bone. I got to the bottom and Nina Kuscsik came out to encourage me. All I could think was, 'I'm not going to walk.' I had never stopped running and been able to finish a marathon walking before. She put me on a trolley. Gave me money. You didn't need money to ride the trolley if you had a marathon number, but we didn't know that.

"So I got on this trolley and a big cheer went up, and it infuriated me because I'm not finishing for the only time in 21 years. But I got a cheer bigger than when I finished!

"Somebody stood up and gave me a seat. This was terrible. Then an-

YOU GOTTA HAVE HEART

In 1973 Terence Kavanagh, M.D., medical director of the Toronto Rehabilitation Center, brought six of his cardiac patients to run Boston. "At the time, that was considered insanity," recalls Ron Lawrence, M.D., founder and head of the American Medical Joggers Association. Begun in the early 1970s, Dr. Kavanagh's program was one of the first attempts to rehabilitate cardiac patients with exercise.

To motivate his patients, Dr. Kavanagh promised that if they trained properly, he would bring them to the Boston Marathon. The group ran at the back of the pack, with a support system that included cardiac nurses on bicycles, much the way militiamen had supported early marathoners. The fastest patient, Herman Robers, ran 4:10. All finished. Nobody died. They made a powerful statement to the world about the relative safety of participating in endurance events.

Dr. Terence Kavanagh (third from right) and his cardiac patients. They trained together and all successfully finished the 1973 Boston Marathon.

AMJA "BANDITS" RUN BOSTON

Given the busy schedules of most doctors, Ron Lawrence, M.D., founder and head of the American Medical Joggers Association (AMJA), believed the time standards were unreasonable. Judi Babb, who served as part-time secretary for the new organization, painted special numbers for the 25 AMJA members who appeared in 1971. They started toward the back of the pack with other so-called bandits who were unable to meet the new qualifying standards.

The following year, in 1972, 55 AMJA runners ran the race. They wore yellow singlets bearing the caduceus symbol of Mercury: twin snakes coiled around a winged staff, the emblem of the medical profession. The crowds soon realized that runners wearing those shirts were doctors. Not immediately recognizing that there was a "J" in AMJA, signifying the group as the American Medical Joggers Association, spectators would shout, "Go AMA!" The organization's high point came in 1979 when 775 doctors ran, more than the number of entrants in any race during the marathon's first seven decades!

Ron Lawrence, M.D., founded the American Medical Joggers Association, which now provides medical coverage for the Boston Marathon—but no pre-race physical.

other person came over with a bag of groceries and gave me orange juice. It was like, 'I'm king of the hill and I'm still six miles from the finish.' I kind of indicated that I wasn't happy with the reception, even though they were being extremely nice. I was so embarrassed.

"By the time I got off the trolley, I figured it was another peak experience. I had gone through all the apologetics about what had happened. I had no idea why I had run so poorly. When I said good-bye to everybody, I decided that I had done my absolute best. Every other time I finished The Boston I must have had something left to cross the finish line, right? But if I didn't finish, it meant I had nothing left. Does that sound like pretty good reasoning?" He chuckled at the thought.

Dr. Sheehan would continue to return to Boston each year to lecture to rooms packed with runners who came to have him explain why they enjoyed running so much. He looked like he always did: A skinny Irishman in a turtleneck sweater, jeans, running shoes, talking without notes, taking the words of Kierkegaard, Nietzsche, Jung and Camus and relating them to the running experience. On November 1, 1993, George Sheehan died a few days short of his 75th birthday. He left an indelible mark upon the race he called The Boston.

The American Medical Joggers Association

One other physician who first ran Boston in the 1960s would leave his mark upon that race. Unlike Drs. Robbins, Cooper and Sheehan, he never ran track in college. Unlike Drs. Cooper and Sheehan, he never wrote a best-selling book. He was a celebrity only to other physicians because he founded the American Medical Joggers Association (AMJA). His name was Ron Lawrence, M.D.

Born March 24, 1926, in the Queens borough of New York City, Dr. Lawrence attended New York University, then the University of

California College of Medicine before moving to North Hollywood to practice as a neurologist and psychiatrist. "I never ran. I never did anything physical," recalls Dr. Lawrence. "I never had time."

He began running in 1967 at age 41, not for competitive reasons but more out of fear. One of his associates died of a heart attack. Dr. Lawrence recalls, "It made me ask myself, 'Is that the way you go?' I looked at the doctors around me. They were smoking, overweight, looking a lot like the Norman Rockwell painting: cherubic face, red cheeks, little girl standing nearby with a little dolly, and the doctor looked 65 but probably was 50. That was the image of the doctor at the beginning of the 1960s."

Dr. Lawrence started slowly, following a program for beginning joggers similar to that offered in Dr. Cooper's *Aerobics*. On his first day of running he struggled to cover even one block.

Within a year Dr. Lawrence was lining up at the starting line of the 1968 Palos Verde Marathon. Walt Frederick, a seasoned competitor, said, "Stick with me. I'll get you through." They finished in 4:24:00. Dr. Lawrence found himself attracted almost sensually to the mystique of the marathon, but he also saw the marathon as an acceptable and achievable goal, a means of getting other doctors interested in exercise so that they could act as role models for their patients.

In 1969 he founded the American Medical Joggers Association as an adjunct to the National Jogging Association, begun by Lieutenant General Richard Bohannon, who had recently retired as Surgeon General of the U.S. Air Force. At the midwinter meeting of the American Medical Association in New York City that year, the group sponsored a run in which 25 doctors participated, including Dr. Sheehan. Dr. Lawrence set as his next goal encouraging doctors to participate in the Boston Marathon. He recalls, "To my surprise, I found that the people in

THE MEDICAL TENT

In supervising medical care each year at the finish line, William P. Castelli, M.D., the white-haired director of the Framingham Heart Study, evokes the Rule of 5:30: If you're still in the medical tent at that hour, he automatically sticks an intravenous tube in your arm to restore lost liquids. "That way, the volunteers can adjourn to the bar of the Copley Plaza before 6:00," he jokes.

One reason marathoners can be cleared out so soon is that those ministering to them have learned to treat their most common medical problem—dehydration—more effectively. "In warm years we sometimes sent a dozen or more runners to the hospital for further treatment," says Dr. Castelli. "Now, we might send one or two."

How many need treatment depends on the weather. In 1982 the medical tent treated 1,700 runners; in 1994 with cooler weather it treated 429, none of whom needed to be sent to the hospital.

The numbers of runners needing treatment also varies with the hour. "Most elite runners are so well-trained that they rarely need treatment," explains Lyle J. Micheli, M.D., a member of the medical team. After 2:30, increasing numbers experience problems. A surge occurs between 2:50 and 3:00. "These are relatively fit runners who have been pushing themselves to break 3 hours." The peak comes near 3:30.

Afterward, although runners continue to cross the line in large numbers, fewer need treatment. "These are recreational runners, who run the marathon at the same pace they train," says Dr. Micheli. "For the most part, they don't get hurt."

After a morning run
Dr. George A. Sheehan
often waxed philosoph-
ical at the typewriter
on his porch in Ocean
Grove, New Jersey.

Boston—Will Cloney and Jock Semple—were not too enthusiastic about the idea."

The Boston Bandwagon

Boston—and running—was about to experience an explosion in numbers. In 1969, 1,152 runners entered the race, 678 of them finishing under four hours. A similar number started the following year when Ron Hill of England set a course record of 2:10:30. Cloney and Semple felt that the narrow Boston course could not tolerate more than those numbers. Runners in the back lost precious seconds, even minutes, between the time the gun sounded and the time they finally crossed the starting line.

Sorting them out at the finish line also seemed an impossible task. In an attempt to keep the size of the field below 1,000, the BAA in 1971 initiated time standards. To enter its race, runners would need to show proof that they had the ability to finish a marathon within four hours. "This is not a jogging race," warned the entry blank. Presumably, this would eliminate the less talented and the less serious—but these were exactly the people, at least within the medical community, that Dr. Lawrence hoped to attract.

By the early 1970s, the BAA had weakened and offered members of the AMJA special privileges, allowing its members numbers without meeting the qualifying standards, which had grown progressively stricter for men through the decade from 4:00 to 3:30 to 3:00 and finally to 2:50 by the early 1980s.

Qualifying for Boston

Rather than limiting the field, the qualifying standards had the opposite effect. Each time the BAA lowered its time standard, it challenged more and more runners to meet those standards. A runner crossing the finish line of another marathon in 2:49:59 or faster immediately made his travel plans to run Boston the following April. In 1979, 7,877 runners met Boston's strict standards and entered the race.

By then, the BAA and AMJA had developed a working partnership. Marvin Adner, M.D., a hematologist at Framingham Union Hospital, suggested to the BAA that AMJA members provide medical support along the course and at the finish line. "We met with Jock Semple, and Jock decided our organization was not that horrible," says Dr. Lawrence. "In the end, he became one of our best friends. His bite decreased. We got to know Will Cloney, and he came to like us, too.

"We worked out a four-hour time limit for our members, which was very liberal at the time. That allowed the AMJA to receive special numbers for which we were quite grateful. We tried not to boast, because some runners resented our getting special treatment. But there's no question that the support we provided added to the quality of the race, and it certainly added to its safety."

In only one year did Dr. Lawrence run fast enough to earn an official number. In 1978, when the time standard was still 3:30, he ran 3:30:05 in the Western Hemisphere Marathon in Culver City, California. Usually, when a runner came that close to its standard in a race where he could plead having been delayed that many seconds in a crowded start, the BAA relaxes its standard—at least slightly. Cloney offered an official number. Dr. Lawrence felt proud to be part of the regular race.

Nevertheless, the presence of the doctors at the Boston Marathon would significantly impact not only that race but other running events. People read about the achievements of the doctors and their lives were changed. The doctors, by their presence at Boston, attested to the inherent safeness of running. No more would the marathon be looked upon as a race that might kill you; instead, it could save your life.

Sex and Sub-terrrr-fuge

I didn't want to run Boston to prove anything. I just fell in love

with the marathon.—*Roberta Gibb*

For the Boston Marathon's first 70 years all of its entrants were men. That was true of almost all marathons, not just Boston. Until then, few women had cared to run 26.2 miles. Or perhaps more correctly, few were encouraged to run that far. After all, sports were for boys.

Women competed in track and field at the Olympic Games of course, but in events no farther than 200 meters. At the start of the 1960s the Amateur Athletic Union (AAU) rules permitted women to run cross-country races as long as 1½ miles. But women did not run road races and certainly did not run marathons.

Or did they? A Greek woman had reportedly run from Marathon to Athens in 1896. Legend suggests her name was Melpomene, although Olympic historians believe her actual name was Stamata Revithi. Supposedly, she trained for three weeks. Refused entry in the Olympic Games, Revithi ran the course before the men, finishing in 4½ hours. During the next 70 years a handful of women ran marathons in France (Marie Ledru, 1918), England (Violet Percy, 1926; Dale Greig, 1964) and New Zealand (Mildred Sampson, 1964). A woman may have run the 1951 Boston Marathon. Canadians talked about a

❦

PAGE 118: In the 1967 Boston Marathon Kathrine Switzer was running comfortably through Natick with friend John Leonard (left) and her coach, Arnie Briggs (490). Her confrontation with the Boston Athletic Association was miles behind her. LEFT: Early women marathoners thought they had to look good as well as run fast. Kathrine Switzer took great care selecting her running uniforms.

"mysterious woman in red" who ran the full distance that year wearing an all-red uniform. But the story seems apocryphal; if she did exist, the woman has never acknowledged her achievement.

Still, women were starting to appear in the marathon, even if briefly. In 1959 one of the Wellesley College students jumped into the race and ran with the men for a time. And a 17-year-old girl, a high school student from Newton, apparently ran the last five miles of the marathon in 1963. But neither of these women seemed to be making a statement. Like other students, they just thought it might be fun to run part of the Boston Marathon. Run a few miles. Get cheered. Laugh about it afterward. Guys did it; why not women?

Why Not Women?

Neither Jock Semple nor Will Cloney, the race organizers, envisioned that a woman might some day want to enter the Boston Marathon. It was not that they believed women incapable of running long distances. Nobody—including most women—much thought about the matter. They just didn't run. In fact, until the start of the 1960s very few males ran once they left school.

By the beginning of the 1960s, however, a few women began to show an interest in distance running. One of them was Sara Mae Berman, whose maiden name was Sidore. She was born May 14, 1936, in the Bronx. While dating her future husband, Larry Berman, Sara Mae often would travel to Boston on weekends to see him run. Larry was captain of the Massachusetts Institute of Technology (MIT) cross-country team his senior year.

Once, as a lark, Sara Mae did some running around the golf course where MIT held its meets. She wore a skirt and blouse and regular shoes. After Larry and Sara Mae married, she sometimes would go to Jamaica Pond in Brookline and sit on the grass while he worked out. "It never occurred to me that I might be able to run, too," says Sara Mae.

Because Larry enjoyed feeling physically fit, he had continued to train after graduation. He competed in road races as well as in cross-country ski meets. One day, Larry suggested his wife run with him. At that time, there were no "joggers"—men or women—to serve as role models. Sara Mae sprinted as fast as she could and by 100 yards was gasping for breath, ears ringing, thinking she was going to die. "I can't run that fast," she told her husband.

"Who told you you had to run fast?" he replied.

The logic inherent in that simple statement would fuel the running revolution: You don't have to run fast. Or even compete. It's enough to merely run. Like many "nonathletic" men of that era who had begun to recognize the potential of their own bodies, Sara Mae soon realized that if she ran more slowly, she could run farther.

By the end of that summer, Sara Mae found herself able to run a full lap around the pond, about a mile and a half. She embraced running as an enjoyable activity but didn't think of herself as a pioneer. Nor did she consider entering any road races, which were the domain of men.

See Sara Mae Run

By 1964 Sara Mae was running 5 miles in near 40 minutes (about an 8-minute-mile pace) but couldn't seem to get under that time. To run 5 miles in under 40 minutes had become a challenge for her, a motivational goal. Larry suggested that if she entered a road race at that distance, the extra adrenaline rush triggered by competition might help her run faster. They chose a 5-mile handicap race in Marlborough, a town west of Boston. "To say that I was self-conscious is putting it mildly," Sara Mae recalls. "There I was in Marlborough, a young matron in my late twenties with three small children and a babysitter to watch them, about to run around in my shorts in the middle of town."

Sara Mae Berman was nervous as she approached the YMCA in Marlborough to enter the race. A number of male runners sitting on the steps watched her approach. She worried about their reactions and whether or not they would accept her invasion of their male domain. "Are you going to run with us?" one asked. Berman conceded that she was. "Great!" the men replied.

After that, she felt more relaxed. Whether aware or not of AAU rules that might have prohibited a woman's entry, race organizers handed Berman a number and offered a favorable handicap as they might to any newcomer. She started in the first group with the older (and slower) men. As the faster runners passed, many offered encouragement. She finished in 38:37, somewhere in the middle of the pack.

Enjoying the experience, Sara Mae ran other road races. Her times improved. At some of the road races where she participated, Sara Mae would see Jock Semple, who attended many of the races as coach of the Boston Athletic Association (BAA) team. Semple gave Berman no special attention. To him, she was simply one of the boys. In 1965 Berman ran a 30-K race in New Bedford, Massachusetts, but failed to finish because of blisters. Yet she never considered running the Boston Marathon.

The next year, however, changed her mind. Sara Mae watched the Boston Marathon from the sidelines, waiting for her husband to pass. Suddenly, one of the spectators asked her, "Did you see the woman?"

"What woman?" asked Sara Mae, shocked that she had not. Paying as much attention to her children as the runners passing, she had failed to see the woman cross the finish line.

The woman was Roberta Gibb. The next morning, Sara Mae read the stories about "Bobbi" Gibb with a combination of pride and envy. "I was thrilled that a woman actually had completed the distance—and that it was publicly verified that she hadn't died doing it—but I was a bit disappointed that I hadn't done it myself."

"I Just Fell in Love with the Marathon"

Blonde, wide-eyed and long-legged, Roberta Louise Gibb had a winsome beauty to her. If you were casting someone to play the lead in a movie about the first woman to finish the Boston Marathon, she would have made an excellent candidate.

Roberta Gibb had been born November 2, 1942, in Winchester, Massachusetts. As a girl she sometimes would pretend she was a horse, cantering around her home. She ran with her dogs, sometimes for an hour or more. In school at the Boston Museum of Fine Arts Gibb began training partly as an excuse to spend time with a member of the cross-country team at Tufts University.

In 1965 she watched the Boston Marathon for the first time. "I saw these guys running and I just fell in love with the marathon. It never crossed my mind whether there were women running or whether I might be the first, but I decided to run the next year's race."

Her runner friend from Tufts was named William Bingay. After graduation he entered the Navy and was sent to San Diego. Gibb drove cross-country in her Volkswagen van, sleeping under the stars. In January they married. And while her husband was away at sea on duty, Roberta Gibb Bingay continued to run.

One day, Bill Gookin, one of San Diego's top competitive runners, encountered Gibb running in Balboa Park. He was surprised at first. "You encountered very few men running back then," he says. "You never saw women." Gookin introduced himself to Gibb and the two fell in step. Gookin was curious as to how far she ran. Gibb described

I ran with Roberta Gibb a while and realized she was
running effortlessly, just for the joy of it. — Bill Gookin

Pioneers

LEFT: Roberta Gibb in 1968. By chance the first woman to run Boston looked like a Greek goddess. **RIGHT:** Sara Mae Berman and Jock Semple announce to the press that women would be allowed to officially enter the Boston Marathon in 1972.

having run from her home near the park to the ferry, which she took to Coronado, then down that peninsula to near the Mexican border and back. Gookin calculated the distance in his mind and figured it to be between 25 and 28 miles.

He recalls thinking, "No way, I can barely do that. Then I ran with her for a while and realized she was running effortlessly, just for the joy of it." Later, he and his brother Ed ran with Gibb on a long workout that went to the top of Black Mountain, east of San Diego. Ed and Bill Gookin both had 10-K times faster than 34:00. Both also had dropped out of marathons and respected the ability it took to run that far. Until that workout, Ed Gookin doubted Gibb. "Halfway down the mountain we lost my brother," smiles Bill Gookin. "He couldn't keep up! After that he became one of Bobbi's biggest defenders."

In February 1966 Gibb wrote the BAA and requested an entry blank for the Boston Marathon. Her request was rejected by Jock Semple, citing the AAU restrictions that prohibited women from running races longer than 1½ miles.

"I was just dumbfounded," Gibb later recounted. "I felt anger and shame and outrage. This is the feeling that you are not going to be allowed to be who you are and do what you can because you are a woman. It never occurred to me not to run."

Bobbi Runs Boston

In April Gibb rode a bus from California to Massachusetts. The journey took four days and three nights. On race morning her mother drove her to the starting line. She had been training in Red Cross nurse's shoes, but they hurt her feet, so she bought a pair of men's running shoes, size six. "I didn't know you were supposed to break them in," recalls Gibb.

She wore a black one-piece bathing suit and over that Bermuda shorts and a sweatshirt with a hood. She pulled the hood tight over her head to cover her long blonde hair, fearful that officials might stop her if she revealed her intentions of running. After the gun sounded she stepped off the curb and joined the men.

Hood or not, anyone who looked closely could see that Gibb did not resemble a male. Other runners soon began to notice her. "Is that a girl?" Gibb heard them asking each other. Gibb remained silent. She did not know whether or not she would be accepted. One of them finally directed the question to her. Gibb conceded what was now obvious.

"Wow," said one of the runners. "I wish my wife would run."

Gibb continued running with the men around her. "I'm afraid to take off my sweatshirt," she told them. "They'll see I'm a woman and kick me out."

One of the men told her, "We won't let them."

Just One of the Boys

After that comment, Gibb felt that a burden had been lifted from her shoulders. For whatever its value she had become one of the boys. She removed the sweatshirt, threw it to the side of the road and ran more comfortably. As runners shifted positions, word spread ahead and behind Gibb that there was a woman in the race. Those officials who might have stopped her—Will Cloney and Jock Semple—were far ahead on the press bus following the lead runners.

Reporters on that bus were oblivious to the fact that the marathon's lead story that day (bigger than four Japanese runners sweeping the top places) was well behind them. Officials checking runners at checkpoints along the route at Framingham and Natick and beyond certainly saw Gibb but did not react. They made no attempt to stop her. She received her loudest cheers as she passed Wellesley College. "The women

GUARDIANS OF THE GATE

As the two individuals most responsible for guiding the Boston Marathon through the turbulent 1960s, both trainer Jock Semple and race director Will Cloney considered themselves protectors of the race's integrity. During this decade, they looked with disfavor on anyone who might disrupt their event—male or female.

This included the "bandits" who joined the race without numbers, running at the back of the pack, along with the characters who wore clown suits, rabbit ears and the like. One runner appeared at the start each year smoking a cigar, mugging for photographers. Another runner of average ability would sprint into the lead for the thrill of leading Boston, even if only for a hundred yards. These antics infuriated Semple. In the mind of Semple the Boston Athletic Association Marathon occupied sacred territory. Its running each April was almost a religious event. Race director Cloney felt much the same. Semple felt these clowns and jesters were mocking his race. He called them cheats. He said, "I can't stand cheats."

Particularly detested by Semple were those unentered who failed to finish, who saw the Boston Marathon as a vehicle by which they could grab some attention and steal glory from the race's legitimate runners. Semple once spotted an unentered runner jogging along in an ape costume. He halted the press bus, got off and slugged him, much to the amusement of reporters.

When women first started to appear at the Boston Marathon, it would take a while before Semple and Cloney realized that they were serious about their intentions and serious about their sport, and not just a new class of glory-grabbers.

were ecstatic," recalls Gibb. "They were screaming."

Gibb cruised across the line after 3 hours and 20 minutes of running, a respectable time for any first-time marathoner, male or female. Only Mildred Sampson of New Zealand had recorded a faster time, running 3:19:00 two years before in her homeland. Most of the marathoning efforts by Sampson and women distance runners in other countries were unofficial, and some question exists concerning Roberta Gibb's exact time.

After Gibb crossed the finish line, another runner offered her a blanket. Governor John Volpe of Massachusetts shook her hand. At first, skeptics refused to believe that a woman could run distances as far as 26.2 miles. Eventually, enough people came forth to state that they had seen her along the length of the course to convince the doubters. Even Semple admitted he had noticed Gibb running soon after the start.

The Boston Athletic Association conceded that maybe Gibb had gone the distance—but that didn't mean they were going to list her as an official finisher. She had not entered. She did not have a number. When Gibb tried to join the men finishers in the cafeteria in Prudential Center where they were eating the beef stew traditionally offered to competitors, she was refused entry. "They said no women allowed," she recalls. She was no longer one of the boys.

Gibb returned to run the Boston Marathon the following two years, finishing as first woman both times. Somewhat to her chagrin, in 1967 the attention of the press shifted to another woman runner who finished well behind her: K. V. Switzer.

"She Did Not Look Like a Boy"

Kathrine Virginia Switzer possessed one item that year that had eluded her predecessor, a race number. In his Scottish brogue Semple would claim later that she and her "co-conspirators" got that number by "sub-terrrr-fuge," that she had disguised her sex by using initials.

But Switzer claimed she obtained it in innocence, that she always signed her name that way. Whichever, the number 261 on the front of her sweatshirt gained her entry to the bull pen on Hopkinton Green. Switzer remembers actually being pushed into the bull pen by race director Will Cloney. "Get in there!" Cloney said, directing her inside.

The bull pen lasted just a few more years—race entries soared, necessitating major shifts in the race's organizational structure, and the bull pen became a relic. So did the idea that the Boston Marathon—or any other running race of 26 miles, 385 yards—was the exclusive domain of male runners.

"I had my makeup on," Switzer recalls. "I wasn't trying to disguise the fact that I was a girl. But it was cold and drizzly, so I had the hood of my sweatshirt pulled over my head." For that reason BAA officials failed to notice the woman with a number lining up to start their race. Cloney and Semple had enough problems caused by the increasing numbers and could not give any one runner close examination. An atmosphere of crisis prevailed. The swelling interest in their race threatened to overwhelm them. It made them touchier and more irritable than usual.

One of the runners that day who did notice Switzer's presence was Larry Berman. He saw Semple walk past Switzer and tell her to move back. "I was standing about 15 feet away," Berman recalls. "Kathy was wearing a gray sweatshirt, but she did not look like a boy. On marathon day Jock was so wound up he didn't even notice that she was a girl."

An Official Entrant

Switzer had been running for several years. Encouraged by her father, Switzer had started to run in order to get in shape for field hockey, a

ARNIE BRIGGS: THE MAN WHO TRAINED K. V. SWITZER

Arnie Briggs remembers the fall day in 1966 that Kathrine Switzer first appeared at the track office at Syracuse University. "Could I try out for cross-country?" she asked. Coach Bob Grieve told Switzer to report to practice that afternoon to run the 5-mile course. After Switzer left, Grieve said to Briggs, "I guess I got rid of her."

But when they started practice, they found Switzer. "We had Kathy jog the freshman course," Briggs recalls. "She did that with no trouble. Then one of the runners took her around the varsity loop."

Grieve told Switzer she could join the team, but the athletic director disagreed. Switzer trained with the team anyway, going for long runs with Briggs. His tales of Boston captivated her. "Arnie, I want to run Boston," Switzer insisted.

Briggs told Switzer that if she could run the full distance in practice, he'd enter her in the marathon. In the spring they ran 26½ miles together. After finishing, Switzer worried: "What if the course was short?" She convinced Briggs to run another 3½ miles. Briggs remembers little after that. He finished in a fog. Switzer slapped him on the back, "Arnie, we did it!" Briggs pitched forward on his face. After regaining his composure, he agreed to take Switzer to Boston.

Sitting in the same track office at Syracuse where he had first met Switzer, Briggs noted that Jock Semple, trainer for the BAA, never spoke to him afterward. "He blamed me for Kathy running Boston." Briggs claims that if officials in the Hopkinton gym had been paying attention, they might never have offered the disputed number.

"The travel permit clearly read Kathrine Virginia Switzer," laughs Briggs. "If they had bothered to read it, who knows what the history of women's running might have been."

Determination

LEFT: Long-distance running came naturally to Roberta Gibb. In 1966 she became the first woman to run the Boston Marathon. CENTER: In 1972, after being granted official sanction to enter Boston, women formed a chorus line for photographers. Posing in Hopkinton are (left to right) Nina Kuscsik, Kathrine Switzer, Elaine Pederson, Ginny Collins, Pat Barrett, Frances Morrison and Sara Mae Berman. Kuscsik won in 3:10:26 with Pederson second and Switzer third. Defending three-time winner Berman came in fifth. RIGHT: Following her win, Kuscsik was led to a private dressing room for the women. Feeling ill, she lay down, laurel wreath still on her head.

sport at which she excelled in high school and college. She started with a mile a day and gradually increased her distance.

At Lynchburg College in Virginia she sometimes trained with the men's track team. Invited by the coach to compete, she ran 5:58 for the mile and 2:36 for the 880, possibly becoming the first woman to run in a men's intercollegiate track meet. She even won a letter.

After transferring to Syracuse University for her junior year, Switzer asked track coach Bob Grieve if she could work out with his team. He gladly accepted her and introduced her to Arnie Briggs. A frequent competitor at Boston, Briggs assisted with the distance runners.

At first Briggs doubted her ability. He came from the old school that believed women did not—and perhaps should not—participate in sports. Eventually, he became convinced of her sincerity, even when Switzer told him that she wanted to run the Boston Marathon.

Briggs hesitated. He knew that AAU rules prohibited women from competing in distance events. Finally, he said that if she could prove to him she could go the distance, he would take her to Boston. In the spring of 1967 Switzer covered 30 miles in one workout to demonstrate her ability. Briggs obtained an entry blank for Switzer. He and Tom Miller, a hammer thrower who Switzer was dating at the time and who later became her husband, made plans to accompany her to Boston as did another Syracuse track athlete named John Leonard. While Switzer waited in the car, Leonard entered the gym to pick up her number.

By now, there was no question about Switzer's ability to run a marathon. She had proved that in practice. She was a registered member of the AAU, a requirement for all runners entering Boston. The BAA had no stipulation on its entry blank that women could not run, although the ban was understood because of AAU rules.

Cloney would say later that he feared that if the BAA circumvented those rules, the AAU might refuse to sanction the Boston Marathon. Without a sanction, the BAA not only would be unable to attract top-ranked foreign runners but fast Americans fearful of losing their eligibility for future international competition might also stay away.

Jock Semple might have looked the other way when he saw Sara Mae Berman participating in local road races, but this was the BAA Marathon. Its integrity was not to be tampered with, not by students who sometimes jumped into the race wearing funny outfits and not by women.

The Woman Revealed

Four miles into the race, Switzer had just passed through the town of Ashland. She was running comfortably, well back in the pack. Roberta Gibb was ahead of her, moving at a much faster pace. Switzer recalls hearing honking as the flatbed truck carrying the photographers came from behind. The runners shifted to one side of the road to allow it and the following press bus to pass.

By now Switzer had shed her outer sweatshirt with its hood, revealing herself as unmistakably female. The photographers spotted her and asked the driver of the truck to slow down, the presence of a woman in the race clearly presenting a photo opportunity.

"I hammed it up," admits Switzer. "I smiled and waved at them. I did not think there was anything wrong with my running in a men's race."

Behind the flatbed truck was the press bus containing Cloney and Semple. After Gibb's appearance the previous year everybody was looking for her or other women. Then one of the reporters announced, "Hey, Jock, it's a girl. And holy smokes, she's wearing one of your numbers."

In his appropriately titled autobiography, *Just Call Me Jock*, Semple would relate his version of what happened. Even though Cloney was the

The crusty Scotsman felt that he was guardian of the Boston Marathon's integrity.

Would doors for women in running have opened without the infamous confrontation between Jock Semple and K.V. Switzer? Certainly, but worldwide publication of these photographs speeded the process. **LEFT:** Race director Will Cloney (center) and trainer Jock Semple (far right), both in dark clothing, rush to confront the running Switzer (261). **CENTER LEFT:** Semple (behind Switzer) tries to reclaim her number as Arnie Briggs (left) defends her. **CENTER RIGHT:** Tom Miller, Switzer's boyfriend (right), gets ready to act. **TOP RIGHT:** Miller brushes Semple aside.

race director, the crusty Scotsman felt that he was guardian of the Boston Marathon's integrity. He admitted to being disturbed that reporters the previous year had paid more attention to Roberta Gibb than winner Kenji Kimihara, but he seemed not to blame Gibb. "I saw her but I didn't chase her," wrote Semple. "She didn't have a number. She wasn't really cheating."

But Switzer had a number, apparently obtained through "sub-terrrr-fuge." "She had tricked me by sending an application with only her initial instead of her first name," wrote Semple. "I used to assign the numbers for the Boston Marathon in between periods of the Bruins and Celtics games. Bobby Orr must have had an outstanding game for me to miss that one."

The reporters on the bus quickly matched Switzer's number with her name listed in the program: K. Switzer. They began to rib Semple.

"Hey, Jock, this 'K' fellow wearing 261 looks pretty good."

"What's her mother call her, Jock," asked another, "Karl?"

This fed Semple's anger. The Scotsman's blustery brogue masked a man who deeply loved the sport of running and the runners who populated it—at least the serious runners. Semple was not yet convinced that a woman could be a serious runner. He still classified women with the students who jumped in and out of the race without bothering to enter.

At that point, he did not know how hard Switzer had trained. Briggs had failed to inform Semple of that fact. If Briggs had done so, Semple might not have been so angry. Of course, he also would not have issued a number to someone entering as K. V. Switzer.

"Get Out of My Rrrrace!"

"Jock shouted for the driver of the press bus to halt," recalls *Boston Globe* reporter Joe Concannon. "He and Cloney went storming outside.

Jock was red-faced and screaming, 'Get out of my rrrrace! Get out of my rrrrace!' "

Cloney always stood in the doorway with the door open so that he could direct the motorcycle policemen ahead of the leaders. He was first to descend when the press bus stopped. The truck carrying photographers also stopped. Cloney and Semple waited to pounce as Switzer and her three companions approached.

Miller was not very large as hammer throwers went, but he was still larger than Cloney. "When I got within five feet of her, he started moving toward me," recalled Cloney. "Not being stupid, I retreated to the press bus. It was at that point that Jock came charging past me."

Concannon recalls: "Cloney tried to run after the woman runner but couldn't catch her. So Semple took after her at full speed."

Switzer recalls hearing footsteps rapidly approaching from the rear. "I turned around and there was Jock," she recalls. "He was shouting at me and trying to grab my number. I pulled away from him. Arnie told him, 'Leave her alone, Jock. I trained her.' I looked at Arnie and thought, 'You know this maniac?' All this time, Jock was shoving me, trying to grab the number on the front of my shirt, which didn't make me very comfortable. I shouted, 'Hey!' "

This was the point when Miller shoved Semple away from Switzer.

"Tom decked him," she says. "Jock went spinning head over feet into the grass."

"I tripped over my shoelaces," Semple would say later, trying to make light of the incident. But that was much later. At the time, he was furious.

Switzer and her three male escorts continued down the road. Semple picked himself off the ground and climbed back on the press bus with Cloney. As they passed Switzer to recatch the front-runners, he swore angrily out the bus window at her.

ABOVE: Joan Benoit Samuelson had plenty of male company during her 1979 win, including George Hirsch (T142), then publisher of *The Runner* magazine. **RIGHT**: Rosa Mota of Portugal ran 2:25:24 in 1990, winning her third Boston Marathon in an astounding hour faster than women a quarter-century before.

Andy Crichton, an editor from *Sports Illustrated* who frequently ran Boston, was on the press bus that year. As he recalls, "After Jock returned to the bus, some of us began to kid him about what happened. Then we realized how angry he was and shut up."

According to Switzer, "At the moment everything happened, I was embarrassed. As I continued to run, I got angry. I had trained just as hard as the men who had entered the race legally. Why shouldn't a woman be permitted to run?"

She continued and crossed the finish line somewhere in the neighborhood of 4 hours. "Nobody in our group wore a watch," says Switzer. "Arnie claimed we ran under 4 hours, but he's probably wrong." Switzer discreetly gives 4:20 as her most likely time.

Four Photos That Changed the World

Switzer had finished nearly an hour after Roberta Gibb, who that day ran 3:27:17. But, while Gibb finished first, Switzer grabbed all the publicity, partly because of Harry Trask, a photographer for the *Boston Herald-Traveler*. Trask usually shot baseball games but on that Patriots' Day was assigned to the Boston Marathon. He recalls: "I was irritated because by the time I got to the office, the baseball photographers had taken all the good cameras."

Trask was riding on the photo truck and saw Semple emerge from the press bus shaking his fist. "Usually, wherever Jock went controversy followed," recalls Trask. "So I decided to climb off the photo truck, even if it meant getting left behind, to see what Jock was up to."

Trask thus was in position when Semple grabbed for Switzer's number. He shot four pictures in sequence, showing Semple lunging, Switzer reacting, then Miller pushing Semple away. Trask's photographs appeared on front pages throughout the world the next day.

The Barrier Crumbles

Switzer did not return to Boston the following year, but Gibb and two other women ran in 1968. Nina Kuscsik finished in about 3:45. Marjorie Fish, whose husband was studying at Harvard Divinity School, finished around 4:45. "Marjorie had not run any road races," recalls Sara Mae Berman. "It was simply a lark for her."

By 1969 Berman finally decided it was time for her to run the Boston Marathon. Sara Mae had delayed that long because she wanted to be certain of her ability to finish. Little did it matter that some of Boston's most illustrious champions (including both Old John and Young John Kelley) had failed to finish in their first attempts. No woman would be permitted that luxury—or so felt Berman.

Gibb retired as an active marathoner after her third Boston, though she continued to run for enjoyment (and would run Boston again in 1983). Running with her husband, Sara Mae Berman finished first in 1969 in 3:22:46. Elaine Pederson, a flight attendant from California, followed in 3:43:00; Kuscsik ran 3:46:00.

In 1970 five women runners ran the marathon, including Kathrine Switzer, back for the first time since her encounter with Semple. Switzer improved her previous time by 45 minutes but finished fifth out of the five in 3:34:00. Berman won again in a course record of 3:05:07 on a chilly day when Ron Hill also set a course record of 2:10:30. The previous year, Berman had placed her dry clothes with those of her husband and changed afterward in a ladies room in the Prudential Building. But by 1970 the BAA had begun to realize that—officially or unofficially—they needed to make at least some provisions for women runners.

Immediately after Berman finished, an official wrapped her in a blanket and began to guide her into the Prudential garage, which then served as the post-marathon collecting area for finishers. This caused Sara

I have always been in great favor of the girls running,

that is, when they do it legally. —Jock Semple

Competitors

LEFT: A tailwind in 1994 pushed Germany's Uta Pippig to a record 2:21:45. **CENTER:** Nina Kuscsik's winning 1972 time was 3:10:26, but she

later broke three hours. **RIGHT:** Patti Lyons (center) should have been happy in 1981, having run 2:27:51 to break the American record, but she and

her sisters felt disappointed that she only finished second to New Zealand's Allison Roe.

Mae to be separated from her husband, who had finished earlier.

Berman recalls: "I thought, 'Good, they're going to have a special place for us, because there were other women in the race.' And I was led to a semidark cave, a changing room for women ice-skaters who skated at the 'Pru'. I don't remember a shower, but there was one light on and a narrow wooden bench between two rows of lockers, and I was so exhausted that I lay down on it.

"The blanket offered some comfort but not much. The room was unheated and I was there for the longest time. I think another woman came in, but I don't remember who. She asked me about what was available there and I said, 'Nothing.' She left so I thought I better go, too. I had no dry clothes because they had been sent with Larry's, except he did not know where I was. Eventually we found each other and went home."

Berman won again in 1971 over Kuscsik. Berman led through the Newton hills only to be passed by Kuscsik on the downhill stretch past Boston College. Berman repassed and moved away, winning by 30 seconds.

Women No Longer Banned at Boston

More and more women runners began entering races previously closed to them. At a race in New York City women were granted legal entry but told to start ten minutes before the men. So the women entrants ignored the gun and sat down on the starting line for ten minutes to await the regular start.

The Road Runners Club of America continued to lobby the AAU for change. At its 1971 convention the AAU finally repealed its rule prohibiting women from running marathons. In 1972, when Boston finally granted women official status, Kuscsik won in 3:10:26. Switzer placed third in that race, Berman fifth.

"Throughout all this controversy," says Switzer, "the men runners always offered support and encouragement. They wanted women to be allowed to run with them. In fact, even Jock Semple changed his mind when he realized women were willing to train as hard to run his race as the men. He came up to me at the starting line of Boston in 1973 and said, 'All right, lass, let's cause some controversy.' He gave me a kiss on the cheek while photographers snapped our pictures."

Semple later wrote, "I have always been in great favor of the girls running, that is, when they do it legally."

Switzer would run Boston eight times, her best time being 2:51:37 when she finished second to Liane Winter of Germany, who set a world record of 2:42:24 that day in 1975. Within a decade, Joan Benoit Samuelson lowered the women's record at Boston to 2:22:43, and Norway's Ingrid Kristiansen set a world mark of 2:21:06, times only a small number of elite male runners are capable of bettering.

Switzer didn't disappear from the sport. She worked as a journalist, then for AMF, coordinating that organization's sponsorship of the national track-and-field championships in 1975 for *masters* athletes. She moved from that position to Avon Products, where she organized a worldwide circuit of women-only races, including the Avon Women's International Marathon, beginning in 1978. With Switzer as its spokesperson, Avon stated its goal as getting a marathon for women included in the Olympic Games. That occurred in 1984, with Joan Benoit Samuelson winning the gold medal in Los Angeles.

There had been no gold medals, however, for Roberta Gibb, who won Boston three consecutive years between 1966 and 1968. And none for Sara Mae Berman, who won the three following years from 1969 through 1971. And none for Switzer, despite the fact that her second-place time in 1975 was third fastest among those women who ran Boston during their first decade of participation. Asterisks would appear beside the names of

Miki Gorman of Los
Angeles was the first
woman at Boston to
break 3 hours with her
1974 victory in 2:47:11.
She raced to victory
again at Boston in 1977.

the first women finishers in record books and press kits, identifying them as unofficial.

At a press conference before the 1994 marathon, during which BAA race director Guy Morse offered preliminary plans for Boston's 100th anniversary, he invited those defending champions in the audience to come up on stage to be presented with special 1996 T-shirts.

During the presentation, Morse looked down in the audience and spotted Kathrine Switzer, who was working with one of the TV networks covering that year's race. "Kathrine," said Morse, "you belong up on this stage."

"I only got second, Guy," Switzer corrected him. But Morse was right. Switzer belonged up on that stage, as did Gibb and Berman, because every other woman who entered Boston afterward would run in their footsteps.

Making up. After a stormy initial encounter, Jock Semple and Kathrine Switzer realized they had much in common, including a love of running and the Boston Marathon.

WOMEN'S MARATHON RECORDS

On two occasions women winning the Boston Marathon established world-best times. Liane Winter's 2:42:24 from 1975 and Joan Benoit Samuelson's 2:22:43 from 1983 were considered world records. Among the men only South Korean Yun Bok Suh's 2:25:39 from 1947 makes the list of records for 26-mile, 385-yard races. (Times recorded before the establishment of that as the official marathon distance are excluded from the list.) Times made on the Boston course no longer qualify for world record consideration because of more stringent regulations. Boston's downhill profile disqualifies it for record purposes.

Time	Runner	Marathon	Date
3:40:22	VIOLET PERCY	London	10/3/26
3:27:45	DALE GREIG	Ryde, Great Britain	5/23/64
3:19:33	MILDRED SAMPSON	Auckland, New Zealand	7/21/64
3:15:22	MAUREEN WILTON	Toronto	5/6/67
3:07:26.2	ANNI PEDE-ERDKAMP	Waldniel, West Germany	9/16/67
3:01:42	ELIZABETH BONNER	Philadelphia	5/9/71
2:46:30	ADRIENNE BEAMES	Werribbee, Australia	8/31/71
2:43:54.5	JACQUELINE HANSEN	Culver City, California	12/1/74
2:42:24	LIANE WINTER	Boston	4/21/75
2:40:15:8	CHRISTA WAHLENSIECK	Dulmen, West Germany	5/3/75
2:38:19	JACQUELINE HANSEN	Eugene, Oregon	10/12/75
2:35:15.4	CHANTEL LANGLACE	Oyarzun, France	5/1/77
2:34:47.5	CHRISTA WAHLENSIECK	West Berlin	9/10/77
2:32:29.8	GRETE WAITZ	New York City	10/22/78
2:27:32.6	GRETE WAITZ	New York City	10/21/79
2:25:41.3	GRETE WAITZ	New York City	10/26/80
2:25:28.7	GRETE WAITZ	London	4/17/83
2:22:43	JOAN BENOIT SAMUELSON	Boston	4/17/83
2:21:06	INGRID KRISTIANSEN	London	4/21/85

Note: Allison Roe of New Zealand ran 2:25:28.8 in New York City on 10/25/81, considered at the time a world record. The course later was remeasured and determined to be 155 meters short.

Red, White and Blue

Chapter Eight

8

There is something very unique about Boston.... It is

Mecca-like.—*Bill Rodgers*

AMERICAN VICTORIES AT BOSTON had become rare in the years following World War II. With improvements in air transportation top marathoners from other countries could travel to Boston more easily. Thus, between 1946 and 1972, Finnish runners won the Boston Marathon seven times and Japanese runners six. Yet, during this same 26-year period, only twice had Americans triumphed in their country's most prestigious road race: John J. Kelley in 1957 and Amby Burfoot in 1968.

Then, in 1973, an unexpected American victory by Oregon runner Jon Anderson signaled the start of a new era. Over 11 years American men would win Boston eight times. Even more remarkable, for six of those victories the winner had been coached by the same individual—Bill Squires.

Lean and lanky, Squires had been a four-time all-American at Notre Dame University, running a 4:06 mile. Graduating in 1956, Squires moved back to his home in Arlington, Massachusetts. He taught and coached at nearby Wakefield High School, where his teams won six state titles. He also continued to compete as a track athlete on the indoor board circuit. Although most Boston Athletic Association (BAA) athletes were road runners, Squires respected Jock Semple, the BAA trainer, and competed wearing the BAA's yellow singlet with its unicorn logo.

❦

PAGE 138: Bill Rodgers crosses the finish line in 1978 for his second Boston Marathon victory. He would win again in 1979 and 1980. LEFT: Jack Fultz ran and won Boston anonymously in 1976. Water had soaked his number, causing it to rip off.

Squires Runs Boston

In January 1960 Squires placed third in a 1,000-yard race in Philadelphia. Several days later he received a telephone call from Herbert Holm, secretary for the New England Amateur Athletic Union (AAU). Holm informed Squires that he no longer could compete as an amateur, as he was being paid to coach, and must surrender his AAU card. "You're now a professional," insisted Holm. Squires thought a moment and requested that Holm permit him to run one last race. "I've always wanted to run the Boston Marathon," said Squires.

"Billy," said Holm, "you're a miler. How far do you think you'll get?"

"One race," pleaded Squires. "Let me run Boston, and I'll turn in my card the next day." Holm finally agreed, leaving Squires only 13 weeks to transform himself from a miler to a marathoner. He shifted the focus of his training from speed work to distance. Instead of 440-yard repeats on the track, he did half-mile repeats. He increased his weekly mileage from 35 to 70 miles. He started doing long runs on Sundays, gradually increasing them from 11 miles to 20. As a final test he ran the New England 30-K Championships in New Bedford, placing fourth.

That Patriots' Day, Squires set his goal as finishing in the top 35, which would earn him a medal. Squires started conservatively. By Wellesley he had moved into medal position. "I had trained on the Newton hills," Squires recalls, "so once I reached that part of the course, my confidence grew stronger.

"My only mistake was that I had failed to familiarize myself with the last stretch. I got to Kenmore Square thinking I had only a few blocks to run but more than a mile remained. That hurt. I was a local boy wearing a BAA shirt, and everybody was cheering me by name. It was painful but fulfilling."

Squires finished 20th in 2:47:46. The following day, he stopped by the AAU office at Boston Garden and handed Holm his card.

"That race was very important to me," says Squires. "It provided a mental perspective for teaching others how to run well at Boston."

The Greater Boston Track Club Evolves

In 1965 Squires began teaching and coaching at Boston State College, winning a National Association of Intercollegiate Athletics (NAIA) cross-country championship his first year. Remembering how much running the Boston Marathon had meant to him, he established a tradition that members of the team would run the BAA Marathon in their senior years. To prepare, the Boston State runners ran long distances during the winter, using indoor meets mainly for speed work. Twice a week they trained on the marathon course, running from Boston College to Wellesley and back, about 14 miles. Squires began to build a marathon empire.

Several of his college runners ran top times. Wayne Frongello ran 2:20:41 and won an NAIA marathon title. Rick Bayko ran 2:20:22; he would finish 13th at Boston. Joe Catalano ran 2:22:45. Using principles learned at the foot of Squires, Catalano later coached his wife, the former Patti Lyons, to several 2nd-place finishes at Boston.

In 1973 a group of runners who had graduated from other colleges that had competed against Squires's teams asked him to coach them. The leader of the group was Jack McDonald, later the athletic director at the University of Denver.

"We started as a group of middle-distance track guys," recalls McDonald. "Boston had a number of clubs for road runners, including the BAA and North Medford Club, but at that time there was nothing for people who wanted to run track."

Although their main interest was middle distances, Squires trained

McDonald and his group in the fall to run long distances and even entered them in road races. They won several club road running national championships on the road. Squires met with the group twice weekly, Tuesdays at the track at Boston College for interval training and Sundays for long runs through the Newton hills. Word spread among local runners and the group grew in size. They took as their name the Greater Boston Track Club (GBTC).

One evening during the fall of 1974 a runner appeared at the track and asked Squires to coach him. Like most fast distance runners, the individual was slightly built. With long blond hair and angular features, he had a habit of squinting quizzically when you talked to him as though weighing each word. He had begun to develop a reputation at local road races, and the previous April he had placed 14th at Boston with 2:19:34. His name was Bill Rodgers.

Rodgers Meets Burfoot

Even as a child, William Henry Rodgers had loved being outdoors: hiking, camping, fishing, hunting with bow and arrow and chasing butterflies with a homemade net in fields near his home. Sometimes he and his brother Charlie would go for long walks. "We were always moving," wrote Rodgers in his autobiography, *Marathoning*. "I became a runner because it suited my personality."

Rodgers started to run seriously at age 15, training by running around the block, two laps to the mile, usually going five laps. If the weather was cold or rainy, he stayed inside. At Newlington High School he trained under coach Frank O'Rourke, who had him do mostly repeat 220s, 440s or 880s on the track. His high school bests were 4:28.8 in the mile and 9:36 for two miles. He won the state cross-country championship his senior year. Graduating in 1966, Rodgers enrolled

AN AMERICAN VICTORY

Despite having made the American Olympic team in 1972 at 10,000 meters, Jon Anderson was not a favorite at Boston the following year. He had run several marathons, but none under 2:20. The starting number (28) assigned to him based on his best time indicated his relatively low status.

Americans had not done well at Boston during the nearly three decades since John A. Kelley's last win. Since 1945 only John J. Kelley (1957) and Amby Burfoot (1968) had been able to blunt the foreign invasion. Thus, in 1973, few expected an American victory.

On a warm day Anderson decided to run with fellow Olympian Jeff Galloway, an experienced marathoner. Galloway and Anderson stayed together through Wellesley, running 1:08 at halfway. Eventually, Anderson left Galloway and passed the front-runners at 20 miles.

"I was surprised that it happened so quickly," says Anderson. "It was an emotional moment. I couldn't believe that I was leading Boston. I couldn't savor my victory in the closing miles because I was afraid someone might catch me. After I crossed the line, I went back to the water fountain in front of the Prudential and jumped in to cool off."

Anderson's winning time was 2:16:03, his second half slightly faster than his first. Although nobody yet realized it, Anderson's upset victory would begin an era in which American men won 8 of 11 races. When the reporters left to file their stories, Anderson asked Jock Semple if he could use a phone in the press room to call his wife. Semple said yes.

Anderson picked up the phone to dial, then Semple caught his eye. "Jon," said the frugal Scotsman, "call collect!"

at Wesleyan University in Middletown, Connecticut.

In doing so, he moved within the aura of Amby Burfoot, two years ahead of him at that college. Burfoot would later go on to become executive editor of *Runner's World* magazine. Also attending Wesleyan at that time was Jeff Galloway, later a member of the 1972 Olympic team at 10,000 meters and after that a founder of a chain of running stores and coach of beginning marathoners.

Galloway was a senior when Burfoot was a junior and Rodgers a freshman. Years later, Squires wondered why Wesleyan cross-country teams never had greater success with three so accomplished runners on campus at the same time, but all three had individualistic personalities and seemed to march (or run) to the beat of different drummers.

Burfoot was the consummate road runner, and for him, winning the Boston Marathon was more of a goal than achieving success as a college athlete. He was one of the early pioneers of LSD (long slow distance) training. He ran twice daily, more than 100 miles a week, but eschewed most of the fast track training popular among runners of that era.

Rodgers previously had looked toward Abebe Bikila, winner of the Olympic Marathon in 1960 and 1964, as his role model. Now he began to think of Burfoot in that same light. "Amby Burfoot seemed to me almost a reincarnation of Bikila, a living, in-the-flesh person I could identify with. He inspired me," says Rodgers.

Burfoot would remember that Rodgers ran with consummate ease. "We ran together frequently, with Bill always a half-stride behind, eyes nearly closed, right arm flapping and light hair bouncing rhythmically to the cadence of the run. It was his relaxation that most amazed me. He seemed to be able to run with almost complete detachment from the mental and physical effort involved."

(continued on page 147)

ANALYZING BOSTON'S COURSE

While preparing athletes to excel in the Boston Marathon, coach Bill Squires minutely analyzed the course. "I probably spent more time looking at the route from Hopkinton than anyone," says the Greater Boston Track Club mentor. He even rolled golf balls along the road to identify its cant. Both for training and strategic purposes, Squires divides Boston into four midcourse segments, not counting the start and finish.

Prelude: Hopkinton to Natick (0–10 miles)

PROFILE: Elevation drops from 462 to 177 feet.

ANALYSIS: Squires sees this stretch as preparing to race. He advises not to run it too fast. "Nobody likes the first mile and a half because it drops so sharply," says Squires, "but after that you have nice, undulating terrain and good footing." ADVICE: Have fun. Take it easy.

1. Natick to Wellesley Square (10–13.1 miles)

PROFILE: Elevation drops from 177 to 137 feet.

ANALYSIS: This segment includes a few mild hills but nothing challenging. Runners need to watch the slant of the road to avoid running on an angle. "There's always two or three wild guys darting out front," he says. "Behind are overmatched runners trying to hang on. Between is the midpack rolling along in control—and that's where your winners come from." ADVICE: Stay alert. Hold position.

2. Wellesley Square to Lower Newton Falls (13.1–16 miles)

PROFILE: Elevation drops from 137 to 49 feet.

ANALYSIS: Other than the opening mile, the drop to Lower Newton Falls is the longest and steepest hill on the course. "The hill lasts three-quarters of a mile," he warns. "You can really destroy your legs if you overrun it trying to stay up." ADVICE: Yield ground cautiously.

3. Lower Newton Falls to Cleveland Circle (16–22 miles)

PROFILE: Elevation rises from 49 to 236 feet, then drops to 147 feet.

ANALYSIS: Squires calls this stretch the Killer Chain. Runners must negotiate a chain of stepped hills culminating with infamous Heartbreak. Then they encounter a sharp decline past Boston College. "Everyone overlooks the first hill before the Fire House," says Squires, "but it sets you up for the tough stuff later. Boston can be won or lost here." ADVICE: Relax on the ups; run the flats and downs hard.

4. Cleveland Circle to Kenmore Square (22–25 miles)

PROFILE: Elevation drops from 147 to 20 feet.

ANALYSIS: This last segment goes downhill, but gently down. "If you keep your concentration, you can run fast while still recovering," says Squires. Opponents who have been softened on the uphills can be dropped during this downhill segment. ADVICE: Keep your focus. Maintain your speed.

Coda: Kenmore Square to Finish (25–26.2 miles)

PROFILE: Flat with a slight incline on Hereford Street.

ANALYSIS: Very few marathons are won or lost in the last mile. Squires's athletes don't train on this part of the course. "There's too much traffic," he says. ADVICE: Concentrate on form. Smile breasting the tape.

Squires made his course analysis to aid runners capable of winning Boston, or placing in the top ten. But the same analysis works for midpack runners attempting to achieve personal bests. "Runners who start behind become frustrated in the first three miles down to Ashland because crowded conditions prevent them from running full speed," says Squires. "But when the course opens up, they have to remain in control, at least through Wellesley. If you can maintain your composure, you'll pass a lot of people in the last half of the race."

Squires adds: "Running the marathon is like a game of chess. Those who have the most pawns win at the end."

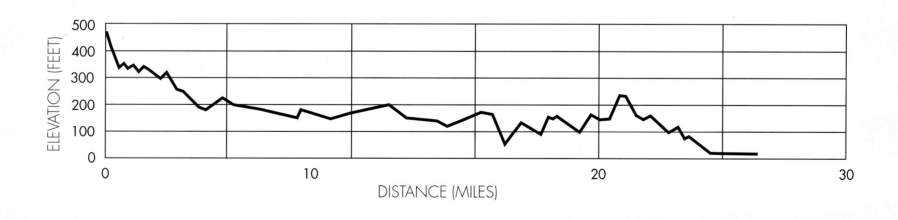

LEFT: Not many predicted Amby Burfoot's victory at Boston in 1968. Shortly after he crossed the finish, he and Jock Semple faced the press together. Burfoot was the first American to win the race since 1957, when Young John Kelley wore the laurels. RIGHT: Burfoot at Boston again in 1993, celebrating the 25th anniversary of his victory.

The pair trained together and eventually roomed together. Preparing for the 1968 Boston Marathon, Burfoot would go for 25-mile runs early on Sunday mornings, too early usually for Rodgers to get out of bed to accompany his roommate. More often, Rodgers joined Burfoot for the last 10-mile loop, providing both companionship and motivation. Burfoot, a senior, would push the pace harder "to keep the soph in his place."

Burfoot remembered one Sunday in the spring of 1968 when Rodgers rose earlier than usual to join him for the full distance. "That psyched me from the start," recalls Burfoot. He ran the first 15 miles harder than usual, but Rodgers still shadowed him. During the last 10 miles, which included a series of hills, Burfoot began to run faster than 6-minute miles. Rodgers didn't falter. Only by mounting an all-out attack over the last 2 miles was Burfoot able to move away from his roommate.

Burfoot finished the workout both exhausted and exhilarated. He stood beside the door to their dorm, soaked with sweat, still breathing heavily and waited two more minutes for Rodgers to complete the run. For Burfoot it was the last great test of his fitness. Within the month, he achieved his goal of winning the Boston Marathon. Later that year, he set a personal record of 2:14:28.8 at the Fukuoka Marathon in Japan, placing sixth. That time was only a second slower than the American record held by Buddy Edelen.

Yet, reflecting back on 1968, Burfoot would seem as amazed with the great potential of his roommate as with his own accomplishments. "Bill's run that morning was the first intimation of a prodigious marathoning talent," Burfoot would write.

Drifting Away

That potential would not reach early fulfillment. Burfoot's graduation left Rodgers temporarily minus a role and road model. "My training

fell off sharply," he recalls. With the Vietnam War, campus unrest had reached a peak. "Whether or not I was going to be running a 2-mile at a Wesleyan track meet was not what I was thinking about." Rodgers quit the track team. He began to smoke, half a pack of cigarettes a day. He hung out at bars, favoring beer or gin and tonic. Completing his new renegade image, he later bought a motorcycle.

The drift continued for Rodgers after graduation in 1970. He applied for status as a conscientious objector to avoid fighting a war he didn't support. To fulfill an obligation to provide alternative service, he moved to Boston and found a low-level job at Peter Bent Brigham Hospital that included wheeling dead bodies to the morgue.

Rodgers's self-esteem sagged. He eventually lost his job at the hospital because of his activist role in trying to organize a union for orderlies. When he returned to the hospital a week later, Rodgers was astounded to discover that handbills had been distributed warning that if he returned, he should be apprehended and the police called. The description offered of Rodgers was of a person dressed in ragged clothes with long hair and a ponytail.

Rodgers thought, "Is that how people see me?" He remembered what it had felt like to be a runner. Then, in 1972, he spent Patriots' Day weekend at Cape Cod. Returning to Boston, he decided to stop and watch the marathon near the finish line. Rodgers sat on the saddle of his motorcycle, a package of Winstons in the upper pocket of his jacket. He knew several of the front-runners and cheered them as they passed. He wondered what it would be like to be running with them.

Rodgers Joins the BAA

That summer, Bill Rodgers was stunned to see Frank Shorter win the Olympic Marathon in Munich. "Americans simply didn't win medals in

FAR LEFT: Frank Shorter (left) was a teammate of Bill Rodgers at the 1975 World Cross-Country Championships in Morocco. Here they run Boston in 1978. CENTER LEFT: Starting Heartbreak Hill at Boston in 1975, Boston Billy had such a commanding lead he could pause to tie a shoe and still stay ahead. CENTER RIGHT: Or walk through water stations to make sure he drank enough. FAR RIGHT: Rodgers won the victory laurels at Boston four times: 1975, 1978, 1979 and 1980. During that same period, he also won the New York City Marathon four times.

the marathon," Rodgers recalls. Shorter had been a student at Yale while Rodgers attended Wesleyan, but Bill couldn't remember racing against Frank.

Shorter's Olympic Marathon victory—the first by an American since John Hayes in 1908—inspired Rodgers to return to competition. He stopped smoking and started to train at the YMCA on Huntington Avenue near his home. Running on the YMCA's tight indoor track, he sometimes told people that he once had trained with a runner who won the Boston Marathon.

That Rodgers returned to form so quickly is a tribute to both his basic talent and his determination. By the end of the year, Rodgers had shifted his running outside and had upped his weekly mileage to 100 miles, most of it slower than 7 minutes per mile. Jock Semple encouraged him and Rodgers joined the BAA.

Rodgers frequented Semple's training room at Boston Garden. "Jock was great to me," he recalls. "There was a terrific excitement at Jock's place. He had photos on the wall of great runners: Johnny Kelley, Amby Burfoot, Finns, Greeks, Japanese and Koreans. Jock had a lifetime love of running. I became immersed in the culture. This was heavy-duty Marathon City. The atmosphere was staggering."

Returning to Racing

Rodgers entered the 1973 Boston Marathon but made the mistake of going too fast on a warm day. Troubled by a sidestitch, he stopped at 7 miles, reconsidered, jumped back into the race and went 21 miles stop-and-go before finally quitting near Boston College.

That year, Bill Squires accompanied his team from Boston State to the marathon. He saw Jon Anderson of the Oregon Track Club running with the lead group. Nobody had picked Anderson to place in the top

WHO IS THAT MASKED MAN?

In 1976, his final year at Georgetown University, Jack Fultz set as his goal qualifying for the U.S. Olympic Marathon Trials. His first Trials qualifying attempt was in North Carolina in January. Although he won the race, he failed to qualify. Heavy winds doomed a March attempt on Long Island, New York. "That's a classic attempt of how disaster creates new opportunity," says Fultz. "If I had qualified for the Trials, I never would have run Boston that year."

Fultz felt confident that Boston's fast field would pull him under his time goal. Starting conservatively, Fultz had no idea of his time or place for the first three miles into Ashland. Gradually through Framingham and Natick he began passing runners who had gone out too fast on a day when on-course temperatures soared into the 90s. In Wellesley a spectator shouted to Fultz: "You're in tenth place!"

Although Fultz doesn't recall accelerating, he continued to pass runners until the Newton hills, when he slid into second place. Fultz took the lead at 18 miles.

This posed a problem for those on the press bus. Because of the heat, spectators used hoses to spray the marathoners. Fultz had been running through showers of water, causing his paper number to become soaked and fall off. "Who are you?" reporters shouted.

Fultz smiled and wouldn't tell them. Noticing Georgetown on his shirt, they guessed he must be Justin Gubbins, Fultz's roommate who entered but failed to start. Fultz smiled again and shook his head no.

He was still smiling as he crossed the line first in 2:20:19, qualifying for the Olympic Trials. Fultz never did attain his ultimate goal of running in the Olympics, but he will remain among the list of Boston Marathon winners forever.

ten. His race number, 28, indicated his relatively low status. Squires recognized Anderson as having been a cross-country runner at Cornell University and a member of the 1972 Olympic team at 10,000 meters. "Anderson was easy to spot," recalls Squires. "He was taller than most of the runners. By Heartbreak, he had just begun to break away. I wondered if he could last to the finish." Paying more attention to his college runners than the leaders, Squires failed to get to the finish line in time to see Anderson win in 2:16:03. Nor did he spot a struggling Bill Rodgers.

Squires and Rodgers had not yet formed their alliance, but Rodgers began to focus his attention on the marathon distance. He won the Bay State Marathon in Framingham in October 1973 with a time of 2:28:12. He ran Boston again the next spring and was running 4th at 20 miles before fading to finish 14th in 2:19:34. He ran the New York City Marathon in September 1974 and led at one point but cramps from dehydration slowed him. He finished 5th in 2:35:59. He also won a marathon in Philadelphia in December in 2:21:57.

But Rodgers felt stuck on a plateau, well below the top runners. He could match stride with them during the early stages of marathons but often faded toward the end. He respected Jock Semple of the BAA, but Semple was better suited to being a trainer than a coach. Jock's work with the Bruins and Celtics along with his duties supervising Boston Marathon entries left him little time to coach individual runners.

That's when Rodgers decided to ask Bill Squires to coach him.

Training Formula for Boston

At first Squires was not eager to accept that role. Although most of his runners trained by running long distance and his college runners used the Boston Marathon as the focus of their senior years, Squires's Greater Boston Track Club was mainly track-oriented. Squires had re-gained his amateur status when the AAU relaxed its rules related to coaches in the mid-1960s and had run the Boston Marathon several times with his college runners (including 1971 when he ran 2:57:51), but he still thought of himself as a track coach.

More important, having competed for the BAA, Squires didn't want to steal one of Semple's most promising athletes. He agreed to allow Rodgers to train with his runners, though not as a member of the GBTC. Rodgers eventually told Semple he was shifting to Squires's club. Semple seemed to understand. He would continue to offer Rodgers rubdowns and support.

Squires changed Rodgers's approach to training. He offered a training menu that included long repeats on the track (half-miles to miles) and distance workouts over the hilly segment of the marathon course that ran through Newton, the same formula for success that had worked for him during his marathon in 1960 and the runners he had coached ever since.

"It was a radical shift from my previous training, which rarely included any speed work," says Rodgers. "One of the unique aspects of Bill Squires and his track program was that he gave his athletes moderate workouts with longer-than-average rest intervals between hard efforts. It had a significant influence on my running career." Another important factor was that with the GBTC, Rodgers could train with other runners of near equal ability for the first time since Burfoot's graduation in 1968.

A Runner Who Floated

To the other GBTC runners Rodgers stood out as unique. Todd Miller recalls Rodgers as "a bit of a flake," sometimes holding his arms out as he approached a turn and swooping around it like an airplane, making accompanying jet engine sounds. Still, his running ability was evident.

"He floated," recalls Jack McDonald. "We were a pounding bunch of half-milers, and it seemed like Bill was our guardian angel, hovering somewhere above the ground."

Pointing Rodgers toward the 1975 Boston Marathon, Squires established a set of interim goals. In training track runners Squires had encouraged them to run the roads; now, in training a road runner he pushed him toward the track. To tune Rodgers's speed, Squires set as one goal running faster than 9:00 for two miles indoors. Rodgers succeeded in doing that, running 8:53 in a special section at the Dartmouth Relays.

Another goal was to increase Rodgers's strength and confidence through a cross-country test. Squires sent several GBTC members, including Rodgers, to Gainesville, Florida, to run the U.S. team trials for the World Cross-Country Championships. Despite having just gotten over the flu, Rodgers qualified for the team by placing fourth, tied with Gary Tuttle. Frank Shorter won the race, but Rodgers found himself running easily beside the Olympic champion at one point in the race. He began to visualize the day when he would defeat Frank Shorter.

The world championships took place that February in Rabat, Morocco. On the day of the race, Squires called a friend at the *Boston Globe* to inquire about race results. The friend told Squires that Ian Stewart of England had won and some American had placed third.

"Who was the American?" asked Squires, expecting that the response would be Frank Shorter.

"Someone named William Rodgers."

Rodgers had run with the leaders, losing by only seven seconds in the final sprint. (Shorter had finished 20th.) The third place by Rodgers was the best finish by an American at the world cross-country meet, although the press paid little attention. Years later, Rodgers would rate his race at Rabat as one of the two best he ever ran. The one he rated best was coming in two months.

A Chance at Winning Boston

Rodgers returned from Morocco with dysentery, yet won the National AAU 30-K Championships in March in Albany, New York, with a record time over Barry Brown of New York and Tom Fleming of New Jersey. Squires believed that Rodgers had a chance at winning Boston.

The two of them discussed race strategy. Rodgers decided that a time of 2:16 or 2:15 might be possible. Squires thought Rodgers might run much faster. Rodgers's performance in Albany suggested a time below 2:14. Dare they think still faster? To think too fast tempted fate.

Several GBTC runners asked Squires what he thought Rodgers might run. Squires considered their question. Finally, he wrote his prediction on a piece of paper, folded it and stuck it behind the windshield visor in his car.

"When you come to practice Thursday," Squires told them, "you can pull the visor down and see how close I came." The number Squires wrote was 2:11.

What It Takes to Win

Was such a prediction realistic? In nearly eight decades at Boston only one runner had run faster: Ron Hill with his 2:10:30 course record in 1970, accomplished on a perfect day, cool with a tailwind. Shorter was the only American to have run that fast. He clocked a similar 2:10:30 while winning the flat Fukuoka Marathon in 1972. Many reporters, noting all the hills, believe the Boston course is difficult. Certainly, any race that is 26 miles is difficult, but under certain conditions Boston can be surprisingly fast. The year 1975 presented such conditions.

Reporting on Boston in *Runner's World*, Hugh Sweeney described the weather: "Temperature on marathon day was somewhere in the high 40s. The trailing westerly wind was strong. And when the wind shifted, as it

(continued on page 154)

Celebrate

LEFT: Joan Benoit Samuelson won the 1983 Boston Marathon in a world-best time of 2:22:43, beating all but 120 of the 5,415 men in the race. **RIGHT**:

She brought a funky nonchalance to her sport, but she also knew how to celebrate—on the victory stand in 1983, she smiled to an admiring crowd.

JOAN BENOIT SAMUELSON: "ALL A LARK FOR ME"

Joan Benoit Samuelson was a freshman at Bowdoin University in Brunswick, Maine, in 1976 when she first became aware of the Boston Marathon. "I read an article about it in the Bowdoin alumni magazine," she recalls. "It sounded like something that I might want to do some day."

Samuelson grew up in an athletic family, learning to ski at an early age. One winter she broke a leg. Afterward, she found herself no longer quite as willing to take the risks necessary for success in skiing. She focused her energy on field hockey and running. She increased the length of her training runs; she began competing in road races. In college she ran cross-country.

In January 1979, her senior year, she traveled to Bermuda to run a 10-K, part of a weekend of racing that also included a marathon. Samuelson won the 10-K on Saturday, then decided to run part of Sunday's marathon as a training run. Feeling good, she kept going and placed second in 2:50:54. "The race seemed easy," recalls Samuelson. "After I returned home, I decided to aim for the Boston Marathon."

In her autobiography, *Running Tide*, written along with Sally Baker, Samuelson writes about the 1979 Boston Marathon: "The runners gathered in Hopkinton, west of Boston, and went through their pre-race routines in the rain—I watched the top runners bounce and shiver with nerves. But it was all a lark for me."

Wearing a turtleneck shirt covering a black singlet with "Bowdoin" on the front, Samuelson had no dreams of glory. "I wasn't there to win. I was there only to run." The favorite on that cold, drizzly day was American Patti Lyons, who had a best of 2:41:31. Lyons trained by running 100 to 140 miles a week. At that point in her career,

Samuelson probably was running only half that amount.

George Hirsch, then the publisher of *The Runner* magazine, had agreed to run with Sue Krenn of San Diego, whose goal in her first Boston was only to run 2:44. After the first downhill mile, Samuelson joined them. Hirsch recalls spectators beside the road telling Krenn and Samuelson that they were leading the women's race.

Hirsch described the action in his magazine: "Soon Patti Lyons passed us, and we lost sight of her. At about ten miles Joan took off her T-shirt, and her pace quickened noticeably; she meant business. She was running easily as we came into Wellesley. Then we heard that Patti was now some 200 yards in front of us—still out of sight."

But Lyons had begun to struggle. Samuelson caught her after 16 miles. "Patti was suddenly just there on the hills," says Samuelson. "She tried to stay with me for a little bit, but it seemed obvious that she had had it. I ran off and left her." Spectators shouted to Samuelson that she was running in first place, although that fact didn't seem to sink in. She ran in a daze: "At that point I was on a mission."

Not knowing the course, Samuelson only had a vague idea of how many miles remained to the finish. Near 23 miles, a spectator ran out of the crowd and offered her a Boston Red Sox cap, which she plopped on her head. With the cap's bill facing backward, giving her a look of funky nonchalance, a grinning Samuelson strode across the line in 2:35:15, a course and American record.

Samuelson returned to Boston in 1981, placing third behind New Zealand's Allison Roe, who set a course record of 2:26:46, and Patti Lyons Catalano, who set an American record of 2:27:51. Samuelson bettered both records with her 2:22:43 two years later.

did on occasion to come from the front or left side of the runners, it served only to cool them. Within a minute or so, it was again blowing from the rear. The skies were occasionally sunny but were usually overcast. The air was dry and crisp. Seldom has there been better weather in which to run a marathon."

The red and white racing singlets normally worn by GBTC members were made of stiff, heavy polyester that clung to the body when wet—okay for half-mile relay legs in the Boston Garden but not what you want hanging on your shoulders for over 26 miles. "Our shirts were made to last forever," admits Squires. "They were not what you would call biodegradable."

Abandoning the team singlet, Rodgers selected a lilac-colored, cotton mesh T-shirt, then used a marker to write on the front BOSTON and GBTC. He wore navy blue nylon shorts. In that age of running innocence, he sported a headband promoting New Balance shoes, despite running in Nike shoes, which had been sent to him by the Oregon Olympian Steve Prefontaine. Neither company paid him for this exposure.

On that cool day, Rodgers also wore what later would become his trademark, a pair of white painter's gloves. His number 14, attached at a crooked angle to the front of his shirt just beneath GBTC, designated his placing from the previous year and guaranteed him a position in the front row. The marathon, despite 2,340 starters that year, still began on Hayden Rowe, a narrow street with a sharp right turn onto Main Street after the first 200 yards that forced runners to sprint for position.

Dueling in a Race

Among the favorites was Tom Fleming of Bloomfield, New Jersey. He had placed second to Anderson in 1973 and second to Ireland's Neil Cusack in 1974. "The one certain thing about Boston," Fleming had said before the race, "is that Bernie Allen will be leading at the 2-mile point." Allen was an English runner who had led during the early miles in 1974 before fading to ninth. Fleming proved correct. Allen surged and opened a 60-yard gap. "I thought I'd have a go at it," Allen said later. He remained in front as the runners passed the 6.7-mile checkpoint in Framingham, even though they were a half-minute behind Ron Hill's record pace from five years earlier.

Rodgers started more conservatively but caught the lead pack after a mile and a half. Hill was in the middle of this pack, his first time back to Boston since his 1970 victory. In addition to his Boston Marathon win, Hill also had won marathons at the Commonwealth Games and European Championships. To psych himself up, Rodgers thought of Hill, who was then 36, as being "over-the-hill." Canadian Jerome Drayton, the 1969 Fukuoka Marathon winner, also ran in the front pack along with Tom Fleming, Steve Hoag of Minnesota, Peter Fredriksson of Sweden, Mario Cuevas of Mexico and Richard Mabuza of Swaziland, whom the *Boston Globe* had picked to win. (Mabuza would finish 38th.)

After Framingham Drayton and Cuevas passed Allen and gained 20 yards on the lead pack. At first Rodgers let them go then, after a mile, decided that the serious racing had begun.

"I love marathoning when this happens," Rodgers would say when describing this moment in his autobiography. "The pace is slow enough for considerable jockeying and rejockeying for position, and there's nothing I love more than to duel in a race. I moved up and joined them."

At nine miles Cuevas began to fade. Rodgers and Drayton stayed shoulder to shoulder. Drayton wore sunglasses, so Rodgers could not gauge his opponent's fatigue level by looking at his eyes. At the 10.4-mile checkpoint in Natick the pair's faster pace had moved them to within two seconds of Hill's record pace.

TRUE 1980 WINNER: GAREAU, NOT RUIZ

Having run a personal record 2:24:45 at the Mardi Gras Marathon in New Orleans in February 1980, Craig Donath of Lombard, Illinois, came to Boston two months later planning to cruise at a slower pace and enjoy the experience. "You see things you don't see otherwise," he says.

Donath, tall with blond hair, started conservatively. Several miles into the race, he found himself running near several of the faster women. One was short with dark hair. She came from Quebec. Her name was Jacqueline Gareau.

"She was petite," Donath recalls. "There was a rush of people at the water stops. Twice, I watched her reach for water and come up empty, brushed aside by bigger guys."

At the next water stop, Donath grabbed two cups and handed one to Gareau. "Merci," said Gareau, who then spoke little English.

Donath had not planned to pace Gareau, but they found themselves running together. He noticed that they passed several other women, but did not know her place until near the Newton hills. Kathrine Switzer, covering the women's race for TV, appeared riding on a camera cart. Donath asked, "What place is she in?"

"She's running first," Switzer replied.

That became certain after they crested Heartbreak Hill and began the long stretch along Beacon Street. "It was pandemonium," says Donath. "She was obviously the leader because of the way people reacted." Checking his watch, Donath realized they were running faster than Joan Samuelson's record pace from the year before. "I pointed to my watch and offered a thumbs-up sign. She smiled."

But as they passed through Kenmore Square with only a mile to go, Donath sensed a change in volume. "The crowd was cheering, but no longer screaming. Suddenly, they had become more polite. I started acting like a cheerleader, waving my hands over my head, 'Why aren't you people going crazy? This woman is winning!' "

Making the final turn toward the finish line, he heard the public address system: " . . . And here comes Jacqueline Gareau of Canada—the second woman."

Donath thought to himself, "Oh no!"

Gareau finished in 2:34:28. She and Donath hugged briefly in the finish chute, then separated. He looked toward the awards platform and saw another woman with a laurel wreath on her head waving to the crowd. Donath couldn't recall that woman passing them. He later saw Gareau standing to one side, arms folded, a look on her face more puzzled than hurt.

The woman accepting the cheers was Rosie Ruiz. She had jumped into the race with one mile to go. Several officials suspected the ruse, but none had the courage to halt the awards ceremony. A week later the Boston Athletic Association (BAA) announced what everybody by then knew: Rosie Ruiz was a fraud. Will Cloney, the race director, asked Ruiz to return her medal. She refused and passed into oblivion.

The BAA invited Gareau back to Boston for a proper awards ceremony, but it seemed a hollow victory. Over the years, Donath and Gareau sometimes would encounter each other at the starting lines of other races. "She'd always give me a hug," says Donath. "We never ran together again. She was getting faster, and I was getting slower."

Gareau says of Donath: "I'll always remember him, this tall, blond guy. We were running the same pace, and he was nice. With all the controversy, he was one of that day's bright spots."

Coaching

LEFT: Bill Rodgers ran the 1975 race in a hand-lettered T-shirt. As Rodgers ran the final miles, Jock Semple gave the word to Rodgers, "Git goin',

lad! Yee'v got a chance for the rrrrecord!" **RIGHT**: After Bill Rodgers joined the Greater Boston Track Club, Bill Squires supervised his training.

Unknown in His Own Town

Rodgers soon heard a woman cheering from the sidelines, "Go Jerome! Go Canada!" The woman may have been Canadian, but it irritated Rodgers to hear a spectator at the Boston Marathon rooting for his rival, a foreigner. "I was an unknown in my own town," Rodgers decided. "Nobody knew me." He would accept the woman's support of his rival as a challenge. He picked up the pace. Drayton fell back.

The press bus hovered nearby. Had the moment of truth arrived? Reporters watched closely, wondering whether this local kid, whom they had ignored in their predictions, could maintain his lead—or was he another Bernie Allen, merely having a go at it? Many a runner had grabbed the lead at Boston, often late in the race, only to lose it.

Jock Semple had faith. He leaned out of the press bus and asked Bill if he wanted to remove his gloves.

"I'm okay, Jock," said Rodgers. He flashed him a smile that bespoke confidence. Rodgers usually trained with the gloves, continuously taking them on and off as his hands grew cold or warm. He kept reminding himself, "This is like a training run. Relax. Relax. Run fast but comfortable."

Watching the race at Wellesley was a young runner who also trained with the GBTC and was coached by Bill Squires, despite being only a junior in high school. Alberto Salazar lived in Wayland, only three miles from the course, but this was his first Boston Marathon to watch. Since several of his training partners from GBTC were running, he wanted to cheer them.

Salazar recalls: "I looked at the runners coming toward me and realized Bill Rodgers was in the lead. I thought, 'I know that guy! I train with him!' It got me all excited. I shouted, 'Come on, Bill!'" Salazar then decided that some day he, too, would run the Boston Marathon.

Downhill Racer

Rodgers would later write: "It had turned into the kind of classic situation that I always thrive on. I like to get in duels with other runners, and if I feel fairly decent, it's turned out that I've won most of them. That's when I run my best. If I get into a duel with someone in the middle of the race, I'm usually able to get away from him and hang on until the end."

But by halfway through the race, Rodgers's dueling partner had vanished. Rodgers glanced around from time to time but could no longer see Drayton. He was running against himself—and the course—and the sometimes deadly impulse of even the best marathoners to self-destruct. "I don't know what made me go to the front," he wrote later. "Sometimes I think I have a suicidal instinct. But once I was there, I figured I'd better go hard to build a lead, so I pushed it down the hills out of Wellesley."

Rodgers excels as a downhill runner. One of his greatest skills is to accelerate on downhill stretches where other runners fear the pounding to their muscles. Light-footed with a capability to seemingly float above the ground, Rodgers simply gathers speed and goes. The first two-thirds of the Boston Marathon course, though rolling, drops from a high point of 462 feet above sea level to a low point of 49 feet at Newton Lower Falls. Rodgers had used this drop to great advantage. At the 17.6-mile checkpoint in Auburndale he now was 38 seconds ahead of Hill's record pace.

At that point, the course takes a sharp right past a fire station and goes onto Commonwealth Avenue and its series of three hills over four miles that culminates with the infamous Heartbreak Hill. Rodgers did not consider himself a good uphill runner. In fact, he preferred to cut speed on the ups to save himself for the downs. There was the danger

"I will never forget rounding the corner and turning onto Boylston Street for the final yards of the race. It's a striking sight."—Bill Rodgers

that if some runner behind was willing to attack the Newton hills, his lead quickly could evaporate. In his first try at Boston he had dropped out after the hills. In his second try he had lost nearly ten places during this stretch.

But during the previous six months under Squires's supervision, Rodgers had trained frequently on these same hills. As he turned the corner onto Commonwealth Avenue, everything looked familiar. The stately homes beside the boulevard. Its grass median strip with the dirt path marking where Squires's runners trained. This was his home course. Rodgers told himself to maintain a steady pace upward, floating off the tops and into the valleys between hills to regain strength for the next uphill push. He turned again to look behind. There was no sign of Drayton or any other runner.

Nevertheless, he ran within himself. He need not panic. Coming to a water station, he stopped to assure himself sufficient liquid then resumed running at his same fast pace. "If I don't stop, I can't drink," explained Rodgers later. "The water just splashes all over me." His shoelace came untied at the foot of Heartbreak Hill. He calmly bent to tie it. "What better place to tie it?" said Rodgers. "It gave me a mental break from the pace, and I only lost 15 to 20 seconds."

Running in the closing miles, he spotted Jason Kehoe, a friend who used to cruise with him during his motorcycle days. "How you doing, Jason?" Rodgers called out. It was an act of controlled bravura.

The Fastest American

Rodgers still kept looking over his shoulder, wondering if someone back there, Drayton maybe, might still challenge him. Somehow that did not worry him. It would only mean that he would have to run harder over the closing miles. He failed to spot Drayton, but it would be easy

WHERE THE MONEY WASN'T

Some of the world's greatest marathoners failed to win Boston— or even run Boston. In the early decades Boston had not yet established itself as a premier event. Then, through the 1920s and 1930s, travel time discouraged most foreign runners.

Air travel solved that problem. In the 1940s a Finnish-American club began bringing two Finns to Boston each year. The Japanese and South Korean governments financed their best runners. But the cash-poor Boston Athletic Association (BAA) offered no help. Not even for American Buddy Edelen, who set a world marathon record of 2:14:28 while living in England during the 1960s. Edelen wanted to run Boston, but had little money. Though Edelen and Jock Semple, the BAA trainer, exchanged letters about his running, he received no help at a time when European race promoters happily paid his expenses. As a result, Edelen never ran Boston at a time when he might have won it several times.

The same can be said about another American great, Frank Shorter. Despite his prominence in the early 1970s, winning the prestigious Fukuoka Marathon in Japan four times and winning Olympic gold and silver medals, Shorter is barely a footnote at Boston. He ran there only in 1978 and 1979 when he was past his prime as a marathoner.

Like Edelen, Shorter ran where the money was—and there was precious little money at Boston through the 1970s. Only in the 1980s would competition from other cash-rich marathons inevitably force the BAA to reconsider its position as an amateur event.

But in the meantime, the names of Buddy Edelen and Frank Shorter remain missing from the list of Boston Marathon champions.

It was the high-water mark of American marathoning.—Greg Meyer

LEFT: An unexpected victory by Oregon runner Jon Anderson in 1973 signaled a new era. Over 11 years American men would win Boston eight

times. RIGHT: The crest of that wave came in 1983 when Greg Meyer became the last American man to win Boston.

160

to miss the other runner because the crowds were pressed so tightly on the street.

Drayton continued in second but stopped running with only two miles to go. Ron Hill, who finished fifth, spotted the Canadian sitting slumped on the curb. "Get going!" shouted Hill. "Get up and walk if you have to, but finish." Other closing runners told Drayton the same, but he would fail to cross the finish line.

Bill Rodgers, meanwhile, reached the pinnacle of success. His winning time of 2:09:55 not only broke Hill's course record but also was the fastest marathon time run by an American.

"I will never forget rounding the corner and turning onto Boylston Street for the final yards of the race," wrote Rodgers. "It's a striking sight. There are thousands of people there, spilling over onto the streets and sidewalks and up on the plaza near the finish line at the Prudential Center. It's all downhill, funneling toward the finish. It still ranks as one of the most thrilling moments of my life.

"On that day, I acquired a sense of what it was like to win the marathon. It was a deeper experience for me than for any other win."

Rodgers would have the wreath placed over his head at the Boston Marathon on three more occasions. After skipping the race in 1976 and losing to Drayton in 1977, he won three more times in 1978, 1979 and 1980. Between 1976 and 1979 he also won the New York City Marathon four times. Bill Rodgers would achieve a career-best time of 2:09:27 winning Boston in 1979, but the first win four years earlier was the one he would remember most. As for the coach who led him to that first victory, Rodgers would not be the only marathoner guided by Bill Squires to mount the victory stand at Boston.

HIGH-WATER MARK

A miler and steeplechaser from the University of Michigan, Greg Meyer moved to Boston in 1978 to train with Bill Rodgers.

Under the direction of Coach Bill Squires, Meyer began doing long runs on the Boston course. He would run 20 miles, beginning with 2 miles at race pace on the Wellesley High School cinder track. Then he would trace the course to Cleveland Circle, circle the nearby reservoir and return to Wellesley for a final mile on the track. "Those hills are not fun running backward," Meyer insists.

Nevertheless, they played an important part of the strategy Squires developed for Boston in 1983. Meyer would not run the uphills nor the downhills hard, but stay in control and accelerate on the flats between, where his track speed could best be used.

Meyer recalls the weather that year as being perfect for fast times: "overcast, cool, a touch of rain, a quartering tailwind." In Wellesley when Benji Durden opened a lead on a downhill stretch, Meyer ignored the move. "It was a gamble," says Meyer, "but we were running fast enough as it was. It's a racing sense: knowing how far you can let a guy go and still reel him in."

Meyer caught Durden at the base of Heartbreak Hill and continued to a 2:09:00 victory. "It was the high-water mark of American marathoning," says Meyer. "I just happened to catch the crest of the wave that day, but after that the tide went out."

Meyer's 1983 victory ended the Decade of the Americans, a period of 11 years beginning with Jon Anderson's 1973 Boston win when American men won 8 of 11 races. Ironically, Anderson also ran Boston again in 1983, his time (2:16:19) only 16 seconds slower than his earlier winning mark. It earned him 34th place!

The Duel

Chapter Nine

9

I had as many doubts as anyone else. Standing on the starting

line, we're all cowards.—*Alberto Salazar*

O N THE THURSDAY BEFORE THE 1982 BOSTON MARATHON, Dick Beardsley watched the evening news on television

at the Sheraton Boston. It showed Alberto Salazar, the race favorite, arriving in town. Reporters swarmed around Salazar

at the airport, thrusting their microphones at him and asking about his chances of victory. Salazar seemed edgy after a long,

cross-country plane ride but displayed a subdued confidence about his ability to win—as well he might.

A National Collegiate Athletic Association (NCAA) cross-country champion from the University of Oregon, the

American-record holder at both 5000 and 10,000 meters and a member of the 1980 U.S. Olympic team, Salazar also was the

world's best marathon runner. He had appeared at the 1980 New York City Marathon for his first race at that distance and con-

fidently—almost cockily—predicted a time of 2:10.

Many close to the sport considered such behavior outrageous, but Salazar was simply being honest. He and his coach, Bill

Dellinger, knew from his training that he was capable of that fast a time and, at age 22, Salazar had no hesitation at stating

that fact. Reporters might have considered Salazar arrogant but he fulfilled his promise. He won the New York City Marathon

in 2:09:41, the fastest debut marathon on record.

❦

PAGE 162: At Coolidge Corner Dick Beardsley attempted to break Alberto Salazar, who had been stalking him through much of the race. LEFT: Salazar finished on fumes and afterward, Beardsley stared in amazement as police helped his rival to the medical tent.

Salazar returned to New York City for his second marathon the following year, again predicting victory, again delivering. He ran 2:08:13, breaking by 21 seconds Australian Derek Clayton's 12-year-old world record. At Boston in 1982 Salazar seemed ready to produce another major marathon victory—perhaps another world record.

Bushwacked by Reporters

Reporters interviewing Salazar at the airport attempted to extract quotes to use in their marathon coverage. Salazar told them that he had first watched the Boston Marathon in high school. He had grown up in Wayland, a suburb north of Wellesley, only three miles from the marathon course. "I resolved to run Boston some day," he said. Yes, he expected to win. Yes, he was aware of the other runners in the field, but he still was confident of victory. No, he didn't want to predict another world record, but he conceded one was possible.

Watching Salazar's TV performance, Beardsley focused on the other runner's statements, looking for motivation. Was Salazar overconfident? Was he too cocky, too arrogant? Did he underestimate his competition, namely Dick Beardsley? Beardsley decided the answer was yes. He respected Salazar for his achievements, but he no longer remained in awe of the world record holder. He believed he could beat him and win the Boston Marathon. Still, he could not overlook Salazar's calm and confident approach to the race.

Had Beardsley been able to peer into the automobile carrying Salazar home, he might have gotten another impression of his opponent. Despite his cool demeanor Salazar usually became very nervous before races. And to make things worse, a knot in one hamstring muscle had surfaced during a hard workout the day before.

Besides, he liked to cultivate an aura of invincibility. He purposely avoided mentioning Beardsley by name during the airport interview. "I thought right from the start that Beardsley would be toughest. I didn't say anything to the press about him because it would have just pumped him up."

Coach to the Front-Runners

Because defending champion Toshihiko Seko of Japan chose not to run in 1982, the number 1 for Boston went to four-time champion Bill Rodgers. Salazar would wear number 2 and Beardsley number 3, based on their fastest marathon times.

But Rodgers, Salazar and Beardsley shared more than fast marathon times. All had been coached at one point in their careers by Bill Squires. As coach for the Greater Boston Track Club Squires had guided Rodgers before his first Boston victory in 1975. Salazar had trained under Squires's supervision while in high school. Now a consultant for New Balance, Squires worked with several of its top runners, including Dick Beardsley.

That his former coach was now guiding his top rival didn't bother Salazar. "Bill Squires had done a lot for me and had gotten very little," says Salazar. "He received no payment, just headaches for working with a high school runner. He deserved all the respect I could give him."

Beardsley Gets Serious

Beardsley had come a long way before meeting up with Squires. Although he played basketball and hockey in high school, he found greater success as a runner. "I enjoyed running," he recalls, "but I didn't expect to make a career out of it." He ran in college but dropped out to manage a dairy farm to earn enough money to get married.

After leaving school, Beardsley did no running for three months, but an article in *Runner's World* about what it took to qualify for the 1980

Olympic Trials in the marathon caught his eye. The qualifying time was nearly ten minutes faster than his college best, but Beardsley accepted that as a challenge. "I quit my job at the dairy farm, moved to the Twin Cities, got work at a Foot Locker store and started cranking out 120 miles a week to get ready for the Olympic Trials." At the Manitoba Marathon the next June he ran 2:21:54, qualifying for the Trials by two seconds.

At the 1980 Trials he ran 2:16:01, running his second half faster than the first. Beardsley already had planned to rent a farm after the Trials, but, crossing the finish line in 16th place, he told himself, "I can't quit now." He decided to run four more years and train for the 1984 Olympics.

After Beardsley's successful run at the Trials the New Balance shoe company invited him to visit its factory in Boston and also run the Falmouth Road Race on Cape Cod, expenses paid. Squires escorted Beardsley during his visit. Beardsley placed well behind the leaders but that didn't seem to discourage New Balance or Squires.

Road running was on the verge of becoming a professional sport. More and more races had begun to offer appearance fees and prize money. Shoe companies, profits soaring during the running boom, had begun to aggressively recruit the fastest runners. At one point Nike had nearly 1,200 runners under contract. Most received only shoes and clothing; a few earned six-figure incomes. Adidas, Brooks, Puma and Tiger (Asics) were among the shoe companies trying to identify and recruit the next Bill Rodgers.

After Falmouth New Balance offered Beardsley a monthly stipend of $500. That was a fraction of what Nike paid Alberto Salazar to run for its exclusive Athletics West team, but Beardsley had won no NCAA titles. He was ecstatic. Even more exciting was the fact that Squires offered to help with his training. "I was stunned that a world famous coach actually wanted to work with me," recalls Beardsley. "He sent me workouts on backs of napkins and torn pieces of paper, and I'd have to call him on the phone to decipher what he meant. It was like Morse code, but he took me to the next level."

At the 1980 New York City Marathon Rodgers placed fifth and Beardsley placed ninth in 2:13:55, another personal record.

During a period of ten months, Beardsley would run seven marathons, including a tie for first in the London Marathon and first at Grandma's Marathon in Duluth, Minnesota, where he ran 2:09:37. These performances put him among the top American marathoners with Salazar and Rodgers. New Balance increased his monthly stipend to $1,000.

A Positive Influence

At the beginning of 1982 Beardsley shifted his training base to Atlanta. "I went there so I could get out of Minnesota's harsh winter, but I also wanted to train on hills to get ready for Boston."

Squires arranged for Beardsley to train with Dean Matthews, who had won the 1979 Honolulu Marathon. Matthews and Beardsley would go for 23-mile training runs. They ran up and down hills, practicing mid-run surges, which were sudden increases in pace that they would use to defeat their opponents.

In March 1982 Beardsley beat Matthews and Benji Durden in a 10-K race, running 29:12. That was nearly two minutes slower than Salazar's best for the same distance, but the time improved Beardsley's confidence because it was achieved on a hilly course. Hills would play an important part of his strategy to defeat Salazar in Boston.

An Uphill Course

Two weeks before the marathon, Beardsley flew to Boston to stay with Squires and complete his final race preparations. They drove to

At Boston in 1982 Salazar seemed ready to produce another
major marathon victory—perhaps another world record.

Talent

LEFT: As a Minnesota high schooler, Dick Beardsley didn't run well enough to attract many scholarship offers—but he soon would improve. RIGHT:
Alberto Salazar, a Massachusetts state champion, was recruited by the University of Oregon. While there, he won an NCAA championship.

Hopkinton so Beardsley could run the first 15 miles of the marathon course. Squires told his runner to hold back, but when the coach looked at his watch, he realized Beardsley was running a seemingly frantic 5:20 pace. "Dickie," shouted Squires, "just relax!" "I am, coach," Beardsley responded. "I feel like I can fly!"

Two days later Beardsley was scheduled to run seven repeats up and down Heartbreak Hill, except a freak April storm covered Boston with a foot of snow. Squires looked out the window and suggested they postpone the workout, but Beardsley insisted he wanted to run. Road conditions were so bad Squires had difficulty driving to the area, so Beardsley jumped out of the car and promised to meet him later at Boston College.

Beardsley remembers the workout: "It was sleeting and snowing and blowing and miserable and cold. I couldn't run the main course on Heartbreak Hill because of the snow, so I ran on the parallel frontage road. I couldn't go very fast. I had to run with my head down, but I ran that workout saying, 'There is nobody out running today! There is nobody who could do this workout! There is nobody alive this tough!' The confidence I got from that one workout is one of the reasons I was able to stick with Alberto at that point in the marathon race."

Because of the snow, Squires sent Beardsley back to Atlanta. Salazar, meanwhile, was completing his preparations in Eugene, Oregon. To test his ability to double at 10,000 meters and the marathon at the 1984 Olympics, Salazar organized a 10,000-meter race featuring himself and world record holder Henry Rono on the University of Oregon track the weekend before the marathon. The race was run in atrocious weather. Rono narrowly beat Salazar. "It was 48 degrees and raining," says Salazar. "We were so cold that neither Henry nor I could mount much of a kick at the end. We ran 27:30. I felt certain I could have run even faster, maybe challenged the world record, under better conditions."

By the Saturday before the Boston Marathon, Salazar felt confident that his tight hamstring would not prevent him from running Boston. He continued to stay with his parents, avoiding the bustle of the race headquarters hotel.

Beardsley, on the other hand, remained in the hotel. His wife, Mary, answered the phone, telling well-wishers that Dick was resting. "I sank into a shell. I didn't want to talk to anybody. I didn't want to see anybody. I wanted to be with myself."

Race Day Dawns

Monday morning he awoke at 7:15. The previous several days had been cool and cloudy with a favorable wind, giving runners hope for fast times. Beardsley opened the curtains and saw a day that was clear and sunny. He moved to the TV and turned on *Today* to check the temperature. Weatherman Willard Scott announced that it would be a "great day for the Boston Marathon, sunny with temperatures in the 70s."

Great day for the spectators, thought Beardsley. He called room service and ordered a hot chocolate and two pieces of toast. Thinking how warm weather might affect his race strategy, he began to drink, both water and Gatorade. At 9:00 a driver from New Balance arrived in a station wagon. Beardsley climbed into the wagon's backward-facing seat. He was crunched among the bags of other runners, but at least he could be alone with his thoughts. "I put on my game face," recalls Beardsley.

An hour later the wagon arrived in Hopkinton. The shoe company had arranged to borrow a house for the convenience of its runners. Beardsley was led to a room in which he could lie down. There was a stereo and a separate toilet.

Alberto Salazar had breakfast at Mel's Restaurant in Wayland. He had worked there in high school as a busboy and dishwasher. Everybody knew him. All the waitresses wanted to talk to Alberto, but the normally shy Salazar didn't mind. He ordered pancakes. Mel told him the meal was on the house. "Leroy the cook came out and wished me good luck," recalls Salazar. "I'm always nervous before races but seeing my old friends made me feel comfortable."

After breakfast he returned home and rested until it was time to be driven to the start by Norm Potochney, his next-door neighbor. The Salazar family planned to watch the race from the finish line. Potochney drove him to the First Congregational Church in Hopkinton, used as a gathering area for the elite runners.

Toeing the Line

About ten minutes before the start, Salazar donned his racing shoes and jogged to the starting line a short distance away. Beardsley also headed for the line but found that the house in which he was staying was farther away than he thought. Boston had a near record 6,689 starters. It seemed as though every one of them was standing in Beardsley's way as he made his way toward the front row. He was living the runner's nightmare where the race was about to begin and he could not reach the starting line. Finally, he took his place beside the other seeded runners. He removed the New Balance T-shirt and warm-up pants he had worn to the line and threw them toward the spectators on the curb.

Salazar stood nearby on the front line, but neither runner remembered doing much to acknowledge each other's presence. It was not from any sense of personal antagonism; each was locked in his own personal battle with his own doubts. Months of training lay behind; 26 miles lay ahead. Salazar's face was impassive but inwardly his stomach was churning; his legs felt so weak he wondered if they would respond once the gun sounded.

Salazar did not fear Beardsley this moment; he disliked focusing on individuals. "The chances that in a race it will come down to you and any one other individual are very slight," he says. "It might be someone entirely different. Anyone can have a good day, or you or the individual you focused on beating can have a bad day. In my experience you're better off worrying about yourself rather than others."

Getting Off the Line

More to fear was the crowded start. Having grown up in the area, Salazar knew the marathon course. Still, he was surprised at how narrow the road appeared with so many runners crowded on it. He reminded himself to hold his elbows out to fend off runners from each side and to take quick and choppy strides at first to lessen the chance of getting clipped from behind.

Starter Tom Brown stood on a platform above the runners' heads. The loudspeaker announced two minutes to go. Salazar began a silent prayer.

Dick Beardsley felt a tap on his shoulder. He turned around and saw Barney Klecker, a friend from the Twin Cities, standing behind him. Klecker was the American-record holder for 50 miles and he also had a 2:15:18 marathon best. "Dick," said Klecker, "good luck. Did you double-knot your shoes?"

Beardsley was puzzled. "What?"

"Your shoes. It's important."

Beardsley didn't like having his concentration broken right before the start. He thanked Klecker but returned his attention to the road before him, now emptying of people and vehicles.

Klecker persisted. "Dick, it's important to double-knot your shoes."

"Barney, leave me alone!"

But within seconds Beardsley regretted being so abrupt with his friend. He turned to apologize but failed to spot Klecker. He looked down at his feet. Klecker was kneeling there, double-knotting Beardsley's shoes!

Shot Out of a Cannon

As Tom Brown fired the starting pistol, it caught Beardsley by surprise. Salazar reacted more quickly. "It was like he was shot out of a cannon," recalls Beardsley, who, nevertheless, quickly recovered. Soon, he was right behind Salazar, five yards back, the two of them already opening a gap on the other runners. "It was like a flock of geese with Al and me at the point of the V," recalls Beardsley.

"I got out a bit too fast, but I was still worried about getting tripped," remembers Salazar. "After we had gone a certain distance, I slowed down and let the others catch up."

The time for the first mile was 4:38—fast but not ridiculously so considering that the course drops sharply in its first mile. "Dick, you're fine," Beardsley told himself. "You knew that the start would be fast."

Worried about the warm weather, Beardsley had been drinking fluids all morning before the race. Once the race began, he continued to drink as much as possible. Beardsley had gone barely a half-mile when he spotted a boy standing beside the road offering runners water. He grabbed a cup from the boy's hand. "As soon as I saw anyone with water," says Beardsley, "I'd grab it and take at least one good swallow and dump the rest on my head."

Salazar, meanwhile, was monitoring his body signals. He made a great effort to reduce the tension he felt but somehow relaxation eluded him. "The only thing I can remember thinking during the first few miles," he told *Runner's World*, "was something Rodgers had said. I always claim that the marathon is just another race to me—and it is, but

Billy insists that some day the marathon can humble you. I thought about that in the first 4 miles. 'Could this be the race that gets me?' I could feel the knot in my hamstring, and I started to think, 'Gee, this must be what Rodgers is talking about.' Here my leg was hurting, and I still had 22 miles to go."

A Stalking Game

The two runners let others move to the front, no one controlling the pace, but all of them moving in a phalanx. Bill Rodgers was among those in the lead pack along with Ron Tabb, Ed Mendoza, Doug Kurtis and Dean Matthews, Beardsley's training partner from Atlanta.

Salazar knew that these early miles were part of a stalking game, the faster runners trying to conserve energy as much as possible, watching those around them, looking for weaknesses that they might later exploit. Lesser runners pushed to stay with the lead pack, hoping the early pace would be slow enough so that they could remain in contention. It was a hot day. Anything could happen. Eventually, inevitably, they would peel off the back of the pack and would be lucky to finish or would finish in times much slower than their personal bests—but, in the meantime, they were leading the Boston Marathon.

Salazar watched some of these runners almost with contempt. He thought they were foolish to dart around ahead of the pack and somewhat resented them for making him work harder. At one point, Tabb and Matthews surged to a brief lead. Matthews was waving to the crowd. "What are those stupid asses doing?" Salazar said to nobody in particular.

The First Ten Miles

Beardsley had been told by Squires to not—repeat, not—take the lead in the first ten miles. Beardsley had no desire to do so. "For the first

Pride

LEFT AND CENTER: Mile after mile, Dick Beardsley hammered Alberto Salazar, trying to break him. Salazar would not break, but neither could he take the lead. Beardsley refused to let him. "It was frustrating to be behind him," Salazar would admit. "It was a matter of pride that I didn't want anybody close to me." **RIGHT:** On the victory stand together, Salazar raised Beardsley's arm to join his in triumph.

five miles, I felt terrible," he would say later. "It was a warm day. The pavement was hot. My feet were on fire. I worried that I would develop blisters." Squires told Beardsley not to worry about the other runners, to focus on Salazar. Beardsley was glad that Salazar was not pushing the pace. Like Salazar, he ignored the early surges by Tabb and Matthews.

For Matthews the surges were a calculated part of his race strategy. He and Beardsley had practiced surging during their long training runs that winter. He hoped that by shifting pace, he could lure Salazar out of his race plan and help weaken him. "At that level, you have to be an initiator," says Matthews. "You'll never win if you let others control the race." He noticed, however, that Salazar remained under control. "Alberto never got entrapped in the surge game. He might have had doubts but he stayed back. Obviously, he had been well-coached."

After Framingham they approached a reservoir. Rodgers tapped Beardsley on the shoulder and pointed toward a couple in a canoe. "Wouldn't you like to be out in a canoe right now?" said Rodgers.

"No kidding," Beardsley replied.

Beardsley continued to grab cups and bottles of water. When not drinking water, he poured it over the billed painter's cap he used to shade his head from the sun. He also carried a sponge in the waistband of his shorts, which he would fill with water and squeeze later onto his legs. Beardsley noted that Salazar was not taking nearly as much water as he. "In the latter stages of the race I'd hand him a water bottle and sometimes he'd take it and sometimes he wouldn't," says Beardsley.

Salazar says, "I took water several times but only a sip each time because I was worried about stomach cramps." Salazar later estimated that he drank as little as 2½ cups of water. He noticed that Beardsley often would keep a water bottle and sip from it for a quarter-mile. Salazar wondered, "Does he really need to drink that much?" After the race

Salazar would decide that the answer was yes and that he would have been wise to have done the same.

Plotting Their Strategies

Up until Natick Dick Beardsley had followed his coach's instructions not to lead during the first ten miles. With that mark now past he decided to surge for 200 meters, as much to stretch his legs and test his speed as to break anybody. With a slight acceleration he moved away from the pack. Only his training partner, Matthews, chose to chase him. When Matthews reached Beardsley's side, Beardsley told him, "Dean, that was only a fake surge. Don't get excited." Relaxing, Beardsley allowed the pack to gather him into its fold.

Continuing to monitor his own body and the movements of those around him, Salazar understood that eventually the race would be between him and Beardsley. He suspected that Squires had carefully instructed Beardsley on the best strategy to defeat him. That strategy, Salazar reasoned, was to beat him on the hills. "I knew Beardsley had been training on Heartbreak Hill," says Salazar. "I knew I had more speed than Beardsley, so his big chance, other than if he could push the pace from the beginning, would be to push the hills and try to break away. My strategy would be not to let him do that. I figured that if I got to the top of the last hill with him, his confidence would lower."

Indeed, Squires had plotted just such a strategy for Beardsley: planning a series of long surges through the hills between 17 and 21 miles that would wear Salazar down and shake *his* confidence. As Beardsley explains: "We figured that if I could be in the lead or within striking distance at the top of Heartbreak Hill, I had a chance to win it. Coach Squires said that if I was with Al at that point, it might get him worried

(continued on page 177)

UPPER LEFT: Bob Hall was a pioneer in wheelchair racing, winning the first Boston Marathon wheelchair competition in 1975. His first racing wheelchair was little better than those used in hospitals. **LOWER LEFT:** In their high-tech chairs, wheelchair competitors move at a pace so fast that runners no longer catch them. **CENTER:** After a bad crash on the steep downhill out of Hopkinton in 1987 the Boston Athletic Association mandated a controlled start for the first mile. **RIGHT:** In 1994 Jean Driscoll of Champaign, Illinois, won her fifth of six consecutive victories.

WHEELERS AND DREAMERS

Bob Hall remembers August 8, 1974, as a pivotal moment in his life. He was then age 23 and had just won a marathon in Toledo, Ohio—not on foot but in a wheelchair. Stricken with polio at ten months, the short-legged Hall could walk, but only with braces or crutches. At Boston State College he began playing wheelchair basketball. He also competed in track, winning national titles at 100 meters and the mile. When several competitors challenged him to enter the National Wheelchair Marathon Championships in Toledo, Hall began training with Bill Squires. In Toledo, Hall won in 2:54:05, the first wheelchair athlete to break three hours.

It was during the drive back from Toledo that Hall decided to participate in the Boston Marathon.

He would not be the first wheelchair athlete to do so. In 1970 Eugene Roberts of Baltimore started an hour before the runners and finished long after them, taking seven hours. Considering that wheelchair athletes now race Boston far under two hours, the times of Roberts and Hall seem embarrassingly slow today, but they used hospital wheelchairs. "We had nothing like the high-tech chairs available today," says Hall.

Before the Boston Marathon in 1975 Hall contacted race director Will Cloney for permission to enter. Stung by the controversy surrounding women the previous decade, Cloney had no wish to start a new war with wheelchair athletes. He welcomed Hall's entry.

At the start Hall positioned himself inconspicuously in the back row. "The fact that I couldn't extend myself physically in the early miles probably saved me toward the end of the race," he concedes.

"It was amazing to see so many spectators every foot of the way. In the final miles it was like a wall of people." Hall finished in 2:58, a minute ahead of Harry Cordellos, a blind runner from California. Between them, they proved there was no limit to the human spirit.

Hall skipped Boston in 1976, concentrating his attention on the Paralympics for handicapped athletes. In 1977 he recruited six others to come to Boston. It became the National Wheelchair Marathon Championships. The "wheelers" started 15 minutes ahead of the runners, thus avoiding the crowded start. Winner Jerome Drayton didn't catch and pass Hall until the Newton hills. Hall won the wheelchair race in 2:40:10; Sharon Rahn of Champaign, Illinois, was the first woman in 3:48:51.

As more and more people in wheelchairs started competing, demand increased for better equipment. Hall formed a company to manufacture racing wheelchairs. Lower, lighter and with self-directing steering systems that allow racers to push almost continuously, the new generation of chairs guaranteed that runners would never catch the wheelers again. Jim Knaub of Long Beach, California, came to dominate Boston, rolling to a record time of 1:22:17 for his fifth win in 1993. (The following year Heinz Frei of Switzerland bettered that with 1:21:23.) Jean Driscoll of Champaign, Illinois, earned her sixth consecutive victory in 1995.

With the wide separation between their times, runners and wheelers now operate in different dimensions, often sharing the same road races and courses and desire for personal achievement, but meeting mostly after the race at the awards ceremonies.

"Boston is the pinnacle," says Hall. "It's the event that showcases our abilities at their highest. Everything else trickles down from there."

Coming through
Wellesley Hills, Dick
Beardsley glances left
to survey the compe-
tition: Bill Rodgers,
Alberto Salazar and Ed
Mendoza. Beardsley
thought Mendoza looked
strongest, but he would
be proven wrong.

about his fitness because that meant I would have stayed with him about 3 miles farther than anyone else in a marathon before."

But as the lead pack moved into Wellesley at 12 miles, the hills remained at least 5 miles away. Until that point, Salazar could wait—and watch.

Mind Games

At Wellesley College women from the school crowded into the streets, forming a corridor so narrow that the entourage of vehicles accompanying the lead runners had to slow to squeeze through. The female spectators shrieked in appreciation of the runners passing their doors. "They were screaming so loudly it hurt," recalls Salazar.

Several of the lead runners offered quick waves of thanks. Most yearned for the relative quiet once the college was behind them, although there was little quiet on the Boston course that year. The unseasonably warm and sunny weather, plus the promise that Alberto Salazar might set a world record, had attracted more spectators than anyone could remember from previous years. Some suspected the number to be as high as two million, although nobody could say for sure. Boston is a sporting event where you cannot count the number of tickets sold.

Nike had a store on the left side of the road just before runners departed Wellesley around 14 miles. In passing, Salazar spotted some familiar Nike employees. Briefly relaxing his concentration, Salazar smiled and waved at them. Beardsley noticed: "It was as though Al was saying, 'This is my turf. This is my territory.' He wanted me to know how relaxed he felt." In response, Beardsley began to wave at spectators on the right. He saw that Salazar immediately got a stern look on his face as though he disapproved.

At that point in the race, Salazar felt anything but good. "My ham-string felt tight through the halfway point, so I had been concentrating on running as easily as possible," Salazar recalls. "But I had not taken much water, a mouthful here, a mouthful there. It was 70 degrees but dry. Since I wasn't perspiring, I hadn't thought much about the heat or the fact that I might be losing fluids. By 13 miles I started to work a little. By 15 it took more effort. By the hills at 17 I had really begun to hurt."

Narrowing the Field

Salazar was not the only one hurting. Doug Kurtis began to fade after 10 miles. He eventually would finish 109th in 2:27:13. Tabb and Matthews failed to finish. Tabb stopped at 13, blaming a new pair of shoes. Matthews dropped out at 14 miles with calf problems. He says, "One minute I was running strong; the next minute I was out of the race."

Beardsley remembers: "Each mile, we'd lose another runner." By mile 15 only Rodgers and Mendoza remained with Salazar and Beardsley.

Near 16 miles Rodgers took a brief lead on the long downhill stretch leading to Newton Lower Falls. Rodgers excelled as a downhill runner, one reason he usually ran well at Boston. But his surge into the lead proved to be a final and desperate gambit. Salazar, Beardsley and Mendoza quickly caught him. Rodgers began to lose contact on the first hill.

It was now a three-man race. Beardsley surveyed the two other runners and himself. "Of the three, I thought Mendoza looked the best, then, all of a sudden, it was like he dropped off the end of the world. One minute he was there and the next minute I looked over my shoulder and couldn't see him." Mendoza would fail to finish.

A Two-Man Contest

As they continued to battle through the four Newton hills, it was now a two-man race. As he had planned, Beardsley picked up the pace, moving clearly in front. They had reached the "moment of truth" anticipated by Salazar, when Beardsley would attempt to destroy him.

"This is it," Salazar told himself. "Don't let him break you! You're better than him!" Salazar kept reminding himself that if he just stayed with Beardsley to the top of the hills, he could win.

Salazar might tell himself that but he was not sure he believed his own words. Beardsley would stretch his lead by several yards, and Salazar would need to fight to gain the yardage back to avoid getting dropped, which would have been devastating psychologically at that point. Mostly, Salazar tried to run just off Beardsley's left shoulder a half-stride back, signaling that he was there and waiting, but sometimes the effort to hold that position was too great, and he dropped to a drafting position immediately behind Beardsley. It was a position he disliked to assume. It wounded his dignity.

"It was frustrating for me to be behind him," Salazar admits. "It was a matter of pride with me that I didn't want anybody to be close to me at that point in a marathon." Salazar had no choice. He was running as hard as he could to stay even. Any time he moved to Beardsley's side as though threatening to take the lead, it only urged Beardsley to run faster.

Beardsley was acutely aware of Salazar's position. "I never looked back," he would say, "but the way the sun was positioned I could see the shadow of Alberto's head. A couple of times the shadow would loom up bigger and I'd figure he was getting ready to jump me so—boom!—I'd take off because I wanted to get the first jump. The shadow never disappeared. I couldn't get rid of it."

Salazar kept telling himself, "There's no way I'm going to lose this race! There's no way I'm going to let him beat me!" Any chances of improving his world record had long ago been forgotten. Salazar later

would admit, "My attitude changed during the race from wanting a fast time to wanting a clear victory to finally just wanting to win." Salazar began to realize that, unless Beardsley cracked soon, it might come down to a sprint on the final straightaway, something he feared despite his seemingly superior speed.

Attacking the Hills

Beardsley was in front doing what he had to do to beat the world record holder: run fast between 17 and 21 miles. The fact that three of Boston's toughest hills were located within that 4-mile span was almost incidental to his strategy. He had trained on those hills in a snowstorm, so he dismissed them. "I didn't even see the hills," Beardsley would say later. "The hills weren't even there to me. I went flying through the hills."

Royce Flippin, a reporter for *The Runner*, had been assigned to watch the race from the Woodland checkpoint at 17¾ miles, where he had a view of the top of the second hill. "At the top of the grade," wrote Flippin, "Beardsley seems unaffected by the ascent. He is still running fluidly, with a faint look of anticipation on his face. Salazar appears hot and fatigued, his jaw hanging slightly open and his head dripping from a recent dousing. But he is on Beardsley's shoulder, and as Beardsley crests the hill and begins to surge down the other side, Salazar goes right with him."

It was Beardsley's strategy to not merely run fast up the hills but to run fast over the crest of those hills, down the back sides and into the flat valleys between the hills. Beardsley felt he could not afford to allow Salazar even a few strides to relax and gather confidence. Thus, he would betray no hint of weakness. He wanted to hammer, hammer, hammer on his rival until he broke.

The pair reached a final rise on the second Newton hill, having covered nearly 18½ miles. At that point, an employee from New Balance popped out of the crowd and attempted to jog with Beardsley for a few strides. He could barely do so but handed the runner a bottle of water, shouting, "Dickie, Dickie, keep it up!"

Beardsley drank from the bottle, carried it for a period, then offered it to his rival a half-step behind. Salazar shook his head.

Beardsley and Salazar rushed over the top of the second hill and into the valley leading to the third, a short hill where a statue in honor of the elder John Kelley would be erected a decade later. Beardsley continued to push but he had not yet broken Salazar.

"I was in the lead," Beardsley recalls, "but I was not leading. Al was right off my left shoulder. But at this point, I could almost feel the crowd come to me and say, 'You're the farm boy from Minnesota. You're about to score a major upset.' Because now we were at a point where nobody had been able to stay with Alberto Salazar before."

The lead pair moved over the top of the third hill and across the short, flat stretch before the ascent onto fabled Heartbreak Hill. Their charge through the hills was at a pace faster than anyone had ever run the Newton hills before. Salazar could only remain near Beardsley by reminding himself continuously, "You're better than him! You just ran 27:30 in Oregon! You can beat him!"

Salazar would say later: "It was a whole different game once we got to the hills. We had been running really slow and from my point that was fine. But once we started up, he began pushing the pace at an intensity that neither of us could continue to the finish. It was a matter of time before either he would break me or he would have to slow down himself."

All Downhill from Here

When they crested Heartbreak Hill, Salazar was not broken. But neither was Beardsley. The duel continued as each looked for a sign of weakness in the other. Beardsley remained in the lead as they began a long descent past Boston College. It is this descent that many runners fear more than the preceding ascents because of the punishing effect that downhill running has on the muscles. The elder John Kelley once referred to this stretch as the Haunted Mile. The ghosts of many runners who at least figuratively had died on this descent were present.

Tom Hart, another reporter for *The Runner*, was stationed by the Lake Street checkpoint near 21 miles. "Beardsley looks stern but still loose," wrote Hart. "Maybe it's only an illusion engendered by the pertly upturned bill of his white cap, but he seems to have more left than Salazar, who runs with an absence of expression to which Raymond Chandler might have done justice in describing a professional killer. Salazar is locked in two steps directly behind Beardsley, and he's not enjoying himself."

But Beardsley wasn't enjoying himself at this point either. Five miles remained and he knew those last miles would not be fun. He also was close to cracking, although he did not want his rival to know it. A sudden move by Salazar might finish him. Beardsley would recall: "I had taken that pounding punishment coming down the long hill after Heartbreak, and my legs bit the bullet. I thought I could break him but he went right with me. He was still there, and I couldn't feel my legs! There was just a numbness from the waist down. I put it on automatic pilot, running just on instinct, putting one leg in front of the other."

One Mile at a Time

Beardsley decided to adapt a mental strategy that would ignore the fact that five miles remained. He would run those miles one at a time, not caring whether there was another, not worrying whether or not tomorrow existed, unconcerned whether any moment he would step into a

DICK BEARDSLEY'S MARATHON RECORD

Date	Race and Location	Time (Place)
8/13/77	PAAVO NURMI MARATHON — Hurley, Wisconsin	2:47:14 (60)
10/9/77	CITY OF LAKES MARATHON — Minneapolis	2:33:22 (7)
6/17/78	NATIONAL JUNIOR COLLEGE CHAMPIONSHIPS — Dowagiac, Michigan	2:33:06 (3)
6/24/78	NORTH DAKOTA MARATHON — Grand Falls	2:31:50 (2)
6/17/79	MANITOBA MARATHON — Winnipeg	2:21:54 (5)
9/9/79	NIKE/OTC MARATHON — Eugene, Oregon	2:20:22 (44)
5/24/80	U.S. OLYMPIC TRIALS — Buffalo	2:16:01 (16)
9/7/80	NIKE/OTC MARATHON — Eugene, Oregon	2:15:11 (10)
10/26/80	NEW YORK CITY MARATHON — New York City	2:13:55 (9)
1/10/81	HOUSTON MARATHON — Houston	2:12:48 (2)
2/1/81	BEPPU MARATHON — Japan	2:12:41 (3)
3/29/81	LONDON MARATHON — England	2:11:48 (1)
6/20/81	GRANDMA'S MARATHON — Duluth, Minnesota	2:09:37 (1)
8/15/81	STOCKHOLM MARATHON — Sweden	2:16:17 (2)
1/24/82	HOUSTON MARATHON — Houston	2:12:42 (2)
4/19/82	BOSTON MARATHON — Boston	2:08:54 (2)
6/19/82	GRANDMA'S MARATHON — Duluth, Minnesota	2:14:49 (1)
10/24/82	NEW YORK CITY MARATHON — New York City	2:18:12 (30)
3/8/87	NAPA VALLEY MARATHON — Napa, California	2:16:04 (1)
6/20/87	GRANDMA'S MARATHON — Duluth, Minnesota	2:22:49 (15)
10/5/87	TWIN CITIES MARATHON — Minneapolis	2:30:06 (45)
4/24/88	U.S. OLYMPIC TRIALS — Jersey City, New Jersey	2:27:21 (45)

At the 1981 London Marathon Dick Beardsley and Norway's Inge Simonson decided in the last mile to tie for first. One year later neither Beardsley nor Alberto Salazar would have agreed to such a tie.

ALBERTO SALAZAR'S MARATHON RECORD

Date	Race and Location	Time (Place)
10/26/80	NEW YORK CITY MARATHON—New York City	2:09:41 (1)
10/25/81	NEW YORK CITY MARATHON—New York City	2:08:13 (1)
4/19/82	BOSTON MARATHON—Boston	2:08:52 (1)
10/24/82	NEW YORK CITY MARATHON—New York City	2:09:29 (1)
4/9/83	ROTTERDAM MARATHON—Netherlands	2:10:10 (5)
12/4/83	FUKUOKA MARATHON—Japan	2:09:21 (5)
5/26/84	U.S. OLYMPIC TRIALS—Buffalo	2:11:44 (2)
8/12/84	OLYMPIC GAMES—Los Angeles	2:14:19 (15)
4/11/92	U.S. OLYMPIC TRIALS—Columbus, Ohio	DID NOT FINISH
5/31/94	COMRADES MARATHON (53.8 MILES)—Durban, South Africa	5:38:39 (1)

Alberto Salazar

breasts the tape in

victory at the 1982

Boston Marathon.

sewer to be carried far out to sea. He accepted any artifice that would allow him to remain in front, because any moment Salazar might fall into his own sewer.

"Okay," Beardsley told himself at 21 miles, "you're leading the Boston Marathon. You've got the world record holder on the ropes. You can hold this pace for one more mile. One more mile! Only one mile to go!"

At 22 miles Beardsley punched the reset button on his mental speedometer. "One mile to go!"

And at mile 23, "One mile to go! You're beating the world record holder. One more mile!"

The runner behind him, meanwhile, continued to employ his own mental strategies. "Once we got off the hills, he slowed down immediately," Salazar recalls. "We let the pace drop four or five seconds," says Salazar. "I began to feel good again." But the moment of truth did not come. Salazar did not move to take the lead—because he could not! Salazar uncharacteristically continued to run in a drafting position behind Beardsley as the two ran single file down Beacon Street through Boston's Brookline district.

Into the Maddening Crowd

Beardsley was having difficulty remaining focused because of the crowd. Running along Beacon Street in the heart of the city, people seemed to press closer and closer. "The crowd noise was so loud that it got to a point near the end when I could not hear myself think," says Beardsley. "It was like standing next to a runway with a jet airplane ready to take off."

Crowd control seemed nonexistent. "Why don't people get out of the way?" he thought. A phalanx of eight motorcycle policemen accompanied them but neither they nor policemen at intersections nor mounted

The crowd noise was so loud it was like standing next to a
runway with a jet airplane ready to take off. —Dick Beardsley

Struggle

LEFT: This was the "moment of truth" so feared by Alberto Salazar. Regardless of his superior 10,000-meter time, he didn't want the race

to come down to a final sprint where both runners had an equal chance of winning. RIGHT: After the duel was over, Dick Beardsley and Salazar

clasped each other in defeat and victory.

policemen along the route seemed to be able to contain the crowd. Huge numbers of people continued to press closer and closer to the point where he feared the long corridor ahead would close, swallowing him and Salazar and ending the race two miles from the finish line. The situation was intimidating.

The large press bus that had accompanied the lead runners from Hopkinton also was having difficulty maneuvering through the crowds. Near 23 miles Beardsley was running on the right side of the road, Salazar behind. Beardsley suddenly found himself engulfed by a large shadow, except it wasn't Salazar. It was the press bus, which threatened to push him into the crowd.

Beardsley remembers the bus coming so close it brushed him on one shoulder. Salazar remembers Beardsley not yielding, remaining on the right and pounding on the bus with one fist in anger to keep it away. Salazar slowed and moved around the bus to the left. He used the incident to allay his own personal doubts. Salazar told himself, "That's foolish. Why waste mental energy worrying about the bus. Simply go around it." Salazar decided that it was a sign that Beardsley was about to crack.

As they crossed painted numbers on the street announcing that they had covered 25.2 miles, Beardsley suddenly felt himself overcome with emotion. "Seeing how far we had come and how little we had left to go almost got the better of me," says Beardsley. "I almost felt weak-kneed. I thought, 'Not only am I running the Boston Marathon, but I am one mile away from the finish and running in the lead with world record holder Alberto Salazar!' I began sobbing to myself, then I thought, 'Dick, get a grip on yourself. You can't break down now. You've come too far. You've got to get refocused.'" At this point, there really was only one mile to go!

Opportunity Knocks

Beardsley thought that he probably had achieved his greatest lead at that point, but a glance over his shoulder told him it was only five meters. Salazar remained right behind him, waiting, like a panther ready to pounce. Beardsley remembered what Squires had told him: "Dick, Alberto doesn't have a great kick, but it's better than yours."

Beardsley decided to go into a long surge and hold it all the way to the finish line. Suddenly, he felt his hamstring cramp. He could no longer push off with his right leg. He would tell reporters later that Salazar detected the limp and jumped into the lead. Salazar later would deny that occurred, saying that he had simply chosen that moment to take the lead. In all probability, it was Salazar's sudden move to the front, forcing Beardsley to react and increase pace, that caused the latter's hamstring cramp.

Regardless, Salazar relentlessly began to pull away. Years later Beardsley would remember Salazar's lead stretching to one block then a block and a half. "Before we made the turn onto Hereford Street, it seemed like he had a two-block lead." The videotape of this point in the race, however, shows that as the pair turned onto Hereford Street, Salazar's lead was exactly 2.8 seconds, barely 20 meters. This, indeed, was a duel of classic proportions.

Gaining on Salazar

Beardsley's hamstring cramp by now had subsided. He and Salazar had two slightly uphill blocks on Hereford before reaching Boylston Street and the final straightaway. Unfortunately, several of the motorcycle policemen accompanying Salazar and Beardsley had drifted into the gap between the runners. At that point, nothing could deter Beardsley. He would run over the tops of the motorcycles if necessary. "Al's lead

Aftermath

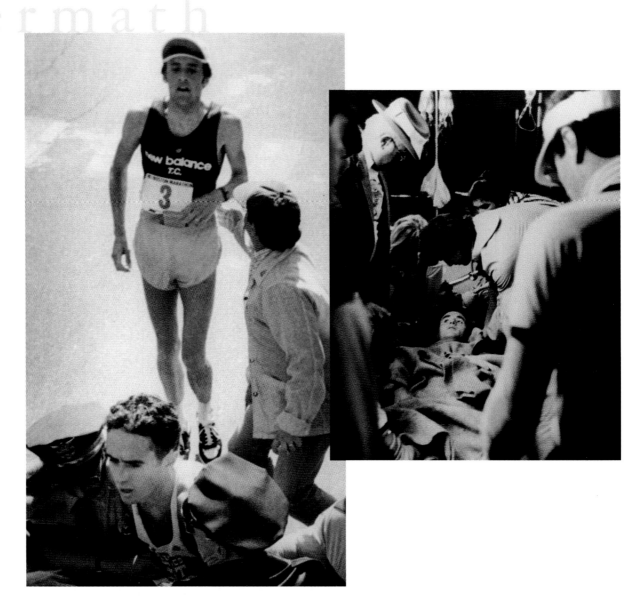

After the greatest
battle in Boston history
since Bunker Hill,
Dick Beardsley was es-
corted to the press con-
ference while Alberto
Salazar was treated
in the medical tent.

started shrinking," Beardsley recalls. "It seemed like every 10 feet he went, I'd go 20. I remember him glancing back, and I don't think he expected to see me that close."

Salazar looked back at Newbury Street, halfway up the Hereford incline. He saw that Beardsley was gaining. The motorcycle policemen also saw Beardsley coming but didn't seem to know which way to go to avoid him.

As Salazar crossed Boylston Street and started a quick right-left zigzag that would take him onto the frontage road paralleling that street, he looked again. Somehow, Beardsley had weaved through the motorcycle policemen without breaking stride. He was there, just off his right shoulder.

Salazar, however, had misjudged the distance. Despite living in Boston, despite having watched the race in high school, despite having visited the finish area before the race, despite having crossed the numbers indicating one mile to go, Salazar somehow was not quite sure how much distance remained once they made the turn onto the frontage road. He would say: "I was thinking, 'There's more than a half-mile to go.' Then, all of a sudden, he was on top of me. I looked ahead and realized, less than 200 meters! That was the exact nightmare situation that I had wanted to avoid. With that much left in a race, anybody can beat you. You might have a lot of energy left but might not be able to turn your legs over. You can get beat."

One Last Sprint

Beardsley remembers relaxing slightly as he pulled even rather than using his momentum to roll forward around Salazar into the lead. But it may not have made any difference. Salazar glanced one more time at Beardsley—and then he accelerated. Very sharply! His arms pumped.

His knees rose. And so at last the duel was won and lost.

"At this point in the race, there wasn't any way in the world he was going to beat me," Salazar later told *Runner's World*. "I don't care if a motorcycle cop had run me over, he was not going to win!" Salazar's sudden sprint propelled him into a ten-meter lead. Beardsley countered with a sprint of his own but could not regain the ground he had just yielded. With the crowd cheering wildly, the two ran the last straightaway almost in lock step, one behind the other, Salazar continuing to glance backward hoping he would not be asked to summon one last sprint. With two strides to go, Salazar attempted to lift his arms in a traditional symbol of victory breasting the tape. He could barely raise them above his shoulders. Time, until that last moment, had seemed almost inconsequential, but the clock above the finish line read 2:08:52, a new course record despite the heat.

Laurels to the Victor

Spent, Salazar almost fell into the arms of two policemen waiting just past the line. Beardsley finished two seconds back in 2:08:54. He, too, raised his arms, half in joy, half in despair. He said, "I can't believe I just ran 2:08 and only finished second!"

The two embraced each other in the finishing chute, mumbling congratulations. Salazar told Beardsley, "Dick, you pushed me harder than anybody ever pushed me. You've made me run harder than I ever have before."

Those words, spoken by two runners who showed each other no mercy, would become part of the legend of the 86th Boston Athletic Association (BAA) Marathon. Their duel became one of the most memorable races—maybe *the* most memorable race—of Boston's first 100 years.

The awards ceremony would be brief. It was over even before third-place finisher John Lodwick crossed the line. Lodwick had started slowly, passing Rodgers in the last mile. Lodwick ran 2:12:01, Rodgers 2:12:38. Rodgers crossed the line looking like he had been placed in a burlap bag and beaten with rubber hammers. When he heard the winning times, Rodgers said, "I can't believe they ran that fast on this hot a day." Sweden's Kjell-Erik Stahl, who never came close to the lead pack, placed fifth in 2:12:46.

The laurel wreath was placed on Salazar's head, the medal draped around his shoulders. Beardsley stood on the stand beside Salazar, nobody denying him that moment, although he would be handed his second-place trophy later. Salazar raised his rival's arm to join his in triumph. "I thought that was a nice gesture," Beardsley would say later.

Ready to Meet the Press

Beardsley and Salazar were sent in separate directions: Beardsley to the media room to give interviews to reporters, Salazar to the makeshift hospital in the parking garage of the Prudential Center to receive medical care. Having taken little water, he was dangerously dehydrated. He felt woozy and his muscles were cramping so badly he could barely walk. He was made to lay down on a cot. The BAA's Jock Semple started to massage Salazar's shoulders. Others massaged his arms and legs. William P. Castelli, M.D., the white-haired director of the Framingham Heart Study and supervisor of the marathon's medical tent, moved to Salazar's side and instructed his aides to begin intravenous injections in both his arms. While the doctor was calm, a nervous television assistant who crowded next to him was not. The assistant told the doctor that they needed Salazar live and in color within 30 minutes since they planned to interview him on national TV.

Having nursed many dehydrated runners back to life, the doctor smiled and told the television assistant, "He'll be ready."

Dr. Castelli positioned two state troopers next to the cot and told them to grab the plastic containers containing intravenous fluid being pumped into Salazar's veins. "Squeeze!" he instructed. In this way, Salazar's dehydrated body absorbed six liters of fluid within 30 minutes. He got off the cot, cramps subsided, head clearer, not able to run 26 miles again for a while, but ready to meet the press.

The Way It Was

Ask Alberto Salazar what his most vivid memory surrounding his Boston victory was and it is none of those moments of truth during its running, not outsprinting Beardsley, not crossing the line first but rather, what happened en route to the press conference.

"Remember, nobody had been able to get hold of me or interview me after I finished," Salazar recalls, the trace of a smile tilting his lips. "As they escorted me toward the press room, there was a phalanx of people, including policemen, on each side. Jock Semple and my grandmother, who was 85 at the time, were in the vanguard of the group.

"My grandmother, especially, was being very protective. People would hedge in wanting autographs, shouting, getting quite aggressive, and she would push them aside. John Linkowski, who was the equipment manager at Oregon, took some photographer who grabbed at me and threw him against the wall. My grandmother got angry. She had a cane and was swinging it in front of her to clear people out of the way.

"We came to a point where a mounted policeman was blocking us. Jock Semple raged at the cop on his horse, 'Get out of the way!' But it was so tightly crowded that the cop couldn't move. So Jock slugged the horse on the leg. And my wife, Molly, was there, and John Linkowski getting red in the face, and my grandmother muttering curses in Spanish and the pandemonium and yelling and screaming, and it seemed so funny that I began to laugh. When I think about Boston, that is what I remember."

Aftermath

The following years would not be easy for either Salazar or Beardsley. On reflection, the 1982 Boston Marathon was the pinnacle of each runner's career. They had pushed each other so hard, destroying each other physically, that afterward there was nowhere to go—except down. "My health problems began after that race," acknowledges Salazar.

Salazar would win his third New York City Marathon that fall but in a slightly slower time (2:09:29) with Mexico's Rodolfo Gomez remaining near him all the way. In the spring of 1983 Salazar chose to run the Rotterdam Marathon rather than defend his title in Boston. His time was respectably fast (2:10:10), but he placed 5th. In 1984 Salazar finished 15th at the Olympic Games in Los Angeles in an even slower time of 2:14:19.

After a battle with various ailments that seemed to defy medical intervention, it would be ten more years before Salazar won another distance race. In 1994 Salazar surprised people who had written him off as a has-been by winning the Comrades Marathon in South Africa.

What Salazar seemed to lose on the road from Hopkinton was his will to push himself almost to the point of destruction. Salazar was always a strong runner but never a graceful one. His winning edge—apart from a high maximum volume of oxygen—came from his ability to endure. In tests at Ball State University in Muncie, Indiana, David L. Costill, Ph.D., had Salazar run on a treadmill to determine his maximum oxygen uptake, the point where muscles cannot absorb any more oxygen from the bloodstream, the point where most top athletes can remain on the treadmill for barely two more minutes. Salazar had remained on the treadmill four more minutes.

It was this will to push through the pain barrier that enabled him to become great and allowed him to defeat others with equal or even greater natural ability. Somehow he had lost that.

The morning after the marathon race, Beardsley received a call at 8:00 A.M. from Jim Davis, the president of New Balance. "Dick, there's a car awaiting you at the front door. It's for your enjoyment."

After Dick and his wife, Mary, dressed, they went downstairs and climbed into a white stretch limousine. They toured Boston, doing the sight-seeing they had avoided while he had conserved energy awaiting the race. Toward the end of the day, they were driven to the New Balance offices. Several executives brought Beardsley into an office and handed him a five-figure contract. "I need time to think this over," said Beardsley, politely handing the contract back.

Beardsley eventually would sign a contract worth $180,000 for three years, but he had achieved the peak of his career. He won Grandma's Marathon two months after Boston in 2:14:49, but an Achilles tendon injury caused him to finish far behind Salazar at New York. In the next decade, Beardsley would become injured in a car crash, nearly have his leg torn off in a farming accident and be hit from behind by a car while training in the dark in Minneapolis.

"It seemed like I could never train for more than six months without getting hurt," Beardsley would say when reflecting on his blunted running career a dozen years after finishing second at Boston. "My body had taken such a beating—not only at Boston but in all the marathons I ran leading up to it—that it no longer would respond."

Beardsley should have been sad, but he had a wide grin on his face. "If there had to be an end, I'm glad it came at Boston."

Ordinary People

10

Chapter Ten

To the spectators, it's a freak show with legs; to the legitimate

runners, it's a test of speed and endurance; and to the

exhibitionists, it's a chance to be a screwball before a ready-

made gallery.—*Will Cloney*

As BILL RODGERS CROSSED THE FINISH LINE IN 1975, Ron Fox, a 42-year-old plastics salesman from Highland Park, Illinois, was struggling through the Newton hills. Fox's finishing time in his first Boston Marathon was 3:19:36—respectable, yet more than an hour behind that of the winner.

Fox recalls being reduced to a near walk on Heartbreak Hill. Around him, everybody else also moved slowly. Despite cool weather, runners grasped desperately at cups of water offered to them by bystanders. A brisk wind sent their discarded cups skittering across the road.

"Look, Daddy," said a young boy standing on the sidewalk, "the cups are moving faster than the runners."

Fox somehow took strength from the boy's comment and continued. The plastics salesman typified the new generation of Boston marathoners much more so than Rodgers. Although Fox had run track in high school, he exercised rarely for several decades as he reared a family and built a career. After reading Dr. Kenneth H. Cooper's book *Aerobics*, he decided to get back in shape. For several years Fox did little more than jog a mile a day on the high school track. Then he met other runners

※

PAGE 188: Long after the winners have crossed the finish line, granted interviews to the press and taken their showers, many more runners continue to cross the finish line. Bill Rodgers once commented: "I can't even imagine what it's like to run for four hours." **LEFT:** Those who finish within five hours now get medals and certificates attesting to their times, but coming up Heartbreak Hill, they'd trade it all for a cold shower.

Life's a marathon. Be in it.
—Seen on a sign along the race route

People

LEFT: Skyboxes on Beacon Street. CENTER: Spectators line the marathon route in 1995.

RIGHT: 26 miles, 385 yards to go.

who competed in road races and started increasing his mileage. Soon, running the Boston Marathon became his goal.

If you talked to others among those who started Boston in 1975, most would offer similar stories of inspiration and achievement.

The Roar of the Crowd

The sponsoring Boston Athletic Association (BAA) regarded the growing popularity of its event almost with horror. In 1964 a record 369 entered. By the end of the decade the number of entrants reached 1,342. Once the numbers passed 1,000, the logistical headaches mushroomed: traffic tie-ups, too few toilets, overcrowding in the starting area and not enough water on the course.

In 1975, with 2,340 men and 52 women starters, volunteers could not process finishers fast enough, causing a backup in the finishing chute. At one point the waiting line reportedly reached back 140 yards. A BAA official walked beside the runners, telling them what their times would have been had they been able to cross the line running.

The BAA began to limit the size of the field. At first, to ensure that everybody had trained properly, the BAA requested in 1970 that they certify their ability to finish a marathon in less than four hours. Jock Semple, the BAA's trainer, considered the standard more than fair, huffing, "I could walk a marathon that fast." In 1971 runners were asked to show proof that they had finished a marathon faster than 3:30 or had run an equivalent time in a shorter road race. By tightening its qualifying standard, the BAA hoped to hold numbers under 1,000.

After the backup in 1975 race director Will Cloney decided to drop the time further to 3:00. Then, in 1979 when 7,357 men and 520 women entered Boston, the BAA imposed a standard of 2:50. Nobody was walking that fast, including Semple, who had placed ninth in 1944 with a time of 2:51:34. Equivalent standards were established for women and *masters* (those over age 40).

Making the Cut

Rather than discourage participation, the standards had the opposite effect. They increased Boston's prestige and added an aura of exclusivity unintended by its organizers. Other than the Olympic Trials, Boston was the only American marathon for which you had to demonstrate your ability to gain entry. Qualifying for Boston became a status symbol among the new breed of runners.

For many runners, then, qualifying for Boston became more important than actually running Boston.

When their qualifying time became known to their running friends, the question would be, "Are you going?" It was never, "Are you going to run Boston?" Boston was understood. The answer to that question was almost always yes. Jo Ann Collier recalls how she felt achieving a qualifying time one year in the Houston Marathon in her hometown: "All I could think of was, 'I get to run Boston!' "

Norb Tatro, an NBC producer and jogger from Chicago, first attended Boston while doing a feature story on a triple-bypass patient who ran the marathon in 1981. "I didn't make any vow to run Boston," says Tatro, "but I did start to run more seriously."

As he increased mileage, Boston finally did become his goal. In his age group Tatro needed to break 3:10. Tatro remembers crossing the finish line at the 1983 Lake County Marathon in suburban Chicago in 3:09:21 with 39 seconds to spare. "I was shaking from emotion. A member of the medical staff asked me if I was okay. I assured him in a trembling voice that I was much more than okay."

Bill Wilson of Livonia, Michigan, also wanted to run Boston but

In what other sport can an average athlete compete
in the same event with the superstars? —Marty McNamara

LEFT: By the mid-1970s hundreds of foreign runners were participating in the Boston Marathon. **UPPER CENTER:** Two American Medical Joggers Association members finish in triumph. **LOWER CENTER:** The thrill of victory belongs to everyone who crosses the finish line, regardless of their times. **RIGHT:** Fred and Paula Palka of Charlottesville, Virginia, ran Boston on their honeymoon in 1983.

found that each time he improved, the BAA toughened its standards. His 3:05:59 at the 1978 *Detroit Free Press* Marathon fell short of the 3:00 qualifying time then in effect. The following year, Wilson ran 2:54:21— but the BAA standard by then was 2:50. Wilson increased his mileage further and dropped his time to 2:47:38, finally qualifying. "I'll always remember the feeling of pride and accomplishment standing at the starting line of the world's most famous marathon," he says.

Marty McNamara of Bradenton, Florida, took nearly 12 years to qualify. He tried first at the Orange Bowl Marathon in 1979 and finally qualified in 1990. By then he had turned 40 and could take advantage of the easier standard for *masters* runners. "Reading about the Boston Marathon in the mid- to late 1970s was one of the main reasons I started competitive running," says McNamara. "It was the World Series and Super Bowl combined. In what other sport can an average athlete compete in the same event with the superstars?"

Tim Dyas of Ridgewood, New Jersey, had trained for the 1941 Boston Marathon in an era when there were no qualifying standards, but that February was called to active duty in the U.S. Army. He served in World War II as a paratrooper, spending two years in a German prisoner-of-war camp. After the war he competed in track at New York University but for three decades forgot about running. He finished his first marathon in 1977 in New York City, running 4:21:54. In 1980 Dyas entered the Jersey Shore Marathon, looking for a Boston-qualifying time. Having just turned 60, he would only need to break 3:30.

Alas, during the race Dyas tripped over a traffic cone. He got up and finished in 3:31:27, but this was short of his goal. At the next meeting of the North Jersey Masters he wondered why one of the members was circling the room asking people for their signatures. Dyas recalls: "Since I was being pointedly ignored, I asked what was going on. I discovered

QUALIFYING FOR BOSTON

Throughout the 1960s the number of runners entering Boston mushroomed from a few hundred to 1,342 in 1969. Hoping to pull numbers back below 1,000, race director Will Cloney introduced qualifying standards, but to no avail.

By 1976 Cloney and Jock Semple tightened entry standards to an imposing 3:00 for men and 3:30 for women and *masters* (those over age 40). But nothing helped. The running boom had begun. The ranks swelled to 7,877 entrants in 1979, with easily a third as many bandits tagging behind. So next year, standards came down to 2:50 for men, 3:10 for *masters* men and 3:20 for women, eventually 3:30 for *masters* women. Numbers dipped in 1981, but by 1982 7,439 entered.

By then, the flood had crested. As the running boom continued through the 1980s, every major city had a marathon. With greater volunteer support the BAA realized it could tolerate fields near 10,000 and decided to relax its qualifying times. For the 100th running, standards for men and women are 3:10 and 3:40 respectively, with progressively easier standards through the later age groups.

Age Group	Men's Times	Women's Times
18–34	3:10	3:40
35–39	3:15	3:45
40–44	3:20	3:50
45–49	3:25	3:55
50–54	3:30	4:00
55–59	3:35	4:05
60–64	3:40	4:10
65–69	3:45	4:15
70+	3:50	4:20

that club members were signing a petition asking that I be accepted in Boston because of my having fallen in the race." The BAA yielded. "Jock and I were basically softhearted when it came to enforcing time standards," admitted Will Cloney, "although we didn't want too many people to know that." At Boston Dyas ran a personal best 3:24:17, placed 15th in his age group and even appeared in the TV coverage.

Why Run Boston?

People run Boston for various reasons. James Jones, a post office employee from Cabool, Missouri, weighed 270 when he started running. After dropping 115 pounds, he ran Boston to celebrate his weight loss.

John Dove, a management consultant from Arlington, Massachusetts, ran Boston to earn credit for a physical education class so he could complete his college degree two decades after dropping out of Oberlin College.

Laura Kearns of Dallas started running because her ex-husband told her she was getting pudgy. She finished her first marathon struggling in at 5:08:29 but eventually she trimmed her time, running 3:07:58 at Boston.

Charlie O'Rourke, a track coach at Somerville High School in the Boston area, ran the 1994 marathon with Lisa Maciel, one of his former runners who had contracted bone cancer her senior year in high school in 1988. She had 14 operations and has only one bone in one leg, but she went on to become captain of the women's track team at Tufts University. Her goal in the marathon was only to break 5:00; she ran 3:57:22. "Lisa went out like a rocket," says O'Rourke. "She had some tough miles midrace but finished strong."

Gary Rauhaus, an electrician from Peoria, Illinois, started to exercise to cope with the stress of rearing four children after his wife died in childbirth. Mostly, he lifted weights at the River City Athletic Club. Working out on a Stairmaster nearby one day was Sally Herman, a nurse.

"We started talking," Sally recalls. "I told him he needed some aerobic work to complement his lifting." They began running together and set as a goal qualifying for Boston. Gary succeeded in doing so at the Twin Cities Marathon, she at Houston. The weekend before the Boston Marathon they married and ran the race on their honeymoon, crossing the finish line together.

Running for Love

Beverly Powers of Roseville, Minnesota, a production planner for a shingle manufacturing company, met her future husband before the 1991 Boston Marathon. She had run recreationally for nine years before deciding to try a marathon. She ran her first marathon at Grandma's Marathon in Duluth, Minnesota, in 1989 and qualified the following year at Twin Cities with 3:29:47. Her sister, Bonnie Welshons, accompanied her to Boston.

On the Saturday before the race, they toured the city, visited the aquarium and the outdoor market at Faneuil Hall and ate pasta in the North End. On Sunday morning Beverly and Bonnie attended services at the Park Street Congregational Church across from Boston Common. After the service, Bonnie suggested to Beverly that she could get her coffee for free if they attended fellowship time in the church basement.

Attending the same service was Ted Rust, pastor of St. Paul's Lutheran Church in Smithville, Ohio, where he also coached high school cross-country.

At the service, Ted noticed Beverly. Impulsively, he scribbled an invitation to dinner on a piece of paper then lost courage and failed to offer it. Spotting her downstairs, he asked, "Are you running the marathon tomorrow, too?" They talked. She gave him her address and said to contact her if he ever decided to run Twin Cities. They parted. Rust looked for her at the pre-race pasta dinner and on race day, but their paths never crossed. He finished in 3:01:25, she in 3:45:25.

Several days later he sent flowers. They exchanged letters and phone calls. He did run Twin Cities that October. Waiting at the airport for him, Beverly said to herself, "I'm going to marry this man." They were engaged in December and married in May. The Rusts named their first child Hope.

Bumping into the Boston Greats

Hope continues to spring eternal among those who head to Boston each April. They find an event changed from its early years when a few dozen runners would run along unpaved roads with militiamen on bicycles offering support.

With the increase in numbers, the Boston Marathon became an extravaganza occupying the long Patriots' Day weekend. Runners jam the hotels in Boston's Back Bay area and crowd into restaurants along trendy Newbury Street or in the North End, where pasta is plentiful and varied.

On Saturday and Sunday they pick up their numbers and attend a mammoth exposition featuring high-tech equipment that turn-of-the-century marathoners never could have imagined. They line up to obtain autographs from their heroes and heroines: Bill Rodgers, Alberto Salazar, Joan Benoit Samuelson. They attend clinics where running experts tell them what to eat and drink before this year's race and how to train for next year's race.

Getting to Hopkinton

On Monday morning runners rise early and stop at the Dunkin' Donuts near the finish line on Boylston Street for one last carbo-load be-

fore catching a bus at Copley Square. Even into the 1970s, Jock Semple would stand beside the buses being loaded with marathoners and accept $2 as payment for the ride to Hopkinton. Semple thrust the money into a gym bag held in one hand. Most often, runners simply dropped their money into the gym bag, overwhelmed that they were passing in front of a legend.

The legend has departed. Runners now show their race numbers before boarding the buses. Larry Rosinski of Toledo, Ohio, was standing in the bus line in 1991 when he suddenly realized he had left his number back in his room at The Farrington Inn, a bed-and-breakfast in Brighton. It was a runner's worst nightmare. Panicked, Rosinski hailed a taxicab. The taxicab driver succeeded in getting back to Copley Square in time to catch one of the last buses. As they arrived back at the Square, the driver said he wanted to write down Rosinski's number just in case he was one of the leaders. Rosinski offered a very large tip.

John F. Joyce still remembers his bus ride to Hopkinton in 1971. One year before, Joyce was working in the Oak Park YMCA in suburban Chicago and spotted an article on the bulletin board. The article told about Joe Pardo, a massage therapist at the Flushing YMCA in New York who had run the Boston Marathon even though he was blind.

Inspired, Joyce began to train and entered the Boston Marathon. On marathon day he boarded the bus for Hopkinton. There were 1,011 entrants that year. He sat next to the window.

Soon, another runner sat beside him. Joyce recalls: "The first thing I noticed was the white cane. When I looked up, I saw a man wearing dark glasses. I took another look. It was him, Joe Pardo from the Flushing YMCA. Out of hundreds of runners and dozens of buses this man sat next to me!"

Joyce introduced himself and told Pardo he was the main reason he

TOP: Bostonians come out to cheer their marathon heroes, even in the rain. RIGHT: Countless gallons of water are poured into the marathoners on race day.

was in Boston for the race. Pardo smiled. It seemed Joyce was not the first person to have told him that.

The two talked during the bus ride—then parted. "Through our talk," Joyce recalls, "it became apparent to me that Joe Pardo recognized no obstacles in his quest for a personal goal. There seemed to be little question in his mind that he would finish the race that day. I wasn't that confident nor were many of the other runners."

Joyce did finish, running 3:12:47. Pardo ran 3:31:00. Joyce, who now works for LifeCenter on the Green in Chicago, continues to run Boston on occasion and continues to be inspired by Pardo. Twenty years later Pardo was no longer running marathons, but he continued to compete in 5-K and 10-K races.

Same Time, Same Place, Next Year

The first buses depart Copley Square at 7:00 A.M., the last buses at 10:00 A.M. Among those first to arrive at Hopkinton High School each year is Doug McKillip of Newark, Delaware. McKillip first ran Boston in 1979 and has run it each year since, staying with his aunt and uncle in Wellesley Hills. Race morning his relatives drive McKillip to Hopkinton, usually dropping him off shortly after 7:30 A.M.

At that time, only a handful of runners have arrived. McKillip walks into the gymnasium and has no difficulty selecting a spot under the basketball backboard at the far end. "This is prime camping ground," says McKillip. "The wall is padded behind the backboard, so you can lean against it." McKillip removes an air mattress from his bag and blows it up. He has been doing this since 1989.

The first buses begin arriving soon after 8:00. Among the early arrivals are Jim Rillema and Marty Povrick from near Detroit and Norbert Peiker and Barbara Dillion from Mansfield, Ohio. They soon join

McKillip under the backboard. They meet each other at Boston in this same manner each year.

"The first thing we ask is how everybody did the previous year," says McKillip. "We never see each other except in the gym, so we wait a year to find out our finishing times. We talk about our training, how fast we ran in our qualifying races and what we expect to do that day. When it's time to head for the line, we wish each other luck and say, 'See you next year. Same time. Same place.' "

As an early camper McKillip enjoys seeing the gym fill with runners. "It's like watching the tide come in," he says. "At first, runners arrive one or two at a time. Then five or six. As the buses arrive, they come in increasingly larger numbers. Spots against the wall go first then seats in the bleachers. By 9:00 floor space begins getting scarce. By 10:00 the gym is a madhouse, wall-to-wall people, runners stepping over other runners. You don't dare get up to visit the toilet without asking your neighbor to save your place. Through it all, most people remain civil and polite—surprisingly so considering how closely we're crammed together."

In earlier days Jock Semple would rumble through the gym soon after 11:00 instructing runners to throw their bags in the buses for transport to the finish. "Starrrrt moving toward the starrrrting line!" Semple would shout in his rolling Scottish brogue. Fifteen minutes later he would reappear, threatening the wrath of several clans if runners did not begin to move. With Semple deceased, such announcements are accomplished on a loudspeaker with considerably less panache. By 11:30 all but a few runners have departed the gym to walk or jog toward the starting line nearly a mile away.

Passing through the parking lot, runners deposit their bags in the buses according to their race numbers. Several hours later upon finishing, they will find the same numbered buses parked in Copley Square. Giving up your warm-up gear as much as 30 to 60 minutes before the start can be a problem on cold or wet days. Vendors at the starting line sell plastic garbage bags to use as makeshift garments—but you have to remember to bring a dollar to buy them. Runners often solve the problem by wearing old clothes to the start, which they discard at the last minute. Each year, Valerie Wilson holds a yard sale at her home on Hayden Rowe in Hopkinton. She says her best customers are runners who buy used clothes to keep warm before the race.

Safe Houses

A few lucky runners have what might be called safe houses. Oklahomans stop at the Oklahoma House only a few blocks from the starting line, where a former Oklahoma family displays the state flag to attract runners from that state.

For others the Kalamazoo House beckons. John and Lenore Tracy, who have relatives from near that Michigan city, typically play host to 30 to 40 runners each Patriots' Day. People from as far away as England and British Columbia and one group from Pittsburgh calling themselves Hot Harry's Runners have visited the Tracys, but most runners are from the area between Kalamazoo and Battle Creek.

Dan Gould, a circuit judge from Kankakee, Illinois, brings a camera with him to Boston each year for the "obligatory starting line photograph." Sometimes it is with the church in the background, sometimes the statue on the green and sometimes the sign saying, "Welcome to Hopkinton: It all starts here." Gould doesn't run with the camera but usually hands it to someone in his group's support crew before entering the starting area. "We capture the 'before' shot with our hair combed," he says, "and later the 'after' shot, when sometimes we don't look so

good even if we feel great." Gould has been recording his Boston memories on film since 1986.

Countdown to High Noon

As noon approaches, runners find their places on the starting grid stretching several hundred yards backward from the line along Hopkinton's Main Street, which is also U.S. 135. The starting grid is defined by snow fences on each side with ropes separating runners into groups according to their qualifying times: fastest up front and slowest behind. Volunteers guard the entrances to each block, repelling those without numbers or those trying to improve their positions (most often to start with a faster friend).

Furthest back are the "bandits," the unnumbered runners who lack official qualifying status. This *lumpenproletariat* is tolerated by the BAA even though they have not contributed an entry fee. The lot of the bandits is not easy, since they will have been granted neither transportation nor access to the gym. (They will, however, be watered along the course, fed after they finish and ministered to should they happen to fall.) Bandits rarely existed back in the 1960s when anyone could enter for a $1 fee, raised only reluctantly at the end of that decade to $2. Nevertheless, bandits have become an integral part of what makes the BAA Marathon a great race. "Spectators lining the course do not discriminate between numbered and unnumbered runners in offering their applause," concedes race director Guy Morse.

A runner dressed as Groucho Marx usually does a brisk business providing special numbers identified as Back-of-the-Pack. Groucho claims not to charge for his ersatz numbers. "The numbers are free," Groucho announces. "Pins cost $1."

At the one-minute-to-go announcement outer garments and garbage bags get flung high into the air or passed from runner to runner to the sides where eventually they will be collected and given to the Salvation Army. (It becomes a contest to see who can achieve the highest throw.) Soon after the start in 1994 Duncan Morris of Salmon Arm, British Columbia, spotted a 1981 New York City Marathon jacket and grabbed it, tying it around his waist. "I'm a born collector," says Morris. Twenty miles later after cresting Heartbreak Hill and feeling the chill wind from the ocean, he was happy to pull the jacket from his waist and don it.

Getting Off on the Right Foot

Once the gun sounds, runners move forward—slowly. Those up front get off fast. Those more than a few dozen rows back get off less quickly. Because of their inferior starting positions, they surrender seconds—or minutes—that they will never retrieve. It may be several miles before many of the marathoners can reach full stride.

Because of the qualifying standards, there are more "fast" runners at Boston than at most other marathons. Runners moving at even sub-3:00 finishing paces find themselves more crowded in the opening miles of Boston than is the case in Los Angeles, Chicago or New York City, where streets are wider and the percentage of runners of near equal ability is lower.

Officials arrange for tables with special water bottles for elite runners, but the near elite who follow behind may have difficulty getting fluids without slowing their paces, something they do only reluctantly. For this reason Boston is not always a good marathon in which to seek personal records.

Houston's Jo Ann Collier recalls reaching for a cup of water before three miles one year at Boston. Another runner reached for the same cup and hit her watch, accidentally stopping it. Although she restarted the watch at the next mile marker, she became frustrated doing the arithmetic each mile, which was necessary to keep track of her pace.

"It was at this point," Collier recalls, "that I began to realize that running in the Boston Marathon was something I had dreamed of for years and that I was not having an enjoyable experience. I decided to forget about my time and just have fun. Moving over to the side of the road, I began slapping the hands of all the kids who reached out." Collier noted that some even thanked her.

Many marathoners draw inspiration from the Wellesley College gauntlet of screaming women. Michael Goldstein of St. Louis considered time spent passing the gauntlet much too brief in 1988. "Two miles down the road, I decided to turn back and run the gauntlet again." Jack Wallace had a different reaction in 1976 when he spotted a bare-breasted girl sitting on the curb. "I lost all my desire to continue."

"Don't Listen to Them, Ma'am"

Joan Ullyot, M.D., author of the first book on women's running, attended Wellesley, graduating in 1961. Unlike many of her classmates, she had never bothered to watch the marathoners pass. "My dorm was at the other end of the quad," says Ullyot, who now lives in Snowmass Village, Colorado. "The race didn't interest me. I had no desire to go watch it."

Running Boston was another matter. Ten years after graduation Ullyot started to jog to allay boredom while her husband played touch football with his friends. Jogging turned into serious running. By 1974 she arrived in Boston to attempt the marathon. Passing her old alma mater, she had tears in her eyes as she heard the cheers of the students. "I had to slow down," she confesses. "You can't run fast with a lump in your throat."

The following year, she found herself running the last six miles with

Support

LEFT: Each year, the race unleashes enthusiasm from spectators. CENTER: For those unable to complete the last miles up Beacon Street, passing streetcars beckon. UPPER RIGHT: "You can do it!" Watching the marathon is not a passive experience. LOWER RIGHT: Marathoning would not be the same without the support of countless volunteers.

Erich Segal, author of *Love Story*. At first Segal failed to recognize her, although she had known him because he was a classmate of her husband at Harvard University. Spectators along the route were shouting encouragement: "Only four miles to go!"

Segal warned Ullyot: "Don't pay attention to them, ma'am. It's four and a half from this corner."

This happened several times again as spectators indicated, "Two miles to go!" or "One mile to go!"

"Don't listen to them, ma'am," Segal insisted.

She eventually corrected him: "Erich, stop calling me ma'am. It's Joan Ullyot!"

Segal said he was pleased to renew an old acquaintance, but within sight of the finish line he began to sprint, pulling away from his companion. Ullyot responded with a sprint herself. She recalls sliding in front of Segal just before they crossed the line.

Segal later wrote about the encounter in a magazine article. He described running with Ullyot in the closing miles and agonizing over whether to treat her as a woman and stay with her or treat her as a competitor and sprint ahead. He finally decided on the latter. "I won," wrote Segal.

After seeing the article, Ullyot wrote Segal, saying that her memory of the finish differed from his. Segal responded, "Joan, you know that I'm a writer of fiction."

You Can Do It!

While spectators sometimes offer wrong information about how many miles remain to run or just how much fun it is to run those last five miles downhill, they nevertheless are part of the support system that keeps runners coming back to Boston—despite the hills.

Running in the 1978 race, Kevin Donahue of Silver Spring, Maryland,

learned he needed the cheers of the crowd. Having started too fast, Donahue found himself reduced to a walk on the first Newton hill. A pudgy youngster on the curb shouted at him, "Keep moving!" When Donahue started to jog, the youngster led the crowd in a cheer.

On the second Newton hill he walked again. An elderly man stepped from the crowd and patted him on the behind, saying, "Come on, son. This is the Boston Marathon!"

Starting to shuffle once more, Donahue began to realize what thousands before had already learned. "Boston is not a race," says Donahue. "It's a state of mind created by a knowledgeable and enthusiastic crowd that doesn't merely watch, it actively participates in the race. Those who cheered me had as much to do with my finish as I did."

Words to Run By

Many competing in the Boston Marathon would remember messages along the way on shirts and on signs. Judy-Arin Krupp of Manchester, Connecticut, recalls spotting a sign written in black marker on a sheet hung from a nursing home in the Newton hills. It said, "Life's a marathon. Be in it." Krupp now runs races wearing a T-shirt with that same message on the back.

Jonathan Beverly, an educator at New York University, had been trying to break 3:00 for the marathon since his junior year in high school in 1980. Ten years later at the Omaha Riverfront Marathon in Nebraska he came within 34 seconds of his 3:00 goal. At Boston in 1994 Beverly passed the halfway point in Wellesley in 1:28 with a lot in reserve but started to crash at mile 22. He began to calculate how much he could slow down and still break 3:00, but his mind wouldn't focus that long. At 23 miles a gust of wind lifted his cap from his head. It was a favorite New York Road Runners Club cap that had served him well in workouts

LEFT: In 1966 Andy Crichton, a *Sports Illustrated* editor, crossed the finish line alone in just over three hours. Today, a runner finishing in that time would share the road with hundreds of other runners. **CENTER:** The finish-line bridge affords 10,000 photo opportunities. **UPPER RIGHT:** Pat Corpora, president of Rodale Books, finishes another Boston. **LOWER RIGHT:** Medals are awarded to runners finishing under five hours.

and races for over a year. "I was too tired to run and chase it," Beverly recalls. He finished in 2:57:27. Afterward, Beverly calculated sadly that he probably could have retrieved the cap and still broken three hours.

The Last Hurrahs

Within the last mile Beacon Street intersects Commonwealth Avenue at Kenmore Square. After passing under an expressway viaduct, marathoners then turn right on Hereford Street for two slightly uphill blocks before making a final left onto Boylston Street. Jack Wallace remembers being passed by John A. Kelley (the Elder) on Hereford Street one year. Wallace had a three-day graying beard. He recalls: "People kept yelling, 'Here comes the old man,' and I thought they meant me." Kelley, then age 66, finished in 3:24:10.

It is on Boylston Street where runners receive their last hurrahs. They finish the final 385 yards on Boylston to continuous applause.

For many, crossing the finish line—no matter how painfully—becomes what George A. Sheehan, M.D., likened to a "peak experience." Veronica Salinas had qualified for Boston in 1988 at the San Antonio Marathon with 3:24:53. Her friends told her, "You are going to Boston!" Salinas went despite an injury that limited her training. Before the start, she found herself in the corral with another runner from San Antonio, who had come with her tour group. She did not know him well, but his name was Pat Riordan. They ran together at an easy pace for the first ten miles. Riordan was running for fun, carrying a camera to take pictures along the course.

At Wellesley Salinas began to pay the price for her lack of training. Even before the Newton hills each step had begun to hurt. "Not only did my left hamstring and calf ache," Salinas recalls, "but my quads on both legs had tightened and felt as though they were being pinched in the grip of a merciless vise." She stopped and stretched. Riordan helped by massaging her calf. She stopped again after the first hill. She walked and shuffled her way to the finish in 4:10:31, much slower than her qualifying time. Somehow, Salinas felt more exhilarated than disappointed. Several weeks later she received a poster in the mail from Riordan that she decided summed up her Boston experience. The poster showed a woman running across a beach. The caption said, "Real winners are ordinary people with extraordinary determination."

The last one to finish Boston each year ordinarily is Dave McGillivray, the technical coordinator for the Boston Marathon. When the BAA offered him that position in 1988, he was faced with a dilemma. "I had run Boston 16 consecutive years, beginning my senior year in high school when I ran as a bandit," McGillivray admits. "I didn't want to break that streak."

McGillivray decided that he would both manage the race and run in it. On race day he arrives in Hopkinton on one of the early buses, supervises arrangements at the start then jumps in a police car as soon as the gun goes off for transport to the finish line. By 6:00 P.M., with most runners across the line, he completes his work and returns to Hopkinton to start his personal Boston Marathon.

Often as many as a dozen of his friends will run portions of the course with him, running in the dark. McGillivray says: "In 1994 my wife, Susan, ran 20 of the 26 miles, which was nice because I was in the worst shape of my life. I had only run five days in five months. It's tough to work on this event and train, too." Chris Lane, one of the officials, remains to time him as he crosses the line, the last official finisher. McGillivray, who once ran coast to coast in 80 days, has a personal record in the marathon of 2:29:58. His best Boston as a late-starting official is 3:03:15, run in 1993.

Spectators not only gain inspiration from watching the tremendous efforts put forth by Boston Marathoners, they also have their own unique ways of watching the race.

Everybody Is a Winner

By the time McGillivray finishes, most marathoners are back resting at their hotels, or celebrating in restaurants, or in cars or planes heading home. The period immediately after crossing the finish line can be both joyful and painful. Wesley Geringer of Black Earth, Wisconsin, recalls boarding a subway train to get back to his parked car after the 1979 race. The train was full, but a woman rose and offered her seat. "That's your reward for running the Boston Marathon," she told him.

Gary Baughman of Livonia, Michigan, received an unwelcome surprise after the 1991 race when he discovered that his car had been towed. Still wearing his finisher's medal, Baughman traced his car to a yard five miles away only to learn it would cost $65 to reclaim the car. Alas, he had only $20 cash and the yard manager refused to take a credit card. Luckily, another individual who also had his car towed recognized Baughman as a marathoner and loaned him the money.

Kara Salvagno had not qualified for Boston in the five marathons she had run but decided to drive from her Trumbull, Connecticut, home in 1992 to watch the race as a spectator. Accompanying Salvagno were her two children, Stephanie, age six, and Craig, age four. "We were touched as we watched the wheelchairs pass on Heartbreak Hill and saw how hard they had to work. We stayed long enough to see John Kelley."

Returning home, they stopped at a roadside restaurant just over the Massachusetts border. A man in his fifties who had run the marathon hobbled slowly into the booth next to them, accompanied by his family. He wore his finisher's medal. As he sat down, Craig rose and moved to shake the man's hand. "You're the winner of the marathon!" announced Craig.

The runner seemed both surprised and embarrassed. "I didn't win the marathon," he said smiling.

To which four-year-old Craig replied, "Oh yes you did!"

Six-year-old Stephanie rose also to shake the man's hand. Salvagno recalls: "By that time, everybody was crying. The man told me, 'I've never been so deeply touched before.'"

Not all runners return home happy. In 1984 Chicago's Peter Elliott (whose personal record was 2:24:19) had a bad race, dropping out of the Boston Marathon at 20 miles. Elliott left for the airport immediately afterward.

With a DNF (did not finish) behind his name Elliott did not feel cheery. He boarded a United Airlines flight on which one of the flight attendants was a runner. The attendant announced, "Anyone who finished the marathon gets a free beer."

As the attendant passed down the aisle, Elliott asked, "How about me? I got as far as 20 miles."

The attendant offered the beer.

Several years later Elliott again was flying United and recognized the same flight attendant. Elliott asked, "Aren't you the one who gave free beers to Boston Marathoners?"

The attendant paused to look at Elliott. "I remember you. You're the one who failed to finish."

Centennial Countdown

The athletes are the center of the event. It is our obligation to provide them with absolutely the very best place to test their athletic abilities.—*Thomas W. Whelton, Boston*

Athletic Association president, 1990-1994

OVER THE YEARS, THE BOSTON ATHLETIC ASSOCIATION (BAA) MARATHON has experienced great change, and—as with so many things in twentieth-century life—some changes have accelerated as the race approaches its centennial celebration.

In 1897 only 15 runners appeared for the dusty trek between Ashland and the Irvington Oval, and for its first seven decades Boston played host to, at most, a few hundred competitors per race. Most marathoners were focused racers in the spirit of Clarence DeMar and Johnny Kelley. They ran to win.

During the next two decades, the tens of thousands who joined the parade were no less interested in performance. For them, however, running in the world's most prestigious marathon was mainly an expression of a fitness-oriented lifestyle. They ran for fun more than glory, and certainly not for money. None was offered by the tight-pursed BAA, which didn't even provide travel expenses for world champions. The club had no funds.

For the first time, Boston's prestige and success seemed threatened by the running boom that it had helped create. More and more people were running new marathons that appeared everywhere: New York, London, Tokyo, Melbourne, Rio de Janeiro. None of these races had traditions to match Boston in attracting name runners. But they could offer money. By the

PAGE 208: Having made the final turn onto Boylston Street, runners confront the final 385 yards before funneling into the finish chute. LEFT: After placing second in 1990 and third in 1991, Germany's Uta Pippig mounted the victory stand in 1994, and again in 1995.

UPPER LEFT: For over 30 years Jock Semple was a mainstay at Boston. **LOWER LEFT:** In memory of Jock Semple, runners wore tartan ribbons in 1988. **CENTER:** Despite a hamstring cramp, Geoff Smith of Great Britain went on to win his second consecutive Boston Marathon in 1985. **RIGHT:** After Rosie Ruiz's deception was confirmed, Jacqueline Gareau of Montreal was officially declared the winner a week after the 1980 race.

mid-1980s long-distance running had become a professional sport with race winners earning prizes of $25,000 or more. The top runners found other races to run each spring rather than run Boston.

For a time, the BAA tried to maintain its race as the last bastion of amateur sports, continuing to offer nothing except a well-honed tradition augmented by the cheers of the world's most appreciative audience. The running community was divided, as were the people of Boston. Some felt Boston should remain pure. Others felt that without professional runners—and management—the Boston Marathon would slide into a backwater from which it might never emerge.

"We were adrift in the 1980s," concedes Guy Morse, who began as a volunteer and was appointed the marathon's first full-time race administrator in 1984. Will Cloney, Morse's predecessor, was among those who had resisted the drift toward professional sports. But the time had passed when he and Jock Semple and a handful of volunteers could manage the marathon out of a training room in the Boston Garden.

The BAA, which had remained largely a paper organization since the sale of its clubhouse in the 1930s, lacked the financial resources to maintain its marathon at the forefront of international sports. Cloney attempted to solve the problem by engaging an independent fund-raiser, but the BAA's Board of Governors disapproved of the arrangement. Cloney retired as race director; Morse soon took charge.

Morse remembers his first day on the job. "They set me up in Boston Garden, one of Jock's old rooms. I opened the door and there was a black rotary telephone sitting on the floor. That was my beginning."

After the 1985 race, Morse helped to convince the Board that for the Boston Marathon to regain its position as the world's premier running event, they would need to offer prize money. Boston never had a lack of potential sponsors wanting to attach their names to the marathon; it was

more the BAA's fear of becoming a commercial carnival that kept those sponsors at bay. Nobody wanted to upset the delicate relationship with the communities through which the marathon must pass. Many wanted Boston to remain an amateur event.

In 1986 the BAA finally signed a ten-year contract with John Hancock Financial Services (renegotiated later to extend to 2003). The contract guaranteed $1.2 million a year in sponsorship funds, goods and services, with Hancock also providing more than 1,000 employee volunteers.

The world's best runners could once more make Boston their top priority. As the countdown continued toward the centennial year, Boston's list of winners expanded to include Olympic champions Gelindo Bordin (1990) and Rosa Mota (1987, 1988, 1990); world record holders Rob de Castella (1986), Abebe Mekonnen (1989) and Ingrid Kristiansen (1986); and a host of fearlessly swift Africans from Ibrahim Hussein (1988, 1991, 1992) to Cosmas Ndeti (1993, 1994, 1995). The 99th running was the first year in the history of Boston that both returning champions, Ndeti and Uta Pippig, repeated their victories.

Yet in many respects Boston has not changed for the individual runner, elite or back-of-the-pack. Prize money doesn't necessarily help you run faster in the 26th mile. You still have to cover the distance from Hopkinton to Boston on foot. There are no shortcuts, either in training or in the marathon itself. Heartbreak Hill continues to punish the imprudent. The weather remains as fickle as ever. The crowds retain their boisterousness. A runner suffering alternating waves of joy, pain, fear and fatigue still can be reduced to tears by a shouted word of encouragement. Boston is still Boston.

Since 1897 a quarter of a million runners have followed in the footsteps of John J. McDermott, and each has a story to tell. In its 100th year Boston remains an inspiration to all.

B.A.A. BOSTON MARATHON

Page 214, CENTER: Each year, the Greek government supplies wreaths of olive branches to crown Boston's champions, such as Cosmas Ndeti, shown in 1994 with his son (named Boston after his father's victory the year before). These branches are cut from the same groves in Marathon where the ancient battle occurred.

UPPER LEFT: Two-time winner Uta Pippig of Berlin, Germany. LOWER LEFT: France's Mustapha Badid won the Men's Wheelchair Division in 1990 in a course record time of 1:29:53.

UPPER RIGHT: Until Italy's Gelindo Bordin won in 1990, no runner had won Boston after winning an Olympic Marathon. LOWER RIGHT: In 1987 Japan's Toshihiko Seko claimed his second Boston Marathon victory, the first being in 1981. PAGE 215: Those who follow behind don't win laurels, yet they, too, experience the thrill of victory.

Only a short stretch of the Boston Marathon course is along Boylston Street, but it is where the long months of training somehow seem worthwhile. The stiffness and soreness from a hard day's work will fade, but memories of this final straightaway will remain forever.

Heroics

Runners participate in the Boston Marathon
for various reasons other than to win a prize or
set a personal record. Most run Boston because
it is Boston—the most famous marathon race
in the world. Even qualifying for Boston is
an achievement, a mark of honor. **PAGE 218,**
LEFT: Large numbers and narrow streets force
Boston Marathoners to run elbow to elbow.
CENTER: John A. Kelley became an inspiration for hundreds of thousands of runners.
He was 80 in 1988 when he finished in 4:26:36.
RIGHT: A runner struggles to finish the 1992
race. **PAGE 219, LEFT:** An exhausted finisher
is helped by race officials in 1992. **RIGHT:**
Each year, Dick Hoyt runs pushing his son,
Rick, who has cerebral palsy. Together, they
have "run" as fast as 2:40:24. Rick enjoys
pointing out that he always finishes one
second in front of his father.

220

PAGE 220: Four champions (clockwise from left): New Zealand's Allison Roe (1981), Great Britain's Geoff Smith (1984, 1985), Australia's Rob de Castella (1986) and Russia's Olga Markova (1992, 1993) all brought a sense of star quality to the Boston Marathon in the last 15 years. **PAGE 221, LEFT:** Germany's Uta Pippig won her second consecutive Boston in 1995. **RIGHT:** Portugal's Rosa Mota gives a hug to Fred Lebow, creator of the New York City Marathon, after her third victory in 1990.

PAGE 222, UPPER LEFT: Cosmas Ndeti was hurting during the closing miles of his win in 1993, but those behind him were hurting more. **LOWER LEFT:** Juma Ikangaa (5) and Ibrahim Hussein (23) led Mustafa el Nechadi (11) and John Treacy (14) through the Newton hills in 1988. **CENTER:** Ibrahim Hussein's victory in 1988 had been the first by an African runner. Soon, Africans came to dominate the race. En route to his third victory in 1992, Hussein (1) ran with Juma Ikangaa (4) and fellow Kenyans Boniface Merende (34), Sammy Nyangicha (37) and Godfrey Kiprotich (behind Hussein). **RIGHT:** Ethiopians Abebe Bikila (1960, 1964) and Mamo Wolde (1968) were Olympic Marathon champions. Bikila (foreground) and Wolde led Boston in 1963, but both failed to win. **PAGE 223:** Ibrahim Hussein of Kenya won his second Boston victory in 1991.

OUT OF AFRICA

For many years no runner from the African continent had won the Boston Marathon. Olympic champions Abebe Bikila and Mamo Wolde came closest to victory. In 1963 the two Ethiopians set a record pace through 20 miles, opening a wide gap from the field before fading to 5th and 12th.

A lack of travel funds caused most Africans to stay home. This changed in the mid-1980s when Boston became a money race.

Finally, in 1988 nine African nations held their Olympic trials in Boston, starting 40 swift runners. As the lead pack began disintegrating through the Newton hills, the swiftest of these Africans emerged: Ibrahim Hussein of Kenya and Juma Ikangaa of Tanzania. Hussein, a former steeplechaser from the University of New Mexico, previously had demonstrated an ability to win, but not to win fast. In four marathon victories, his fastest time was 2:11:01. Hussein's starting number 23 at Boston indicated his relatively low status.

After dropping Ireland's John Treacy, Hussein and Ikangaa ran side by side down Beacon Street and until the final turn onto Boylston Street. Ikangaa edged briefly into the lead, Hussein trailing, but with 100 yards to go the Kenyan shot past his Tanzanian rival for a one-second victory—the tightest finish in Boston's history. Hussein's time was 2:08:43. He would win again in 1991 and 1992. Ethiopia's Abebe Mekonnen won in 1989.

Hussein's victories inspired Kenyan Cosmas Ndeti, who trained by running to school each day when he lived at home on his father's farm. Ndeti won three consecutive victories, beginning in 1993. Both the glory and the money given to Boston winners will no doubt continue to attract Africa's best.

Boston

John J. McDermott was the first to cross the finish line in 1897. Since then, over 200,000 have finished at Boston. Who could have foretold a century ago how time would change the humbly begun Boston Athletic Association Marathon? And who knows what another century of running will bring?

OPPOSITE: The finish chute at the 1994 race. **ABOVE:** The lead pack races along Route 135 in the 1987 race. **RIGHT:** Runners at this point in the 1995 race were already thinking about the centennial year.

IN THE FALL OF 1992 I appeared at an awards banquet for a Chicago Marathon training class headed by Brian Piper and Bill Fitzgerald. I chatted with several runners who told me their plans to run Boston—in 1996! They wanted to be there for Boston's centennial celebration. I was intrigued by the idea that these guys already were anticipating an event nearly four years away, and I began to realize the significance of this anniversary.

A month later, I traveled to Emmaus, Pennsylvania, and had lunch at Fitness House, Rodale Press's quaint company restaurant, with Sharon Faelten, a managing editor in the book division. Joining us was Cassandra Alleyne, then trade sales marketing director for Rodale Books.

Sharon and I were just finishing work on a book, and inevitably, the conversation drifted around to the next project. I mentioned my conversation with the Chicago runners, and thinking out loud, said, "We ought to do a book to commemorate Boston's 100th anniversary." It was a galvanizing moment for the three of us, and we began planning the project. Before long, Cassandra and I visited Boston to inform the Boston Athletic Association's race director, Guy Morse, of our plans. Although it was only 1993, the BAA already had a centennial planning committee.

While eagerly awaiting official approval for the project, I attended the 1993 Boston Marathon as a reporter and spotted Pat Corpora, president of Rodale Books, sitting outside Hopkinton High School. Pat is a serious and accomplished runner who regularly runs Boston. I didn't want to badger him an hour before his race. Anticipating my concern, he looked at me intently and announced: "We're doing the book!"

That settled, I began the daunting, but enjoyable, task of examining 100 years of marathon history. Lee Jackson was assigned as the book's editor. Lee and I would work very closely over the next two years. Among my many books, I can't remember one in which there has been less friction between editor and writer.

At the start of the summer, I visited Indiana University on a writing assignment and met runner and journalism student Geoff Thurner. Geoff mentioned his unsuccessful search for a summer internship that year.

"How'd you like to go to Boston?" I offered.

As a result of that encounter, Geoff spent a good part of his summer at the Boston Public Library researching the long history of the marathon, dating back to 1897. Geoff also ran along the marathon course, stuffing questionnaires into mailboxes, while I placed a notice in *Runner's World* asking readers for their favorite Boston stories. We received hundreds of replies from those who had run or watched Boston over the years, and in one way or another, they have all enriched this book. One who wrote after spotting the notice was Maureen Erbe, a book designer and marathoner from California. Fortuitously, we later chose her company, and Senior Designer Rita A. Sowins, to provide the design that gives this book its elegant look.

Throughout the project, the BAA extended full support. Whenever I visited race headquarters on Clarendon Street, I always enjoyed chatting with Guy Morse, Gloria Ratti and other members of the staff, but I must single out for praise Jack Fleming, who handles the organization's public relations. Jack and I enjoyed a spirited contest to uncover facts and trivia about Boston. Jack would call with information about the original starting pistol. Later, I would one-up him by locating a vanished race champion from a half-century past. Also, Gina Caruso at the BAA graciously shared their collection of Boston Marathon memorabilia with the publisher.

As one who had first run Boston in 1959, this book was a dream project. It allowed me to renew acquaintances with old running companions, many whose names appear in this book. All offered details of

Bostons past and present, and I owe them my thanks.

Apart from those who shared their memories, many others contributed greatly to this book during its production stage. Photo researcher Andrea Schulting located many of the photographs that make this book unique. At Rodale Press I was helped immensely by art director Debra Sfetsios and photo editor Susan Pollack, who worked tirelessly to manage and track the numerous photographs that tell the story of Boston so eloquently. Copy editor John Reeser checked details throughout the book.

I want to thank my associates at *Runner's World* for their support over the years, particularly publisher George Hirsch and executive editor Amby Burfoot, who was kind enough to supply a foreword for this book.

I also owe a great deal to my wife, Rose, who has waited patiently beside many a finish line for me to appear. In 1964, the year I ran my fastest marathon, she didn't accompany me to Boston but stayed home with our three young children. Soon after crossing the finish line, I borrowed a dime from Jock Semple and rushed to a phone booth in the lobby of the Hotel Lenox. Hearing my happy voice, Rose looked at the clock on the wall. Knowing the marathon began at noon, she said, "You must have run well."

I would not have run so well nor written quite so well without her support over these years, or the support of our three children: Kevin, David and Laura.

I've searched my memory for when I first became aware of the Boston Marathon. Certainly, I must have read about the event in the sports pages in high school—but when did I decide to run it?

Before my senior year at Carleton College, I ran my first road race, a 15-κ in Chicago. The winner was John DiComandrea of the Boston Athletic Association. Did he plant a seed? Several years later, I was in the

U.S. Army stationed in Stuttgart, Germany, and trained with the BAA's Dean Thackwray. Dean placed fifth at Boston that spring and made the Olympic team. We had many conversations about Boston, but it would be three more years before I entered. I was offered lodging by Bill Squires, whom I had competed against in college. Bill claims he first ran Boston in 1960 because I bet him a case of beer he'd never do so. (He also claims I never gave him the beer.)

During my conversion from track athlete to road runner, I was aided by Ted Haydon, coach of the University of Chicago Track Club, as well as my companions at that club, including Gar Williams, Harold Harris, Arne Richards and Dick King. When I ran my fastest time at Boston, I was coached by Fred Wilt

Looking back on my years in running, I take pride at having been present in 1958 at the Paramount Hotel in New York City when a small group, led by Browning Ross, founded the Road Runners Club of America. I tip my runner's cap (lightweight polyester mesh) to those race directors within and without that organization who make running the roads so enjoyable today.

I come to the end of this writing task feeling both exhausted and exhilarated, much as I have felt on many an occasion after a 26-mile, 385-yard race. The Boston Marathon has beckoned runners like moths to a candle since the year 1897. May the next 100 years at Boston prove as much fun as the first 100.

MEN'S OPEN, 1897–1995

Year	Name/Home	Time	Year	Name/Home	Time
1897	JOHN J. MCDERMOTT, New York City	2:55:10	1931	JAMES "HINKY" HENIGAN, Medford, Mass.	2:46:45
1898	RONALD J. MACDONALD, Cambridge, Mass.	2:42:00	1932	PAUL DEBRUYN, Germany	2:33:36
1899	LAWRENCE J. BRIGNOLIA, Cambridge, Mass.	2:54:38	1933	LESLIE S. PAWSON, Pawtucket, Rhode Island	2:31:01
1900	JAMES J. CAFFERY, Hamilton, Ontario	2:39:44	1934	DAVE KOMONEN, Ontario, Canada	2:32:53
1901	JAMES J. CAFFERY, Hamilton, Ontario	2:29:23	1935	JOHN A. KELLEY, Arlington, Mass.	2:32:07
1902	SAMMY MELLOR, Yonkers, New York	2:43:12	1936	ELLISON M. "TARZAN" BROWN, Alton, Rhode Island	2:33:40
1903	JOHN C. LORDEN, Cambridge, Mass.	2:41:29	1937	WALTER YOUNG, Verdun, Quebec	2:33:20
1904	MICHAEL SPRING, New York City	2:38:04	1938	LESLIE S. PAWSON, Pawtucket, Rhode Island	2:35:34
1905	FRED LORZ, New York City	2:38:25	1939	ELLISON M. "TARZAN" BROWN, Alton, Rhode Island	2:28:51
1906	TIMOTHY FORD, Cambridge, Mass.	2:45:45	1940	GERARD COTE, St. Hyacinthe, Quebec	2:28:28
1907	TOM LONGBOAT, Hamilton, Ontario	2:24:24	1941	LESLIE S. PAWSON, Pawtucket, Rhode Island	2:30:38
1908	THOMAS MORRISSEY, New York City	2:25:43	1942	BERNARD JOSEPH SMITH, Medford, Mass.	2:26:51
1909	HENRI RENAUD, Nashua, New Hampshire	2:53:36	1943	GERARD COTE, St. Hyacinthe, Quebec	2:28:25
1910	FRED CAMERON, Amherst, Nova Scotia	2:28:52	1944	GERARD COTE, St. Hyacinthe, Quebec	2:31:50
1911	CLARENCE H. DEMAR, Melrose, Mass.	2:21:39	1945	JOHN A. KELLEY, Arlington, Mass.	2:30:40
1912	MIKE RYAN, New York City	2:21:18	1946	STYLIANOS KYRIAKIDES, Greece	2:29:27
1913	FRITZ CARLSON, Minneapolis	2:25:14	1947	YUN BOK SUH, South Korea	2:25:39
1914	JAMES DUFFY, Hamilton, Ontario	2:25:01	1948	GERARD COTE, St. Hyacinthe, Quebec	2:31:02
1915	EDOUARD FABRE, Montreal	2:31:41	1949	KARL GOSTA LEANDERSSON, Sweden	2:31:50
1916	ARTHUR ROTH, Roxbury, Mass.	2:27:16	1950	KI YONG HAM, South Korea	2:32:39
1917	BILL KENNEDY, Port Chester, New York	2:28:37	1951	SHIGEKI TANAKA, Hiroshima, Japan	2:27:45
1918	Military relay race held because of World War I		1952	DOROTEO FLORES, Guatemala	2:31:53
1919	CARL LINDER, Quincy, Mass.	2:29:13	1953	KEIZO YAMADA, Japan	2:18:51
1920	PETER TRIVOULIDAS, Greece	2:29:31	1954	VEIKKO KARVONEN, Finland	2:20:39
1921	FRANK ZUNA, Newark, New Jersey	2:18:57	1955	HIDEO HAMAMURA, Japan	2:18:22
1922	CLARENCE H. DEMAR, Melrose, Mass.	2:18:10	1956	ANTTI VISKARI, Finland	2:14:14
1923	CLARENCE H. DEMAR, Melrose, Mass.	2:23:37	1957	JOHN J. KELLEY, Groton, Connecticut	2:20:05
1924	CLARENCE H. DEMAR, Melrose, Mass.	2:29:40	1958	FRANJO MIHALIC, Yugoslavia	2:25:54
1925	CHARLES "CHUCK" MELLOR, Chicago	2:33:00	1959	EINO OKSANEN, Helsinki, Finland	2:22:42
1926	JOHN C. MILES, Sydney Mines, Nova Scotia	2:25:40	1960	PAAVO KOTILA, Finland	2:20:54
1927	CLARENCE H. DEMAR, Melrose, Mass.	2:40:22	1961	EINO OKSANEN, Helsinki, Finland	2:23:39
1928	CLARENCE H. DEMAR, Melrose, Mass.	2:37:07	1962	EINO OKSANEN, Helsinki, Finland	2:23:48
1929	JOHN C. MILES, Hamilton, Ontario	2:33:08			
1930	CLARENCE H. DEMAR, Melrose, Mass.	2:34:48			

WOMEN'S OPEN, 1966–1995

Year	Name/Home	Time		Year	Name/Home	Time
1963	AURELE VANDENDRIESSCHE, Belgium	2:18:58		1966	ROBERTA GIBB, Winchester, Mass.	3:21:40
1964	AURELE VANDENDRIESSCHE, Belgium	2:19:59		1967	ROBERTA GIBB, San Diego	3:27:17
1965	MORIO SHIGEMATSU, Japan	2:16:33		1968	ROBERTA GIBB, San Diego	3:30:00
1966	KENJI KIMIHARA, Japan	2:17:11		1969	SARA MAE BERMAN, Cambridge, Mass.	3:22:46
1967	DAVID MCKENZIE, New Zealand	2:15:45		1970	SARA MAE BERMAN, Cambridge, Mass.	3:05:07
1968	AMBROSE "AMBY" BURFOOT, Groton, Conn.	2:22:17		1971	SARA MAE BERMAN, Cambridge, Mass.	3:08:30
1969	YOSHIAKI UNETANI, Japan	2:13:49		1972	NINA KUSCSIK, South Huntington, New York	3:10:26
1970	RON HILL, Cheshire, Great Britain	2:10:30		1973	JACQUELINE A. HANSEN, Granada Hills, Calif.	3:05:59
1971	ALVARO MEJIA, Colombia	2:18:45		1974	MICHIKO GORMAN, Los Angeles	2:47:11
1972	OLAVI SUOMALAINEN, Otaniemi, Finland	2:15:39		1975	LIANE WINTER, Wolfsburg, West Germany	2:42:24
1973	JON ANDERSON, Eugene, Oregon	2:16:03		1976	KIM MERRITT, Racine, Wisc.	2:47:10
1974	NEIL CUSACK, Ireland	2:13:39		1977	MICHIKO GORMAN, Los Angeles	2:48:33
1975	BILL RODGERS, Jamaica Plain, Mass.	2:09:55		1978	GAYLE BARRON, Atlanta	2:44:52
1976	JACK FULTZ, Arlington, Virginia	2:20:19		1979	JOAN BENOIT SAMUELSON, Cape Elizabeth, Maine	2:35:15
1977	JEROME DRAYTON, Toronto	2:14:46		1980	JACQUELINE GAREAU, Montreal	2:34:28
1978	BILL RODGERS, Melrose, Mass.	2:10:13		1981	ALLISON ROE, Takatuna, New Zealand	2:26:46
1979	BILL RODGERS, Melrose, Mass.	2:09:27		1982	CHARLOTTE TESKE, Darmstadt, West Germany	2:29:33
1980	BILL RODGERS, Melrose, Mass.	2:12:11		1983	JOAN BENOIT SAMUELSON, Watertown, Mass.	2:22:43
1981	TOSHIHIKO SEKO, Japan	2:09:26		1984	LORRAINE MOLLER, Putaruru, New Zealand	2:29:28
1982	ALBERTO SALAZAR, Wayland, Mass.	2:08:52		1985	LISA LARSEN WEIDENBACH, Battle Creek, Mich.	2:34:06
1983	GREGORY A. MEYER, Wellesley, Mass.	2:09:00		1986	INGRID KRISTIANSEN, Oslo, Norway	2:24:55
1984	GEOFF SMITH, Liverpool, Great Britain	2:10:34		1987	ROSA MOTA, Porto, Portugal	2:25:21
1985	GEOFF SMITH, Liverpool, Great Britain	2:14:05		1988	ROSA MOTA, Porto, Portugal	2:24:30
1986	ROB DE CASTELLA, Canberra, Australia	2:07:51		1989	INGRID KRISTIANSEN, Oslo, Norway	2:24:33
1987	TOSHIHIKO SEKO, Japan	2:11:50		1990	ROSA MOTA, Porto, Portugal	2:25:24
1988	IBRAHIM HUSSEIN, Kenya	2:08:43		1991	WANDA PANFIL, Poland	2:24:18
1989	ABEBE MEKONNEN, Ethiopia	2:09:06		1992	OLGA MARKOVA, St. Petersburg, Russia	2:23:43
1990	GELINDO BORDIN, Milan, Italy	2:08:19		1993	OLGA MARKOVA, St. Petersburg, Russia	2:25:27
1991	IBRAHIM HUSSEIN, Kenya	2:11:06		1994	UTA PIPPIG, Berlin, Germany	2:21:45
1992	IBRAHIM HUSSEIN, Kenya	2:08:14		1995	UTA PIPPIG, Berlin, Germany	2:25:11
1993	COSMAS NDETI, Machakos, Kenya	2:09:33				
1994	COSMAS NDETI, Machakos, Kenya	2:07:15				
1995	COSMAS NDETI, Machakos, Kenya	2:09:22				

A 717   Commonwealth Ave. from Massachusetts Ave., Boston, Mass.

IN MY RESEARCH FOR *Boston*, whenever possible, I interviewed people who had been part of the events described. These firsthand sources are obvious from the text. My search extended back to those who had run Boston as early as the 1920s, including Johnny Miles and John A. Kelley.

Nevertheless, printed resources played a major role as well, including the major Boston newspapers, such as the *Globe* and the *Herald*. Over the past three decades magazines such as *Runner's World* and *The Runner* provided excellent sources in their articles on the Boston Marathon. Before that, Browning Ross's *Long Distance Log* covered Boston but mainly listed results. *Sports Illustrated* (frequently) and other national publications (rarely) also cover Boston and were helpful for specific observations.

Surprisingly, very few books have focused entirely on the Boston Marathon. Others offer sections on Boston, including biographies of those who have run the race. Most fascinating to me was Clarence DeMar's sparse autobiography. Tom Derderian's recent history proved to be an effective research tool as well.

We are all beneficiaries of our sources. Following are those books that proved most valuable during my writing and may be of interest to readers:

BENOIT, JOAN, WITH SALLY BAKER. *Running Tide*. New York City: Alfred A. Knopf, 1987.

BLAIKIE, DAVID. *Boston: The Canadian Story*. Ottawa, Ontario: Seneca House Books, 1984.

CUMMING, JOHN. *Runners & Walkers: A Nineteenth Century Sports Chronicle*. Chicago: Regnery Gateway, 1981.

DEMAR, CLARENCE. *Marathon: The Clarence DeMar Story*. Tallahassee, Florida: Clearwinds Publishing, 1992.

DERDERIAN, TOM. *Boston Marathon: The History of the World's Premier Running Event*. Champaign, Illinois: Human Kinetics Publishers, 1994.

FALLS, JOE. *The Boston Marathon*. New York City: Macmillan, 1977.

FIXX, JAMES F. *Jim Fixx's Second Book of Running*. New York City: Random House, 1980. Chapter on Pheidippides.

HIGDON, HAL. *Fitness after Forty*. Mountain View, California: World Publications, 1977. Chapter profiling Dr. Ken Cooper.

HIGDON, HAL. *On the Run from Dogs and People*. Chicago: Henry Regnery, 1971.

HOSLER, RAY, ed. *Boston: America's Oldest Marathon*. Mountain View, California: Anderson World, 1980.

LEWIS, FREDERICK, AND DICK JOHNSON. *Young at Heart*. Waco, Texas: WRS Publishing, 1992. Chapter on John A. Kelley.

MANDELL, RICHARD D. *The First Modern Olympics*. Berkeley, California: University of California Press, 1976.

MARTIN, DAVID E., AND ROGER W. H. GYNN. *The Marathon Footrace*. Springfield, Illinois: Charles C. Thomas, 1979.

NASON, JERRY. *The Story of the Boston Marathon*. Booklet published by the *Boston Globe*, about 1966.

ROBBINS, CHARLES. *Charles Robbins' Scrapbooks: Running with the Best since 1936*. Available from Frontrunner, North Kingstown, RI 02852.

RODGERS, BILL, WITH JOE CONCANNON. *Marathoning*. New York City: Simon and Schuster, 1980.

SEMPLE, JOCK, WITH JOHN J. KELLEY AND TOM MURPHY. *Just Call Me Jock*. Waterford, Connecticut: Waterford Publishing, 1981.

WILLISTON, FLOYD. *Johnny Miles: Nova Scotia's Marathon King*. Halifax, Nova Scotia: Nimbus Publishing, 1990.

HAL HIGDON PARTICIPATED IN HIS FIRST Boston Athletic Association Marathon in 1959, running with the leaders through Wellesley, but dropping out at 22 miles. Five years later, Higdon led through 19 miles before being passed by eventual winner Aurele Vandendriessche. Higdon held on for fifth (first American), clocking a personal best 2:21:55. Higdon once dreamed of winning the Boston Marathon. That never happened but he has continued to return to Boston both as a competitor and reporter since 1959. Former race director Will Cloney credits Higdon for his suggestion in 1967 that the BAA provide certificates for those finishing under four hours. In 1963 Higdon's *Sports Illustrated* article ("On the Run from Dogs and People," later expanded into a 1971 book by the same name) sparked the upturn in numbers at Boston the following year and helped inspire the running boom that followed.

He ran eight times in the Olympic Trials between 1952 and 1968, his best a nonqualifying fifth in the 3000-meter steeplechase in 1960. He won that same event at the 1975 World Veterans Championships, setting an American *masters* record of 9:18.6 that remains unbroken two decades later. He also won world *masters* titles in 1977, 1981 and 1991.

Although runners know Higdon best for his insightful articles on training and racing as senior writer for *Runner's World*, he has worked full time as a freelance writer since 1959, covering subjects as varied as politics for the *New York Times Magazine*, science for *National Geographic*, business for *Playboy* and aviation for *Air & Space Smithsonian*. His most recent running books include *Run Fast* and *Marathon: The Ultimate Training and Racing Guide*. In addition to running titles, his 28 previously published books have included *The Crime of the Century* (about the Leopold and Loeb case) and *The Horse That Played Center Field* (a children's book made into an animated TV special by ABC).

One of the founders in 1958 of the Road Runners Club of America (RRCA), Higdon received that organization's Journalism Award in 1980 and also was named to the RRCA Hall of Fame. In 1986 Higdon was a finalist in NASA's Journalist-in-Space program to ride the space shuttle. Most recently, in 1995 the North American Ski Journalists Association presented him with its Harold Hirsch Award for his ski columns in the *South Bend Tribune*. Higdon also writes a running column for that newspaper, syndicating it to regional publications.

He lives on the lakefront outside Michigan City, Indiana, and coached four years at the local high school, directing his girls cross-country team to fifth at the state championships in 1992. They won the title the two following years.

His wife, Rose, hikes, bikes, skis and supports him in his running and writing. She co-authored one book with him about her Italo-Albanian heritage: *Falconara: A Family Odyssey*. They have three children and six grandchildren.

At the centennial 1996 Boston Marathon, Higdon plans to run his 100th marathon—his 18th at Boston.

LEFT: Having once made Boston's top ten, author Hal Higdon still felt proud to finish 7,558th in 1995.

NOTE: *Italic* page references indicate boxed text. **Boldface** references indicate photographs and illustrations.

LEFT: Everybody has dreams. For many, Boston is one.